OXFORD ENGLISH MONOGRAPHS

General Editors

CHRISTOPHER BUTLER   STEPHEN GILL

DOUGLAS GRAY   EMRYS JONES

ROGER LONSDALE

A Store of Common Sense

GNOMIC THEME AND STYLE IN OLD ICELANDIC
AND OLD ENGLISH WISDOM POETRY

Carolyne Larrington

CLARENDON PRESS · OXFORD

1993

Oxford University Press, Walton Street, Oxford OX2 6DP

Oxford New York Toronto
Delhi Bombay Calcutta Madras Karachi
Kuala Lumpur Singapore Hong Kong Tokyo
Nairobi Dar es Salaam Cape Town
Melbourne Auckland Madrid
and associated companies in
Berlin Ibadan

Oxford is a trade mark of Oxford University Press

Published in the United States by
Oxford University Press Inc., New York

British Library Cataloguing in Publication Data
Data available

Library of Congress Cataloging-in-Publication Data
Larrington, Carolyne.
A store of common sense: gnomic theme and style in Old Icelandic
and Old English wisdom poetry / Carolyne Larrington.
—(Oxford English monographs)
Includes bibliographical references and index.
1. Didactic poetry, English (Old)—History and criticism.
2. Literature, Comparative—English (Old) and Old Norse.
3. Literature, Comparative—Old Norse and English (Old) 4. Gnomic
poetry. English (Old)—History and criticism. 5. Old Norse poetry—
History and criticism. I. Title. II. Series.
PR215.L37 1992
829'.1—dc20 92–11139
ISBN 0–19–811982–8

Printed in Great Britain
on acid-free paper by
Bookcraft Ltd.,
Midsomer Norton, Bath

ACKNOWLEDGEMENTS

I am most grateful to Christ Church for the Research Lectureship which enabled me to complete the main part of the thesis on which this book is based, and for their generous funding of research trips to Iceland. I wish to thank the other members, both past and present, of the Norse seminar group in Oxford for lively discussions of many matters, both related and unrelated to this work: in particular Guðrún Nordal, Peter Robinson, and Ian Shiels, the *Kolbítar*, Richard North, now of University College, London, and Alan Davey.

Mr Dennis Horgan of St Catherine's College first awakened my interest in Old English; Professor Eric Stanley kindly supervised the Old English chapters and made many helpful suggestions. Dr John Blair and Mr Peter Dronke suggested useful references.

My warmest thanks must go to Ursula Dronke, who inspired me with enthusiasm for Old Norse when I was an undergraduate, who suggested this engrossing subject, and who, as supervisor, has brought her unique energy, good humour, and insight to the study. Thanks are due too, to Professor Douglas Gray and Mr Rory McTurk, who, as thesis examiners, suggested a final shape for the book, and to Dr Paul Acker of the University of St Louis, whose comments were of invaluable assistance in the final revision stages.

Finally, love and thanks to John Davis, whose encouragement, support, and—ultimately—bribery, has contributed, more than he realizes, to the completion of this study.

C.L.

St John's College, Oxford
1991

Betri byrði
berrat maðr brauto at
en sé manvit mikit . . .

A better burden
can no man carry on the road
than a store of common sense . . .

(Hávamál)

CONTENTS

ABBREVIATIONS

AION-SG	*Annali dell'Istituto Universitario Orientale, Napoli, Sezione Germanica*
ANET	*Ancient Near Eastern Texts*, ed. J. B. Pritchard, 3rd edn. (Princeton, NJ, 1969)
ANF	*Arkiv för nordisk filologi*
AM	Arnamagnean
AnM	*Annuale Medievale*
APS	*Acta Philologica Scandinavica*
ASE	*Anglo-Saxon England*
ASPR	The *Anglo-Saxon Poetic Records*, ed. G. P. Krapp and E. V. K. Dobbie, 6 vols. (New York, 1931–53).
BGDSL	*Beiträge zur Geschichte der deutschen Sprache und Literatur*
BGDSL(H)	— (Halle)
BGDSL(T)	— (Tübingen)
Bp.	*Biskupa sögur* (Copenhagen, 1858–78)
B-S	*Handwörterbuch des deutschen Aberglaubens*, ed. H. Bächthold-Stäubli (Berlin, 1927–42)
B-T	*An Anglo-Saxon Dictionary*, ed. J. Bosworth and T. N. Toller (Oxford, 1882–98)
Bwf.	*Beowulf*, ed. F. Klaeber, 3rd edn. (Lexington, Mass., 1950)
CL	*Comparative Literature*
DC	*Disticha Catonis*, ed. J. Wight and A. M. Duff (Loeb Classical Library; London, 1934)
Dronke, *PE*	U. Dronke (ed.), *The Poetic Edda* i. *Heroic Poems* (Oxford, 1969)
EETS	Early English Text Society
ELN	*English Language Notes*
Evans, *Hávamál*	D. A. H. Evans (ed.), *Hávamál* (London, 1986)
Evans, MCS	D. A. H. Evans, 'More Common Sense about *Hávamál*', *Skandinavistik*, 19 (1989), 127–41
Ex. Max.	*Exeter Maxims*
Fritzner, *Ordbog*	*Ordbog over det gamle norske Sprog*, ed. J. Fritzner, 3 vols. (Kristiania, 1883–96)
Grein, *Sprachschatz*	*Sprachschatz der angelsächsischen Dichter*, ed. C. M. W. Grein (Heidelberg, 1912)
Hansen, *SC*	E. T. Hansen, *The Solomon Complex* (Toronto, 1988)
Háv.	*Hávamál*
HMS	*Heilagra Manna Søgur*, ed. C. R. Unger, 2 vols. (Kristiania, 1877)
ÍF	Íslenzk Fornrit
JEGP	*Journal of English and Germanic Philology*

KLNM	*Kulturhistorisk leksikon for nordisk middelalder*
KS	A. Heusler, *Kleine Schriften*, ii. (Berlin, 1969)
LP	*Lexicon Poeticum Antiquæ Linguæ Septentrionalis (Ordbog over det norsk-islandske Skjaldesprog)*, ed. S. Egilsson; 2nd edn., ed. F. Jónsson (Copenhagen, 1916; repr. 1966).
MÆ	*Medium Ævum*
Mar.	*Maríu saga*, ed. C. R. Unger (Kristiania, 1871)
MGH (SS)	*Monumenta Germaniae Historiae* (Scriptores)
MLN	*Modern Language Notes*
MM	*Maal og Minne*
NF	Nordisk Filologi
NLH	*New Literary History*
NM	*Neuphilologische Mitteilungen*
NQ	*Notes and Queries*
NS	new series
OED	*Oxford English Dictionary*
ON-IL	*Old Norse-Icelandic Literature: A Critical Guide*, ed. C. Clover and J. Lindow, Islandica 45 (Ithaca, NY, and London, 1985)
PBA	*Proceedings of the British Academy*
PCPhS	*Proceedings of the Cambridge Philological Society*
PMLA	*Publications of the Modern Languages Association of America*
RES	*Review of English Studies*
Saxo	Saxo Grammaticus, *History of the Danes*, ed. and tr. P. Fisher and H. E. Davidson, 2 vols. (Cambridge, 1979).
SBVS	*Saga-Book of the Viking Society*
S-G	H. Gering, *Kommentar zu den Liedern der Edda*, nach dem Tode des Verfassers herausgegeben von B. Sijmons, 2 vols. (Halle, 1927–31)
SGL	*Samling af Sweriges Gamla Lagar*, ed. H. S. Collin and C. J. Schlyter, 12 vols. (Stockholm and Lund, 1827–77)
Shippey, *PW*	T. A. Shippey, *Poems of Wisdom and Learning in Old English* (Cambridge and Totowa, NJ, 1976)
SI	*Scripta Islandica*
Sig. sk.	*Sigurðarkviða in skamma*
Skm.	*Skírnismál*
SNF	*Studier i nordisk filologi*
SP	*Studia Philologica*
SS	*Scandinavian Studies*
Stj.	*Stjórn*, ed. C. R. Unger (Kristiania, 1862)
STUAGNL	Samfund til Udgivelse af Gammel Norsk Litteratur
TMM	*Tímarit máls og menningar*
Vkv.	*Vǫlundarkviða*
von See, *CS*	K. von See, 'Common Sense und *Hávamál*', *Skandinavistik*, 17 (1987), 135–47

von See, *Edda*	K. von See, *Edda, Saga, Skaldendichtung: Aufsätze zur skandinavischen Literatur des Mittelalters* (Heidelberg, 1981)
Williams, *GP*	B. C. Williams, *Gnomic Poetry in Anglo-Saxon* (New York, 1914; repr. 1966)
ZDA	*Zeitschrift für deutsches Altertum*
ZfdPh	*Zeitschrift für deutsche Philologie*

INTRODUCTION

SOME PRELIMINARY OBSERVATIONS AND DEFINITIONS

This book is a study of the principal wisdom poems in Old Icelandic and Old English; its purpose is to demonstrate the breadth of interests, and the rich stylistic variety of these poems, and to reappraise their aesthetic value and continuing validity in the societies which preserved them.

Genre

The beginning of knowledge is the observation of how things are; the beginning of law, the observation of how things ought to be. Wisdom poetry, typically embodying either or both kinds of observation, is an archaic genre: wisdom texts are to be found among the earliest preserved writings in many literatures. In Sumerian, for example, the earliest preserved tablets, dating from around 2500 BC,[1] contain hymns and instructional works, while in Greek, the *Theogony*, a mythological poem, and *Works and Days*, an agricultural instruction poem, both ascribed to Hesiod, are contemporary with Homer,[2] dating from about 700 BC. In Old English and Old Norse, poems presenting information about human society, the natural world and the gods, or concerned with rules for human conduct, form a considerable — and probably early[3] — part of the extant literary corpus. Wisdom texts not only provide examples of different kinds of literary production: the instruction, the agricultural calendar, the 'mirror of princes', but also, because of their antiquity and range, influence several other types of literature. Thus wisdom material frequently plays an important role in elegy, epic, or in mythological poetry.

A wisdom poem may be defined as a poem which exists primarily to impart a body of information about the condition of the world, for example the Old English *Exeter Maxims*,[4] or about the past, as in the Norse mythological poems *Vafþrúðnismál* and *Grímnismál*.[5] Its intention may be to give advice, guiding on the basis of experience, as in the Old English *Precepts*, or the greater part of *Hávamál*. Such poems may be called wisdom poems, since their main purpose is to present different kinds of wisdom, while *Reginsmál* and *Fáfnismál* can hardly be so called, since they are only partly concerned with information of an arcane sort: their chief interest is in the adventures of the hero Sigurðr.[6]

Poetic Form

Such an ancient genre as wisdom poetry is likely to have un-evennesses and inconsistencies: problems of vocabulary and interpretation frequently occur. Moreover, the wisdom poem is agglutinative in form: one group of maxims or sayings will tend to attract others to it, even if the new material deals with a different subject, or is of a different type. Concerns of poetic decorum are irrelevant to wisdom poetry: if a gnome is recognizably true or useful, it may legitimately be included. Thus wisdom poems tend to be sprawling and compendious: with no structural limitations upon their length, they become infinitely elastic. Hesiod, for example, having completed his calendar of agricultural tasks, turns to discussion of the best season for seafaring in order to bring into *Works and Days* an account of his own voyage, when he won the tripod at a festival in Chalcis (650–62).

The gnomic tradition was constantly revised and refreshed; verses which were no longer comprehensible or which contained obsolete notions would drop out; new ideas, in the case of Old English taken from Christian teaching, could easily be inserted. Thus the problems of coherence and unity which characterize the reading of wisdom verse are largely problems inherent in the genre itself.

The Gnome

Wisdom poems characteristically consist of logically separate parts combined together by one or more poets or 'redactors'.[7] These parts may be of various kinds, gnome, precept, or existential statement, and any of them may be elaborated into an extended descriptive or explanatory passage, as in the portrait of the Frisian's wife in the *Exeter Maxims*. The first problem of analysis is thus: how does one define the individual units of wisdom which commonly constitute a wisdom poem?

Here we may except from discussion for the time being such distinct material as spells and charms, magical and runic lore, and the mythological instruction which formed an important part of wisdom for the non-Christian writer, such as we find in the later verses of *Hávamál, Vafþrúðnismál,* or Hesiod's *Theogony.* We are left with a substantial body of admonitions and observations, such as are defined, in the most general possible terms, by Aristotle:

> a gnome is a statement not relating to particulars, as, for example, the character of Iphicrates, but to universals; yet not to all universals indiscriminately, as, for example, that straight is the opposite of crooked, but to all such as are the objects of (human) action and are to be chosen or avoided in our doings.[8]

While Aristotle here provides a working definition of the 'human gnome'; the type which appears in the works of Hesiod, his definition would exclude some of the types of gnome which are found in Germanic literature. As we shall see, such universals as 'straight is the opposite of crooked', which Aristotle rejects, are considered appropriate subjects for wisdom verse in Old English. Aristotle's definition fits much better the gnomic material of *Hávamál,* which concerns itself primarily with human society.

In *The Growth of Literature,* the Chadwicks augment Aristotle's definition with a description of those gnomes which are less concerned with human action in its moral aspect. These are of a type which:

> relates to the properties or characteristics not only of mankind in general and of various classes of mankind, but also of other beings, objects, natural phenomena, etc. The gnomes of this type may in general be regarded as the results of observation, and are not capable of being converted into precepts. Under this type it will be convenient to distinguish gnomes relating to (a) human activities or experiences in which no choice or judgment is involved, (b) the operations of Fate (death) and the gods, (c) all other gnomes belonging to this type — the characteristics of beings etc. other than human.[9]

Thus the gnome typically deals with both the human and non-human in contexts where moral implications may be either absent or present.

Terminology

Modern English principally uses the following categories to distinguish between the forms in which wisdom may be found:

'proverb', 'precept', 'gnome', 'maxim' and 'sententia'. Other terms are: 'adage', 'saw', 'aphorism' and 'apophthegm'. The proverb is most easily differentiated from the other types in modern English. The *OED* defines 'proverb' as: 'A short pithy saying in common and recognized use; a concise sentence, often metaphorical or alliterative in form, which is held to express some truth ascertained by experience or observation and familiar to all; an adage, a wise saw.' Thus the adage and the saw may be regarded as identical to the proverb, distinguished by its brevity and fixed form, and which must be in common currency. A native speaker can decide relatively easily what is proverbial in a living language, but how is 'common currency' proved in Old Norse or Old English?

In his discussion of the problem of proverbial material in *Hávamál*, Heusler shows that a proverb can only be definitely identified as such if similar proverbs can be found in texts from different geographical areas, so that the one instance cannot have been a direct influence upon the other:

> Ein vorgefundenes Sprichwort is mit Sicherheit nur da zu erschließen, wo das Gegenstück ausser dem Verbreitungsgebiet der eddischen Sittengedichte liegt und auch der sprachliche Ausdruck Zusammenhang heischt.[10]

> One can only conclude for certain that a proverb existed previously, where the occurrence is outside the area of dissemination of the Eddic moralizing poems and where the verbal expression also suggests a connection.

'Kǫld eru kvenna ráð' (Cold are the counsels of women) is an example of such a proverb, since it occurs independently in both Old Norse and Middle English texts.[11] Wessén's analysis[12] of the proverbial material in *Hávamál* shows the difficulty of proving an expression to be proverbial, for many of the instances he adduces could be examples of so-called 'geflügelte Worte' (literally, winged words), quotations from a text which subsequently achieve proverbial status. He has to content himself with assuming that certain brief and pithy lines in *Hávamál* are of proverbial origin, although they cannot be so proven by Heusler's criteria.

Often we cannot be certain that a phrase was in 'common and

no comment on metaphorical nature

recognized use', but the wording or metaphorical nature of a statement suggest it might have been proverbial in origin, for example 'brigð eru útlenda orð' (untrustworthy are the words of foreigners) in *Hugsvinnsmál* 47; in this study the term 'proverb-like statement' will be used in such cases.

The *OED* defines the 'precept' as: 'A general command or injunction; an instruction, direction, or rule for action or conduct; especially an injunction as to moral conduct; a maxim. Most commonly applied to divine commands.' The term 'precept' may then be reserved for admonitions relating to human conduct. These are typically expressed in the imperative, as in the Old English poem *Precepts*, or the *Loddfáfnismál* section of *Hávamál*. Such precepts may demand a course of action, if there is an element of moral choice to be found in the context, as in *Precepts*. Alternatively, a precept may point out the advisability of a certain course of action, using a modal verb, such as *skal* in *Hávamál* 83: 'Við eld skal ǫl drekka, | en á ísi skríða . . .' ([One] is to drink ale by the fire, and slide on the ice . . .).

'Gnome' and 'Maxim' are more-or-less interchangeable in meaning. The *OED* defines 'maxim' as: 'A proposition (especially in aphoristic or sententious form) ostensibly expressing some general truth of science or of experience', and the 'gnome' as: 'A short pithy statement of a general truth; a proverb, maxim, aphorism or apothegm'. As the above definition shows, 'aphorism' and 'apophthegm' are not distinguished from 'maxim' in usage.

'Maxim' is generally understood as being identical with 'gnome', a term borrowed into English from Greek in the sixteenth century. 'Gnome' is characteristically though not exclusively used to denote observations about the natural world,[13] while both 'gnome' and 'maxim' are used of such pieces of wisdom that are not defined as proverbs or precepts above. The word 'sententia', also applied in this context, is defined as a 'thought or reflection' by the *OED*; it is usually employed in literary discussion interchangeably with 'gnome' and 'maxim'.

Grammatical markers of the gnomic

In an early study of Old English wisdom verse, B. C. Williams[14] draws attention to certain 'gnomic indicators' — grammatical markers which indicate to the audience a concisely expressed thought worthy of memorization and application in daily life.

Such grammatical markers may be adverbs of time, characteristic verbs, such as OE *gerisan* (it is fitting), or the modal OE *sceal* / ON *skal;* the present-future tense also signifies the gnomic mode. In both Old English and Old Norse, the gnome is given universality and emphasis by time markers, such as OE *nefre*, 'never', OE *a* (ON *æ, ey*), 'always', or OE *oft* (ON *opt*), 'often'. In gnomic usage *oft* is frequently equivalent to *a* in meaning, and may be translated as 'generally'; but *oft/opt*, unlike *a/æ* allows for the occasional exception.[15] An example is *Exeter Maxims* 35 (cf. also *The Seafarer* 106): 'Dol biþ sē þe his dryhten nāt, to þǣs oft cymeð dēað unþinged;' (Foolish is he who does not know his lord, to him death generally comes unexpectedly).

The 'sceal/bið *problem*'

The modal OE *sceal*, ON *skal* is the most common gnomic marker in the two languages, but in Old English the gnomic present form *bið* is frequently found in alternation with *sceal*. In recent criticism of the Old English *Maxims* (both *Exeter* and *Cotton*), scholars have sought to clarify the difference in usage between *sceal* and *bið*. Critics have tended to appropriate the two verbs as schematic indicators of those oppositions or contrasts which they believe to be inherent in the poems. Thus for P. B. Taylor:[16]

> The *bið*-maxims focus on the immutable conditions of the universe and are framed in the form of an equation or identity, of the type 'wyrd bið swiðost' . . . The *sceal*-maxims, on the other hand, embody expressions about what should be, how things should function.

For L. C. Gruber,[17] the distinction between *sceal* and *bið* seems to lie in the different views either type of gnome offers of the relationship of the human and divine, whether it is the 'immanence' or the 'transcendence' of the Christian God that is under discussion.

A convincing distinction between *sceal* and *bið* must account satisfactorily for the fact that in apparently identical contexts the *Exeter Maxims* poet uses *sceal* where the *Cotton Maxims* poet uses *bið*. In *Exeter Maxims* 71–4, the poet uses *sceal* in the series of gnomes beginning 'forst sceal frēosan' (frost must freeze), while in *Cotton Maxims* the poet uses *bið* for the nature gnomes in 5b ff. of the type 'winter bið cealdost' (winter is coldest). The subjects of both series — the propensities of natural things — seem identical.

M. Nelson's study of the meaning of the two modals[18] concludes that *sceal* and *bið* have both distinct and overlapping semantic functions, ranged along a scale whose ends are 'ought' and 'is'. Thus *bið* (and similarly *is*), has a unique property: 'a respectful verbalization of what everyone knows to be true', but it also shares the meanings 'must', 'is typically', and 'is essentially' with *sceal*. The meanings 'ought always', 'ought', and 'is appropriately' are assigned to *sceal* alone, as in 'Scyld sceal cempan' (a shield is appropriate for a warrior).[19] These distinctions convey through their subtlety a flexibility of expression available to the Old English poet, but now no longer easily accessible to the modern reader, for the variation between the two verbs is as much a question of aspect as of meaning.

N. Howe's recent study of Old English wisdom poems makes this point independently of Nelson:

> To insist on an invariable sense for *sceal* deprives the poem (*Cotton Maxims*) of its interest and its value. Although these maxims do employ a regular syntax, this frame allows for significant variation in meaning. And it might be argued that in this fact lies the true wisdom of the poem, through its syntactic regularity it teaches one to draw significant parallels, but in its use of the gnomic verbs, it also warns that parallelism does not inherently reflect correspondence.[20]

In summary then, while Old English *sceal* often carries an implication of obligation, this implied obligation need not always be active in a given context, such as in the series in *Exeter Maxims* of the type: 'Forst sceal frēosan', which Nelson would translate as 'It is appropriate that frost should freeze'. If overtones of obligation are to be perceived here, they might be explained by reference to a higher power, to which the natural phenomena are subject: the frost has an active duty to perform, to freeze water, while in the *Cotton Maxims*, 'winter bið cealdost' (winter is coldest) is an existential fact.[21]

In the human context, *sceal* and its Old Norse cognate *skal* generally bear the meaning 'ought to', exemplified by the Old English gnomes on the conduct proper to a warrior.[22] These gnomes are close to the precept, as defined above, in their function. However, while the precept is normally expressed by an imperative, implying a speaker and a listener, a statement using *sceal* sets up an ideal standard of conduct, independent of the audience addressed. Its members may aspire to the ideal themselves or be enabled to recognize the ideal in others. *Biδ* is invariably used where the subject of the gnome is God: 'God ūs ēce biδ' (God is eternal for us) (*Exeter Maxims* 8b). Possibly the overtones of obligation which *sceal* carries are inappropriate to a human comment on the Divine. *Biδ* with the implication 'is essentially' tends to be found where natural processes are involved, as in the *Cotton Maxims* series (5b ff.) but there is no real consistency of usage even in this context.

Sceal and *biδ* then tend to be distributed according to context; human activity will usually be expressed by *sceal*, while *biδ* is more likely to be found in relation to God or the natural world.

The subjunctive forms *scyle* and *skyli* are found in Old English and Old Norse as occasional variants of *sceal* and *skal*. In his discussion of *The Wife's Lament* 42ff.,[23] Leslie regards the moods of the verb *sceal* in gnomic verse as being 'differentiated with respect to human behaviour, *sceal* being preferred to list fundamental qualities and *scyle* to indicate desirable qualities'. He compares *The Seafarer* 109–11, *Hávamál* 90, 93, and *The Order of the World* 17, 98.

But Leslie's distinction does not hold good for *Hávamál*. In 90 the subjunctive expresses the series of unreal — and increasingly absurd — conditions with which the love of women with crafty hearts is compared, nor in 93 is the subjunctive used to express articularly 'desirable qualities'. Wessén, however, finds the variation between *skal* and *skyli* in *Hávamál* to be significant:

> Om man jämför de båda grupperna med *skal* och med *skyli* i sin helhet med varandra, framgår det ganska tydligt, att *skal* uttrycker en mer ovillkorlig fordran eller en allmänt vedertagen regel, som man ej för avvika från, *skyli* däremot ett mera modest råd: man bör . . . man bör icke.[24]

> If one compares the two groups with *skal* and with *skyli* in their entirety with one another, it becomes quite obvious that *skal* expresses a more unconditional demand or a generally established rule, from which departures are never found, *skyli* on the other hand [expresses] a more modest counsel: one ought . . . one ought not.

This distinction is certainly valid for some of the different usages in *Hávamál*, for example, the use of *skyli* in 1. In 93, the use of the subjunctive expresses, rather tentatively, the unusual idea that the wise man may be more susceptible to female beauty than the fool; while in 94 the thought is more dogmatic and commonplace: love makes fools out of the wise; the idea of the verse is 'en allmänt vedertagen regel', and thus is expressed through skal.

In a recent article,[25] C. Karkov and R. Farrell have shown how heavily punctuated the gnomic passages in *Beowulf* are in contrast to the normally light punctuation to be found in Old English manuscripts. They plausibly suggest that, together with the modal markers, 'bið', 'mæg', and 'sceal', such pointing clearly indicated the 'importance and weight' of the gnomic passages, the equivalent perhaps of the pointing hand symbol drawing attention to *sententiae* of note in Renaissance books.

Vocabulary

Wisdom poetry employs a varied vocabulary to denote intellectual qualities and activities.[26] The fine distinctions which such adjectives as ON *fróðr*/OE *frod*; ON *snotr*/OE *snottor*; ON *horskr*, *hugalt*, *vitandi*, *spakr*, and *kuðr* (all occurring in *Hávamál*), and OE *wis* and *gleaw*, all meaning 'wise', may once have embodied are now lost to us, as are the different kinds of mental attributes rendered by *hygecræft*, *geþoht*, *giedd*, *geþonc*, *mod*, *ræd*, *hyge*, *snyttro*, and *modgeþoncas* in the *Exeter Maxims*. Nevertheless, the existence of such a wealth of terms indicates an interest in the mind and psychological attributes which predates the importation of classical theory with the coming of Christianity. Study of vocabulary in chapter 3 reveals significant differences between the lexis of *Hávamál* and the Christian *Hugsvinnsmál*, while the different intentions of the Old English *Exeter Maxims* and *Cotton Maxims* is crystallized by the use of some sixteen different words belonging to this semantic field in the *Exeter Maxims*, where the *Cotton Maxims* yield just two: *wisdom* and *hycgean* (to think). This difference indicates why E. T. Hansen's recent book, *The Solomon Complex* (1988), is able to make full use of the *Exeter Maxims* in arguing that Old English wisdom poetry is essentially a self-reflexive, self-conscious, and introspective form, but is unable successfully to incorporate the *Cotton Maxims* into her schema.[27]

Previous Criticism

Wisdom poetry suddenly became a focus of critical attention in both Old Norse and Old English in the 1970s as K. von See's *Die Gestalt der Hávamál* (1972) and T. A. Shippey's *Poems of Wisdom and Learning in Old English* (1976) opened up different areas of debate. Von See's aim was twofold: to present *Hávamál* as a coherent single work, and to prove that this work had been produced by a thirteenth-century editor. The 'pure heathen' wisdom of *Hávamál* had been infiltrated by Christian and classical notions, von See argued. His position has sparked off a lively debate with D. A. H. Evans, the most recent editor of the poem, and R. Köhne.[28] While I share von See's theory of a series of authors arranging and adapting the material in *Hávamál*, I remain unconvinced by the parallels which he adduces in Christian and extra-Scandinavian writing, parallels which this study examines closely.

Shippey's rehabilitation of Old English wisdom verse has been less controversial, although this assertion cannot go un-challenged: 'It was once the fashion to juxtapose *Maxims* and the Old Norse *Hávamál*; but one finds nearly as much by reading the *Maxims of Ptahhotpe* . . . or indeed the collections of anthropologists from Nigeria or New Guinea.'[29] The question Shippey begs here is exactly what we *do* seek from a comparative reading of wisdom verse. The aim of this book is neither to spot 'parallels' or 'influences', nor to evolve an ur-Germanic model of wisdom discourse, but rather to characterize the poems, to explore the different contexts in which gnomic material is deployed, and to illuminate cultural differences between Old Norse and Old English.

E. T. Hansen's challenging study of Old English wisdom poetry seeks to demonstrate its contiguity to issues of paramount interest to modern literary theorists, arguing that 'the wisdom poem is characteristically concerned with the nature, function and value of its own discourse, as well as the extratextual consequences of that discourse'.[30] The study is partially successful in this, focusing on the frameworks in which gnomic verse is presented, and it bravely rehabilitates lesser-known poems such as *Menologium* and *An Exhortation to Christian Living*. But Hansen fails to establish a mode of reading for the bulk of the poetry, the discrete, sometimes incoherent, gnomes and sequences of gnomes which

constitute the *Exeter* and *Cotton Maxims*, and pays scant attention
to the *Rune Poem*. Chapter 1, and the first section of chapter 4, in
this book offer close readings of *Hávamál* and the *Exeter Maxims* as
case studies of the problems presented by the genre. In the first
instance, the disparate elements of *Hávamál* are effectively unified
through complex narrative strategies and the figure of Óðinn; in
the second, once the initial dialogue framework is abandoned,
problems of unity and coherence cannot be overcome.[31]

Notwithstanding the substantial differences in the two traditions,
both Old Norse and Old English wisdom poetry raise similar
questions:

1. Is it possible to determine how great a part of the extant texts
   in the two literatures is pagan in origin? How has this material
   been modified by Christianity? What was the validity of early
   texts for succeeding generations?
2. What is the poetic value of these texts? What kinds of poetic
   device are used to present wisdom, and what are the principal
   artistic features of these poems?
3. The gnomic mode is not restricted to didactic, educational
   poetry; it has diffused into other genres. How does it influence
   elegy, epic, and heroic poetry?

Chapter 1 provides a close reading of the primary Norse text,
Hávamál, demonstrating the skilful structural integration of the
pragmatic, social wisdom with the other kinds of knowledge in
Hávamál, both runic and magical. Chapter 2 explores how every
type of wisdom must be drawn together to complete the education of the hero, Sigurðr. The problematic relationship of
Hávamál to *Hugsvinnsmál* (the Icelandic translation of the *Disticha
Catonis*), and the characteristics of this Christian text, are the
subject of chapter 3, responding to the views of K. von See. The
range of Old English wisdom poetry is examined in chapter 4,
with particular regard to the contrasts which this substantially
Christian verse affords in style and structure with the material of
the Edda, and, in chapter 5, to the powerful hold which Nature
exerts over the imaginations of the Old English poets. In chapters
6 and 7, analysis of the influence of wisdom verse on other poetic
genres reveals the continual presence of a gnomic 'key' through
which the themes of elegiac and heroic poetry are related to
universal experience and social norms.

Far from being platitudinous moralizing, the wisdom poems of the two literatures reveal themselves as comic, ironic, dramatic, and grandiose by turns, exploring a gamut of themes unequalled in any other genre.

Notes

1. S. N. Kramer, *The Sumerians* (Chicago, 1963), 224.
2. Hesiod, *Works and Days* ed. M. L. West (Oxford, 1978), 31.
3. See E. G. Stanley, 'The Oldest English Poetry Now Extant', *Poetica*, 2 (1974), 1–24.(repr. in *A Collection of Papers with Emphasis on Old English Literature*, ed. E. G. Stanley Toronto, 1987, 115–38).
4. Although the *Exeter* and *Cotton Maxims* are also known as *Maxims I* and *Maxims II*, I use the titles suggested by the poems' manuscripts. It is important to keep in mind the codicological contexts in which the poems occur, especially in the case of the *Exeter Maxims*, but also in the *Cotton Maxims*, as J. K. Bollard suggests, 'The Cotton Maxims', *Neophilologus*, 57 (1973), 179–87.
5. Although *Vafþrúðnismál* and *Grímnismál* are examined by J. de Vries in 'Om Eddaens Visdomsdigtning', *ANF* 50 (1934), 1–59, they are not strictly gnomic verse. For a reading of the poems as wisdom poetry, see my Oxford D.Phil. thesis, 'Old Icelandic and Old English Wisdom Poetry: Gnomic Themes and Styles' (1988), ch. 2.
6. This book is concerned only with verse: the many instances of proverbial usage in the sagas and proverb collections lie beyond its scope.
7. For the term 'Redaktor', one who compiles, and may or may not compose parts of, a gnomic poem, see K. von See, *Die Gestalt der Hávamál* (Frankfurt-on-Main, 1972).
8. Aristotle, *Rhetorica* II, in *Collected Translated Works* xi. tr. W. Rhys Roberts (Oxford, 1946), 21, 1–16.
9. H. M. Chadwick and N. K. Chadwick, *The Ancient Literatures of Europe* (*The Growth of Literature*, i) (Cambridge, 1932), 377.
10. A. Heusler,'Sprichwörter in den eddischen Sittengedichten', *Zeitschrift des Vereins für Volkskunde*, 25 (1915), 108–15; ibid. 26 (1916), 42–54 (repr. *KS* 292–313. See here, 293.
11. Kǫld eru kvenna ráð' (Cold are women's counsels) or a similarly expressed proverbial sentiment occurs in *Vǫlundarkviða* 31; Chaucer's *Nun's Priest's Tale* viii 3256; *Proverbs of Alfred*, ed. O. Arngart (Lund, 1959), ll. 336–9; and *Njáls saga* ch. 116. See B. J. Whiting and H. W. Whiting, *Proverbs, Sentences and Proverbial Phrases from English Writings Mainly before 1500* (Cambridge, 1968), s.v. 'rede'.
12. E. Wessén, 'Ordspråk och lärodikt; Några stilformer i *Hávamál*', *Septentrionalia et Orientalia: Studia Bernardo Karlgren dedicata*, Kungl. Vitterhets Historie och Antikvitets Akademiens Handlingar, 91 (Stockholm, 1959), 455–73.
13. See K. Jackson, *Studies in Early Celtic Nature Poetry* (Cambridge, 1935).
14. Williams, *GP*, 8.
15. See Stanley, 'The Oldest English Poetry' in particular 121–2.
16. P. B. Taylor, 'Heroic Ritual in the Old English Maxims' *NM* 70 (1969), 387–8.
17. L. C. Gruber, 'The Agnostic Anglo-Saxon Gnomes: *Maxims I* and *II*, *Germania*, and the Boundaries of Northern Wisdom' *Poetica*, 6 (1976), 32.
18. M. Nelson, ' "Is" and "Ought" in the Exeter Book *Maxims*', *Southern Folklore Quarterly*, 45 (1984 for 1981), 113.
19. *Ex. Max.* 129a.
20. N. Howe, *The Old English Catalogue Poems.*, Anglistica 23 (Copenhagen, 1985), 164.
21. See Hansen, *SC*, 306, n. 11.
22. See below, ch. 7.1.

23. R. F. Leslie, *Three Old English Elegies* (Manchester, 1981), 57. NB P. L. Henry's contention that 'scyle' in *Wife's Lament* 42 is to be read as a prayer or wish: 'may he . . .', in *The Early English and Celtic Lyric* (London, 1966), 101.

24. E. Wessén, '*Hávamál*, Några stilfrågor', *Filologiskt Arkiv*, 8 (Stockholm, 1959), 17.

25. C. Karkov and R. Farrell, 'The Gnomic Passages of *Beowulf* NM 91 (1990), 295–310.

26. M. Godden examines OE theories of, and terminology for, the mind and its attributes in 'Anglo-Saxons on the Mind', *Learning and Literature in Anglo-Saxon England: Studies presented to Peter Clemoes on the Occasion of his Sixty-Fifth Birthday* (Cambridge, 1985), 271–298.

27. See my review in *MÆ* 58 (1989), 319–20.

28. The issues addressed by von See in *Die Gestalt der Hávamál*, and '*Disticha Catonis* und *Hávamál*', *BGDSL*(T) 94 (1972), 1–18 (repr. in *Edda*, 27–44), continued in 'Probleme der altnordischen Spruchdichtung', *ZDA* 104 (1975), 91–118 (repr. *Edda*, 45–72), are debated by R. Köhne, 'Zur Mittelalterlichkeit der eddischen Spruchdichtung', *BGDSL* 105 (1983), 380–417 and by D. A. H. Evans, firstly in his introduction to *Hávamál* (London, 1986), to which von See replied in CS. Evans's response, MCS is followed by von See's *Duplik* in the same issue of *Skandinavistik*: *Skandinavistik*, 19 (1989), 142–8.

29. Shippey, *PW*, 47

30. Hansen, *SC*, 178

31. How far this constitutes a failure in poetic terms is discussed below at ch. 4.1.

1 *HÁVAMÁL*

1.1 INTRODUCTION

Óðinn as Patron of Norse Wisdom Verse

Other gods, Hœnir and Lóðurr,[1] of whom we know very little, may share with Óðinn in the creation of mankind, but the Alfǫður is unique among the Old Norse gods in his continuing interest in the fates of individual humans. Óðinn nurtures and educates his protégés until the time comes to sunder the bond and take the hero to Valhǫll. He teaches men: instructing Sigurðr in battle-omens, speaking in *Hávamál* to illustrate the truth of maxims about drunkenness or sexual relationships, or displaying his own compendious knowledge in *Grímnismál*. As a wanderer in disguise, Óðinn visits giants and men, both teaching and augmenting his wisdom.

Hávamál shows how Óðinn first acquires some of his wisdom: poetic inspiration, runes, and spells. Other Eddic wisdom poems depict the god testing out and demonstrating his wisdom, passing it on to others. Thus the wisdom poems of the Edda are under Óðinn's aegis: his is the figure that unites them all.

Manuscript and Textual History

Hávamál is a composite poem, the work of a number of poets and editors over a long period of time.[2] In addition to the manuscript divisions, signalled by large initial letters at 111 and 138, scholars have often found it convenient to divide the poem into different sections, according to the style and subject-matter of the strophes:

    I: The Gnomic Poem, 1–103.
   II: The 'Gunnlǫð Episode', 104–10.
  III: *Loddfáfnismál*, 111–37.
  IV: *Rúnatal*, 138–45.
   V: *Ljóðatal*, 146–64.

Questions of dating and authorship in a composite poem are problematical. Although the Codex Regius manuscript is written in a single hand dated to around 1270, linguistic differences between the poems indicate that they are of varying ages, and several theories have been suggested regarding how the poems might have been transmitted before they were collected together. The currently prevailing view is that of G. Lindblad,[3] first put forward in 1954, that the Codex Regius collection was compiled from a number of independent pamphlets, in which some of the poems were already combined. Lindblad shows that clear palaeographic and linguistic boundaries exist between the mythological poems on one hand, and the heroic poems on the other. Of *Hávamál* specifically, he argues from a number of linguistic peculiarities[4] that the poem was transmitted separately from the other mythological poems.

D. A. Seip[5] argues from the poems' many Norwegianisms that they were transmitted from Norway to Iceland in written form. This theory would accord well with Lindblad's pamphlet theory, but it has also been shown that Norwegianisms survive in many other Icelandic manuscripts where no question of Norwegian origin obtains.[6] The most recent editor of *Hávamál*, D. A. H. Evans, accepts Lindblad's findings, and seems persuaded that, in *Hávamál* at least, the Norwegianisms, such as the custom of cremation alluded to in 70 and the 'bautarsteinar' (memorial stones) of 72, are best explained by a theory of Norwegian origin for the Gnomic Poem, which would pre-date the settlement of Iceland.[7] However, given the variety of material contained in the poem, there is no reason to suppose that all the verses of *Hávamál* were necessarily composed in Norway.[8]

Date

Eddic poetry is notoriously difficult to date: the continuance of pagan tradition beyond the Conversion and the antiquarian interests of later writers make it impossible to determine the relative age of the poems. If *Hávamál* is truly pagan, composed before the Conversion of Iceland, it would be at least three hundred years older than the manuscript in which it is found.

The case for dating *Hávamál* from before the written period is based on assumptions about the pagan nature of the poem. The absence of any reference to Christianity, and the self-seeking social ethics would not have been tolerated in a Christian society; thus it has been argued that the poem could not have been composed after the Conversion. Nor, it is thought, would the account of Óðinn's self-sacrifice in 138–9, with its uncomfortable parallels with the Crucifixion, have been incorporated in a poem composed by a Christian author. In addition to these arguments, the citation of 76 and 77[1-3] — 'deyr fé, deyr frændr' (cattle die, kinsmen die) — in the last verse of Eyvindr *skáldaspillir's* elegy for Hákon the Good, *Hákonarmál, c.*960,[9] together with the poem's many Norwegianisms, seems to favour an early date for the Gnomic Poem.

Recently, however, there has been a tendency to advance the date of *Hávamál's* composition well into the written period. The impulse towards the composition — or compilation — of the poem is thought to have been provided by Continental literary sources.[10] Parallels between *Hávamál* and biblical and classical texts have been noted, while other scholars have suggested that *Hávamál* was compiled during a period of antiquarian interest brought about in part by the *Snorra Edda.*[11]

At present, we have no conclusive proof of the date of the composition of *Hávamál* in its present form, or of the age of its constituent parts. Scholars have argued, with equal vigour, that the mythological and mystical parts have attracted the gnomic material and hence are older, and exactly the converse: that the gnomic poem is the 'original' *Hávamál* and has served as a kernel around which the more recent mythological material clusters.

Authorship

The problem of the authorship of *Hávamál* is linked to that of its date and genre. If the poem dates from before the literary period, then it is probable that the material was compiled by several different poets, or, conceivably, the Gnomic Poem is an aggregation of verses belonging to a common folk stock. If the poem is from the later literary period, then the probability that there was a single author responsible for *Hávamál* in its present form becomes stronger.

Critics of *Hávamál* have occupied themselves chiefly with the question of authorial intention; whether we are to regard the poem as (i) a more-or-less random agglomeration of material, (ii) as a collection of verses, mechanically arranged by a *Sammler* (Schneider),[12] or (iii) as the work of a *Redaktor* (von See),[13] who brought to bear on the disparate material a considerable literary and aesthetic intelligence, deliberately shaping and ordering the verses to present a coherent and unified poem — using poetry already in existence and verse of his own composition.

Since the publication of von See's *Die Gestalt der Hávamál*, it has become clear that theory (i) can no longer be satisfactory as an account of the poem. There are passages in the Gnomic Poem where the transition from one thematic area to another is clumsily achieved, for example, between 14 and 15, or where there is some lack of smoothness in passing from one section to another: for example, the problematic transition from the solemn hieratic tone of 111 to the more down-to-earth, practical advice of 112. Nevertheless, none of the attempts to restore the original *Hávamál* by excision, or by rearrangement of the Codex Regius stanzas has been convincing — no subjective ordering imposed on the material by a nineteenth- or twentieth-century scholar can have the authenticity of the Codex Regius's scribe's arrangement of the verses.[14] The revision attempts have ultimately had the result of demonstrating the superior validity of the original.

The positions of Schneider and von See are not dissimilar, the main difference between them being the extent to which each estimates the *Redaktor* to have been aiming consciously to create an artistic unity from the 'Spruchhaufe' of the raw material. Von See builds on Schneider's excellent analysis of the verbal and thematic links between the verses, and Schneider himself has to admit the skill of the *Sammler* in creating a striking and atmospheric opening to the poem. Neither writer has been able, however, to establish a critical method by which 'original' verses and those composed by the *Sammler/Redaktor* can be distinguished.

The *Redaktor* theory is finally unsatisfactory because it does not attempt to explain in what form the material of *Hávamál* existed before its 'final' shaping. I contend that there was a body of folk-wisdom, not yet in metrical form, a body which can be sensed as a living, pulsing, gnomic background to all Germanic poetry — not just verse specifically intended as didactic. There is a gnomic 'key' which sounds in other genres, both in Old Norse and Old English, as this study will demonstrate. Norse folk-wisdom formed the basis for the sequences of *ljóðaháttr* verses, already linked by verbal repetitions, or by theme,which constitute the Gnomic Poem of *Hávamál*. This poem was constantly shaped, revised, and refreshed with new material from the folk-stock by a succession of poets, working mainly, though not necessarily exclusively, in the oral medium. Comparison with wisdom material from the Ancient Near East shows how a sequence of verses, organized around the theme of table-manners, translated into various languages, but still recognizable, could travel through different cultures in the course of centuries. Part of *The Instruction of Amen-en Ophet*, an Egyptian text 'which may be securely dated pre-1100 BC',[15] is taken over wholesale into the Hebrew Proverbs 22: 17–23: 12, compiled around the seventh century BC, and 'with an astonishing continuity of tradition'[16] is found in the Apocryphal Ecclesiasticus 31: 12–18, a Greek translation of a Hebrew compilation, in 132 BC. Similarly, in his edition of *Works and Days*, West shows how Egyptian and Hebrew wisdom material appears in Hesiod's *Works and Days*; not as a result of direct literary influence, but of 'general cultural diffusion'. As long as the truth of the verses remained valid, they were incorporated into wisdom writings.

The synthesis of social wisdom and Odinic myth which *Hávamál* represents could have been made as early as the late pagan period: the *Þórsdrápa* of Eilífr Goðrúnarson[17] shows how pre-Christian poetry could be used for highly sophisticated literary purposes. The poem's accomplishment need not argue a later date.

The composite 'author' of *Hávamál* is thus to be regarded, to quote T. S. Eliot, as:

> Both one and many; in the brown baked features
> The eyes of a familiar compound ghost
> Both intimate and unidentifiable.[18]

1.2 SOME WORKING ASSUMPTIONS

The following section is an analysis of *Hávamál* in which I seek to illuminate the major thematic movements, and demonstrate the development of thought through verbal and logical links.

A number of preliminary assumptions must be made to provide a conceptual basis for the analysis. First, the term 'audience' comprises both spectators at oral recitations of *Hávamál* and readers of the text in manuscript. *Hávamál* is very much a text for performance, a vehicle for suspense, grandeur, realism, and comedy, full of dramatic potentiality and swift change of tone; it must have been recited many times in halls similar to the one represented in the opening section. The impulse towards realism generated by the identity of *locus* and text should not be underestimated; the opening section would have had an extraordinary immediacy.

Secondly, I refer to a single poet/*Redaktor* as the narrative voice: he is only the last in a series of such poet/*Redaktors*.[19] How much of the current text might have been composed by this last poet and how much reworked from earlier versions cannot be determined on the basis of the text,[20] nor should speculation about the relative age of *Hávamál's* constituent sections distract us from the task of constructing a reading of the text as it stands.

The poem has a sole narrative voice, which I designate as 'the poet'. The voice is that of a constructed persona who is not necessarily identical with the poet/*Redaktor*: a 'first level'[21] voice which comments, warns, prescribes, and commands. At times this voice may use the first person pronoun 'ek', noticeably in 47 ff., to recount anecdotes from its past experiences which are germane to the theme of the gnomes. At other times, signalled by mythological allusion, the narrative voice assumes the identity of Óðinn; towards the end of the poem, the assumed identity becomes paramount, as the focus moves from human social wisdom to divine mystery and magic. In other, earlier verses, the use of 'ek' leaves open the question of the speaker's identity: both the narrative persona and Óðinn may be intuited.[22]

1.3 AN ACCOUNT OF THE GNOMIC POEM, 1–103

The Opening Movement, 1–5

(1) *Hávamál* begins with no formal introduction, nor framework, not even of the most briefly delineated kind, such as we find in *Hugsvinnsmál* or in the Old English *Exeter Maxims*. Instead the audience is plunged with startling immediacy, into a situation familiar, no doubt, to everyone in medieval Iceland: that of a traveller arriving at a farmhouse filled with unknown people:

Gáttir allar	All the entrances,
áðr gangi fram,	before one goes forward,
um skoðaz skyli,	should be scrutinized,
um skygnaz skyli;	should be spied out;
þvíat óvíst er at vita,	for there is no knowing for

| hvar óvinir | certain, whether enemies |
| sitia á fleti fyrir. | are sitting ahead in the hall. |

The first note of the poem, sounded by the subjunctive forms of the first lines, is one of hesitancy and uncertainty. The entrances, also serving as exits in case of trouble, are to be checked before the traveller even enters the hallway. He does not even know for certain whether enemies, already inimical to him, or as yet unknown, still to be made, an alternative posited later in the poem[23] — are waiting for him inside the hall. Thus the first verse sounds the ground theme of the introductory section of the poem: the necessity for wariness in all unfamiliar circumstances and the continual recurrence of such situations throughout life.

(2)   Now the poem's focus moves, almost cinematically, following the man who pauses at the door and looks carefully about him, through the doors to the hall inside. 'Gefendr heilir!' (Blessed be the giver(s)) are words of greeting, partly begging, partly sycophantic to the host(s), and, as if we are looking over the traveller's shoulder, the next lines reflect the reactions of the other people already in the hall: 'Gestr er inn kominn! hvar skal sitia siá?' (A guest has come! where is he going to sit?) showing first a slight tremor of surprise and excitement at the new arrival, and then interest in the social implications of the event — what is the newcomer's status *vis-à-vis* those already present? Will he be conducted to a seat of honour, or only shown the bare minimum of hospitality? Lines 4–6 represent the words of the prescriptor and commentator posited in 1, who grows naturally into the speaker of advice, words informed by a wry awareness that the traveller will find more than he bargains for at the fireside.

(3–5)   The traveller reaches the warmth of the hearth, and apparent security: warmth, food, and dry clothing are offered in the next verses. The outer world is briefly evoked in 3 'um fiall farit' (travelled over the mountains), but then the focus of attention passes from basic necessities — warmth and water — to the more civilized, even courtly requirements which a host ought to provide: a towel, change of clothes, a friendly welcome, and respectful silence, should the guest wish himself to speak — 'endrþǫgu' (reciprocal silence).

Stanzas 3–5 are linked together by their anaphoristic openings

(Eldz/Vitz/Vatz er þǫrf) (Fire/Water/Wits are necessary),
progressing from an emphasis on the physical requirements of the
traveller to the enumeration of less tangible needs: the importance
of alertness in society and a quick understanding of when to speak
and when to remain silent, lest, among cultivated people, one
should make a spectacle of oneself — 'verða at augabragði'.

Stanzas 1–5 form an introit that has a symbolic quality: the
generalizing effect of the gnomic tone, 'eldz er þǫrf', 'vits er
þǫrf', gives a resonance to this opening section, suggesting that
the frame of reference here is broader than the everyday situation
described.[24] The fearful approach to a new place, as well as the
desire for warmth, food, and water, parallel closely the experiences and needs of a new-born baby. The entry to the hall may be
read on both a literal and a symbolic level: the traveller
approaches the hall with trepidation, but also with an overwhelming need for that which may be found within: physical
comforts and human companionship. Enter he must for there are
advantages in this: 'dælt er heima hvat' — no wisdom is gained
from staying at home with the comfortable and familiar. We never
learn where the traveller has come from; the sole important fact is
that of his entry into the hall, finding himself thrust into an already established society where his individual qualities are as yet
unknown, just as a child comes into the world, equipped with
nothing but potentialities.

With 5 the introduction to the poem is complete: the traveller is
in the hall and his immediate physical requirements are made
known. Seated at table, he waits to see what will befall him next,
whether he will be made into an 'augabragð' (laughing-stock) by
those already present, who may perceive him as uncultivated.
Though the focus of the poem moves now to the qualities
necessary to a man in society, so that he may come through
unscathed — 'þurrfiallr' (30[6]), the tangible goods of the first
verses: fire, food, clothing, and water are never completely
forgotten. They reappear, both as literal objects, and, more
significantly, as sources for imagery throughout the Gnomic Poem
and *Loddfáfnismál*, under both positive and negative aspects. For
example, fire and flame appear as metaphors for bad friendship
and for the benefit of sociability in 51 and 57; food and drink
symbolize friendship in 52, 66, and 67; clothing symbolizes both
friendship and humanity in 41 and 49.

In the Hall, 6–9

(6) After the evocation in 5 of a man's embarrassment at his own awkwardness of wit, outclassed in good company, the problem is expressed in impersonal, gnomic terms in the first lines of 6 — a piece of didacticism that seemed to the author of *Hugsvinnsmál* a useful half-strophe for his own poem.[25] The verse warns against too much arrogant confidence in one's own perspicacity, so that vigilance slackens. The best protection when one is coming to a feast is to be 'horskr' (wise) and 'þǫgull' (silent): the importance of silence in the testing situations ahead is a theme constantly returned to in the first thirty verses.

(7) The guest is shown in the midst of the social group: 'til verðar kømr'. In a comparatively relaxed situation, compared with the tension of the opening stanzas, the guest's senses are nevertheless sharply alert, 'með þunnu hlíoði', and, as in 13, he looks about him, 'augum skoðar'. The wariness is still present, albeit in a minor key.

(8–9) These verses are linked by the contrasting 'Hinn' and 'Sá' (this man and that man); one of the goals of wisdom is introduced — happiness. In order to be 'sæll', a man must be self-reliant: 'lof' and 'líknstafi' (esteem and favour) must be acquired through a man's own good qualities, rather than as a result of another's partiality:

ódæla er við þat	very difficult is it with respect to that
er maðr eiga skal	which a man shall possess
annars brióstom í.	in another's breast.

$$(8^{4-6})$$

The contrast between 'sér' (for oneself), 'siálfr um' (by oneself), and 'annars brióstom í' provides another variation on the theme of relying only on oneself, for it is difficult to lay claim to 'lof' and 'líknstafi'; either to be certain that one is regarded as praiseworthy by others, or to win an admission of one's worth from someone else. Self-respect may be a surer gauge of one's merit than the partialities of others. Once 'lof' is gained, it must be preserved throughout the rest of one's life by one's own efforts (siálfr um). One should not rely on advice from others who may not know best, for finally, as 95 tells us, 'Hugr einn þat veit | er býr hiarta nær' (the mind alone knows what lies close to the heart).

Drunkenness, 11–14

(10–11)   Linked together by identical first halves, the deliberate
balance of 8^6 and 9^6 develops into the absolute identity of the
refrain in these two verses. Stanza 10 reiterates the advice of 5:
sharp wits are of most value when one is travelling. If the hall is a
microcosm of human society, then we may also interpret the road
'braut' as near-allegorical: the journey made on it is the journey
through life itself. 'Manvit' is not mere common sense, but rather
innate intelligence, comparable with Kynde Wit in *Piers Plowman*.[26]
Stanza 11 provides a transition to a specific focusing on drunkenness: the worst companion a man can take with him on life's
journeys. Thus a connection between innate knowledge and drink
is established, in preparation for the Odinic concerns of 13 and
14.

(12)   The themes of 'braut', 'manvit' and 'ǫl' (beer) are woven
together in 11, 12, and 13, bound by the comparatives 'betri'
(better) of 10 and 11, 'verra' (worse)in 11, 'færa' (fewer), 'fleira'
(more), and 'gott' (good), twice-repeated in 12. Thus a hierarchy
of values is established: ale is good in itself, but too much is 'verra
vegnest' (worst provision for the journey). 'Manvit' is better even
than liquor, despite the paradox explored in 13 and 14, that, for
Óðinn, alcohol was the source of a knowledge that could not
otherwise be acquired. This finely integrated series of comparisons prepares for the irruption of the mythic into the hitherto
human domain of the poem.

(13–14)   A new voice is heard, an 'ek' who reveals himself as
Óðinn. Once again a traveller enters a dangerous hall, in a
narrative which both looks back to the beginning of the poem,
and anticipates the fuller account of Óðinn's adventure with
Gunnlǫð in $10^{3–6}$. The illustration of the dangers of drunkenness
with this anecdote is strangely paradoxical; while the preceding
verses have warned of the risks involved in excessive drinking, and
its deleterious effect on human intelligence, the anecdote alludes
to a tale in which drunkenness works for the advantage both of
Óðinn and mankind. Had not Óðinn consumed the divine mead
to excess, 'ofdrykkia', the precious gift of poetry would never have
been brought to the gods and to men. Thus the advice of 11 and
12 is contradicted by the beneficial effects of drunkenness for
Óðinn. Not only does Óðinn succeed in drinking the intoxicant

without losing his 'manvit', he actually returns from the mead-drinking with an enhanced 'geð', giving a double meaning to 14⁴⁻⁶.²⁷

því er ǫlðr bazt	in this case is ale-drinking best,
at aptr uf heimtir	when each man takes home
hverr sitt geð gumi.	afterwards his own intelligence.

If we did not know the full history of the mead-winning from Snorri's account in *Skáldskaparmál*, we might well take 13–14 at face value, as an allusion to a lost tale in which Óðinn is led into danger through excessive drinking while visiting a hostile hall. The poet relies on the audience's knowledge of the complete story, just as the *Beowulf*-poet assumes a close familiarity with Scandinavian tradition and legend on the part of his audience.

Such contradictions as this, between advice given and the effect of an allusion, occur elsewhere in the Gnomic Poem. A similar contradiction is to be found in the series of verses dealing with relationships between men and women. The view of human activities taken by the poet is deliberately partial, so that a dictum valid for one situation, that women cannot be trusted (84), may be countered by another: that men are equally untrustworthy (91).

The episode then was not attracted mechanically to its present position by the drunkenness theme of 11 and 12.²⁸ Rather the precise placing of the allusion in context illustrates the care with which the poet has constructed the work. Stanzas 13 and 14 belong to a different order of poetic intensity from 11–12; the image of the 'óminnis hegri' is of a higher poetic quality than the earlier verses with their easy tone and confident contradiction of established authority, yet the entire sequence is so well integrated that it is impossible to determine whether 13/14 represent older material used as a citation, or whether 11–14 were composed by the poet.²⁹

Some Kinds of Folly, 15–18

(15) A sharp thematic break from the topic of drunkenness and withdrawal from the casual familiarity of the 'ek' in 13/14 follows. No previous hint has been given of a princely circle, the 'þióðans barn' of 15², or of fighting: 'víg' in 16³. In comparison with the tight construction, and controlled development of theme which the Gnomic Poem offers up to 14, this section shows a relaxation of poetic method, a circling round some of the themes already

established: 15, for example, returns to the theme of the importance of silence, last considered in 7, while the second half of the verse takes up again the subject of happiness from 8 and 9.

(16–18) The first of these two verses glances briefly at new topics: cowardice, the inevitability of death, in contrast to the ideal 'vígdiarft' (bold in battle) 'þióðans barn' in 15, and 'gumna hverr' (every man) who should be cheerful even though death awaits him. A new, sarcastic tone is heard; the futility of the coward's attempts to avoid danger and the behaviour of the fool at a feast are precisely observed. In language both imitative and effective, the poet evokes the fool's gaping mouth — 'Kópir afglapi' (the fool stares about), while the placing of 'uppi' at the beginning of the line enacts the speed with which the limitations of the man's intelligence are exposed when his tongue has been loosened by drink. With 'geð' in 17[6], there is a return to one of the preoccupations of 12–14, the nature of men's minds. The fool quickly makes known the quality of his intelligence, while 18, looking back to 5[1–2], suggests that the experience of travel, bringing one into contact with different people, and different types of 'geð' best equips a man to discern what kind of a mind another has.

Moderation in Food and Drink, 19–21

(19) In contrast to the 'afglapi' (fool) at the feast (17), 19 demonstrates how one should act in company. Moderation is advised not so much for its own sake, but, it is implied, because immoderate behaviour will be criticized by others; both the heavy drinker and the unsociable guest who refuses to drink at all are more liable to be accused of 'ókynnis' (bad manners) than the man who drinks a moderate amount and goes early to bed.

(20–1) Unless his intelligence prevents him, 'nema geðs viti', the gluttonwill eat himself into lifelong trouble, laughed at by judicious society. The most important consequence of over-eating, as of drinking too much is making a poor social impression, appearing 'heimskr' (foolish). In the next verse, the failure of human mental control is contrasted with the self-control of animals, who leave the pasture when they have had enough to eat.[30]

The Foolish Man's Behaviour in Society, 22–29

(22) Leaving behind the subject of physical overindulgence, the next section reveals other kinds of behaviour by which a wretched

or foolish man may be recognized. 22 takes up the unpleasantness
of mockery, first mentioned in 20³. Where 20³ evokes the misery
of the butt of mockery, the 'augabragð', 22 shows that the man
who scoffs at everything is an equally wretched creature, so
lacking in self-knowledge that he does not realize that he himself
is by no means perfect. 'Vamma vanr', is found frequently in
Christian writing[31] meaning 'free of sins'; that 'vǫmm' has non-
Christian resonances is indicated by its use in *Sonatorrek* 22 in a
similar collocation 'vamma varr' (wary of faults).[32]

(23–5) The wretched 'vesall' man may be so blinkered, and so
anxious to gain a cheap laugh that he jeers at everything he sees.
In 23, the foolish 'ósviðr' man lies awake all night worrying: both
22 and 23 describe types who are the opposite of those in 15,
neither 'þagalt' nor 'glaðr' (silent and cheerful). Stanzas 24 and
25 are linked by a refrain, as were 10 and 11, as well as by theme.
Stanza 24 deals with an ordinary social situation, recalling the hall
of the introductory section, where the over-confident fool sits with
the wise 'með snotrom'. He thinks that each of them is his friend
simply because they laugh with him, yet behind his back he is slan-
dered without his knowledge. In 25, the scene is laid at the Þing,
where the friendship of the 'viðhlæiendr vini' (the friend who
laughs with you) is put to the test and found to be spurious: no
one will plead on the fool's behalf. A similar situation is the
subject of 62, where the man who comes into a crowd 'með
mǫrgom' and has no one to speak for him, hangs his head like an
eagle over the sea. However, in 62, there is no implication that
the man's friendless state is the result of his own folly, unlike 25,
where the fool has misjudged the situation.

(26–7) Variant situations are offered: 24 and 25 have shown the
fool who believes himself to be popular because everyone smiles
at him, while 26 depicts the man who thinks that he can escape
humiliating attention by skulking in a corner. He would do better
to consider how to answer when the others in hall begin to test
him with questions ('freista hans firar'), an ordeal warned of in 2.
In formal terms, 27 completes this series of verses with another
warning against self-confidence. If, when he is being questioned
('freista hans firar' again), a man says too much, he will reveal his
stupidity more surely than if he had remained silent.

(28–9) The theme of question and answer continues. Wisdom
resides both in knowing how to answer, and how to question

others — an idea repeated in 63[1-3]. The second half of the verse
appears to have no particular connection with the first half: it
declares that people can never conceal 'því er gengr um guma',
which may mean 'that which overcomes men' (as in 94) or 'that
which is said about men'.[33] The gist is that people can never keep
secrets; interestingly the second half of 63 makes much the same
point. Stanza 29 reiterates the observation of 27, but makes a
general comment on the over-quick tongue 'hraðmælt tunga',
rather than limiting the reference to the fool.

These verses (22–9) are mainly concerned with moderation in
speech, yet this idea is not conveyed by a bald statement such as
'It is better to speak neither too much nor too little.' Rather this
section of the poem operates by positing different courses of
action and demonstrating their probable results. Thus the
limitations of each course becomes clear: the man who skulks in a
corner trying to avoid conversation is deluding himself if he
thinks that he can escape attention (26), while the man who
prattles endlessly (27) soon reveals himself as a fool. By placing
the alternatives beside one another, the proper course for the
wise man emerges gradually, becoming apparent to the audience
by a process of deduction. Now each member of the audience can
assess whether he is 'ósnotr' (foolish) or 'fróðr' (wise) according
to the definitions offered in this section.

Mockery, 30–32

(30)   Mockery, first mentioned at 5[3-4], and touched on in 22,
reappears. The 'hraðmælt' tongue in 29, which brings trouble to
its owner unless kept in check, may also, we infer, be guilty of
thoughtless mockery. The mischief-makers in hall, whose attempts
to make newcomers look foolish by questioning them have been a
cause for anxiety in the preceding verses, are at fault.[34] The verse
complements 5[3-4]: where the earlier verse warned that the
ignorant man will become a laughing-stock among the wise 'með
snotrom', this stanza criticizes those who mock for sport. Yet the
mockers serve a useful purpose, for a man's true qualities are only
elicited in conversation as the emphasis of the second half of the
verse shows. The man who thinks himself wise merely because he
has not been shown to be foolish, is guilty of self-delusion. Stanza
28, as also 63, stresses the importance of knowing how to question
the wise man; such questioning, we may suppose, is the best way

of discovering the true nature of other people: 'hverio geði I stýrir gumna hverr' (18⁴⁻⁵).

(31–3) The setting for 30 is once again a social occasion, a visit to friends or kinsmen; the generalized observations of the previous section give way to a more precise location. The ground shifts slightly in 31: mockery of others is particularly unwise if you do not know for certain the qualities of your victim, for you may be making yourself a dangerous enemy. Stanza 32 remarks that even people who are normally well-disposed (gagnhollir) to one another can become quarrelsome at a feast; a truth documented by numerous incidents in the sagas.[35] Stanza 33 leaves mockery and argument behind, prescribing behaviour proper to the man who is intending to make a visit. Although eating early in the day is normally desirable, the visitor should delay his meal, so that he does not arrive at his host's absolutely famished, unable to make conversation while he is busily gobbling his food. 'Snópir'(gaze hungrily about) has an almost onomatopoeic quality, as does 'kópir' (goggle) in 17¹, and 'snapir ok gnapir' (snapping and stretching forward) in 62¹.

Friendship, 34–52

This section of *Hávamál* comprises one of the largest thematic groups in the Gnomic Poem: friendship lies at the very heart of the poem. Earlier warnings about caution, wariness, moderation, silence build now to an articulation of a counter-urge to forge links with others, a revolt against the need for restraint, and tension in one's relationships with others. The verses in this section are linked by a thematic similarity, yet without duplication; although almost twenty verses treat the theme, each offers an individual variation. For example, 42 and 45 appear to be almost identical in sentiment. However, the first of these verses assumes that a friend is to be taken at face value until treachery is proven; deceit may be undertaken against a friend when he has been the first to act dishonestly. The second allows that suspicion alone offers sufficient grounds for entrapping the friend in deception. The logical connections between one verse and the next are relatively simple to trace as the poet allows his complex vision of the nature of friendship to unfold.

Some friends have appeared already in the Gnomic Poem: the first and most trustworthy is native wit 'manvit mikit' in 6⁹, 10, and

11, while unreliable friends have been sketched in 24 and 25. The understanding of life as a journey informs the Gnomic Poem throughout, and, to some extent, *Loddfáfnismál.* The image of the road is first used in 10 and 11 ('brautu at'), although 'um fiall farit' (travelled over the mountains) in 3[6] is arguably the first reference to the journey, a solitary experience with no specific goal, contrasting with the communal existence in the hall, signifying man's activities as a social being. Having established the basic oppositions of hall: road, man in society: man alone, the poet is free to play with them. The road image is elaborated in 34 with an elusive irony:

Afhvarf mikit	It is a great detour
er til illz vinar,	to go to a bad friend's,
þótt á brautu búi;	though he live on the way;
en til góðs vinar	but to a good friend's
liggia gagnvegir,	there are direct routes,
þótt hann sé firr farinn.	though he has gone far away.

(34)

Two types of 'braut', the 'afhvarf' and the 'gagnvegir' are sketched, along which a man may travel in life's journey, yet, paradoxically, these allegorical paths do not correspond to the literal distances involved. The metaphor of the difficult path is varied once again in the reprise of the friendship theme in *Loddfáfnismál* (119). Here the channels of communication become blocked through neglect, the 'hrís' representing the obstacles and misunderstandings which arise. The road image in 34 prepares for the anecdotes drawn from the wayfarer's experience in 47 ff.

(35) The visitor is urged to go on his way in due time and not to outstay his welcome. The prescriptive, pragmatic tone of 33 returns, warning bluntly that even the 'liúfr' (beloved) can become 'leiðr' (hateful) if he lingers too long. This useful formulaic pair[36] reappears in 40, sounding a minor theme in this section. The opposition underlies the contrast of good and bad friends in the verses which follow, hinting at the possibility of transformation in human relationships. The 'liúfr' friend of 35 could become 'leiðr'; the possessions which one hoards up for those one loves can fall into the hands of an enemy; the friend who seems so affectionate has become an enemy by the time six

days have passed (51). Stanza 35 marks the close of the 'guest in hall' theme; from here the poem broadens out into the larger landscape of the farm 'bú' and the plain 'vǫllr' of 36–7 and 38[2].

(36–7) The emphasis hitherto on receiving the hospitality of others is counterbalanced by a paradigm of independence. A friendly visit 'til kynnis' (to kinsfolk), — although fraught with the possibility of being ridiculed — is all very well, the poem implies, but too much dependence causes an inner bitterness:

blóðugt er hiarta   bloody is the heart
þeim er biðia skal   of the man who has to ask
sér í mál hvert matar.   for food on every occasion.
                                              (37[3–6])

The minimum standard of living which a man needs for his own self-respect, 'halr er heima hverr' (everyone is someone at home) repeated twice for emphasis — is exemplified with the precision of Yeats's nine bean-rows: two goats and a rope-thatched roof are sufficient.

(38) Another abrupt change in tone follows these confident assertions of the value of independence: 38[37] returns to the cautious, defensive tone of the opening stanzas. There the unknown danger lay indoors in the hall, now the danger is out on the open road. References to weapons and fighting are few in Hávamál; less open forms of aggression — backbiting and mockery — have been the concern until now.

(39–40) Stanza 39 seems to link back to 37, for the implication of l. 2 'svá matar góðan' (so generous with food) is that only a generous man is likely to provide for the man with no means of support sketched in the earlier verse. This wry look at the wealthy man, who nevertheless always accepts any gift offered, leads into a more general consideration of generosity in 40: one should be generous with one's property, for what one has saved up for the 'liúfr' may end up in the hands of the 'leiðr'. Stanza 40 sounds the first note of the crucial theme of instability which runs throughout the second half of the Gnomic Poem. At first it is riches and property which are seen to be fickle — 'svá er auðr | sem augabragði | hann er valtastr vina' 78[3–6], but this understanding merges in 85–7, 89[38] into a perception of everything as undependable, from women to boiling kettles, from snakes to princes. 'Orztírr' (reputation) and 'dómr' (fame) (76[4],

77[6]) are left isolated as the only exceptions to this general rule.
(41–2)   The admonition to generosity in 40 flows into an illustration of gift-giving, an actualization of the general observation:

> Vápnum ok váðom   With weapons and garments
> skolo vinir gleðiaz —   should friends gladden one another —
> þat er á siálfum sýnst;   that is most manifest;
>
> (41[1–3])

Gifts must both be given and received if a friendship is to endure.
Simple gift-giving is expanded into the notion of a more complete
reciprocity in 42 where the second half — with an unexpected
cynical twist — urges the repayment of laughter (presumably a
false *bonhomie* — as in 46[3]) with laughter, and 'lausung við lygi'.
(43)   The idea of 42[1–2] that one should be a friend to one's
friend, is now developed further. The verse plays with further
possibilities, as if constructing a table of possible relationships:
one should be a friend to one's friend's friend, but not to one's
enemy's friends.[39] The fact that 'vinr' and 'óvinr' share the same
root permits a deft verbal switching between the two oppositions,
almost too quickly for the audience to be able to untangle the
meaning of 'óvinar vinar vinr' and to decide whether this is a
desirable or undesirable state to be in.
(44–6)   Another, deeper kind of reciprocity, necessary to keep
friendship alive is now suggested: not only should gifts be ex-
changed, but also ideas and confidences: 'geðs skaltu við þann
blanda' — literally 'you should mix your mind with his'. Frequent
visits also keep the friendship alive, looking back to 34 and the
metaphor of the short cut, as well as forward to *Loddfáfnismál* 119.
Stanza 45 returns to the bad friend, whose friendship may yet,
paradoxically, be turned to some good. Speaking fairly and
thinking falsely 'fagrt/flátt' are recommended as policy with the
false friend, a dissembling which men employ with women,
according to 91[4–6]:

> þá vér fegrst mælom   then we speak most fairly
> er vér flást hyggiom;   when we think most falsely;
> þat tælir horska hugi.   that entraps the wise mind.

Stanza 46 almost repeats 45, except that laughter, as in 41, is
seen as an appropriate response to the false friend, linking back

to the 'viðhlæiendr vini' of 25[1] and 26[1]. With this the problem of
the bad friend is left behind, for the verses which follow regard
friendship as an absolute good, contrasting it, not with enmity or
falseness, but with the loneliness of the solitary traveller. The
preceding verses have been detached, judicious, pragmatic to the
point of cynicism in tone; now emotional floodgates are opened,
climaxing in the final rhetorical question of 50.

With the change in tone comes a change in perspective: for the
articulation of the deeply personal perception of the overwhelming need humans have for one another's company, the
poet adopts the first person pronoun 'ek'. From the opening
stanzas, where an unknown man enters the hall — 'Gestr er inn
kominn!' — the possibility of an Odinic presence has been
available to the poet, for Gestr[40] could be an Odinic name as well
as 'guest'. Thus in 47 and the verses which follow: 'ek' represents
both the 'poet', an experienced speaker, such as we find in *The
Wanderer*, recounting anecdotes from his own travels in order to
illustrate a general point, and also Óðinn (the referent of 'ek' in
13 and 14), who wanders in disguise, seeking wisdom wherever it
may be found.[41]

(47) The evocation of loneliness in 47 is rendered in explicitly
human terms:

Ungr var ek forðom,	Young I was long ago,
fór ek einn saman;	I journeyed all alone;
þá varð ek villr vega;	then I went astray on the paths;
auðigr þóttumz	rich I thought myself
er ek annan fann;	when I found another;
maðr er mannz gaman.	man is the delight of man.[42]

The verse depicts an absence of friendship, a deprivation of
companionship — emphasized by the alliteration of the first line
on 'einn' — which recalls the situation of the friendless man
forced to travel alone in the Old English *Exeter Maxims*.[43] 'Manvit
mikit' may be better than riches in a difficult situation, according
to 10, but a companion is wealth indeed.

(48) This verse veers away from the subject of friendship; just
such a sharp break as at 15. The first half sums up the findings of
the previous section in the matter of generosity: ultimately it is the
generous, and — in a return to the views of 15 — brave man who
has the best life. The second half offers a contrasting picture of

the unhappy lives led by the coward, always terrified (as in v.16), and the miser anxious about the gifts he must give in return for those received.

(49) Back on the 'vǫllr', out on the plain, the poet tells how he gave his clothes to two *trémenn*.[44] The gift delights them, increasing their self-esteem by improving their appearance — 'rekkar þat þóttuz'. The moral which the poet draws from this, 'neiss er nøkkviðr halr' — the naked man is ashamed — may be interpreted in the light of 41 and 44: the giving of clothing is a symbol of friendship: 'vápnom ok váðom | skolo vinir gleðiast'(with weapons and clothes should friends make one another glad) 41[1-2]. The *trémenn* are thus drawn into the web of reciprocal relationships which constitutes society: the gift makes the wooden men human. Their delight is not so much in the finery, but in the simple fact that they have a friend to give them gifts. Similarly, the *trémaðr* in *Ragnars saga* speaks some verses lamenting his neglect; formerly the sons of Ragnar would sacrifice to him, but now: 'hlýr hvorki mér | hold né klæði' (nor protects me flesh nor clothing) (20[6-8]). The implication seems to be that previously the *trémaðr* was given clothes as part of a sacrificial ritual.

(50–1) The 'þǫll' (fir) of 50 is as bereft of protective covering as the *trémenn*: it has neither bark nor needles. Structurally identical; wooden, upright, and naked, the fir is a *trémaðr* to whom no one has given 'váðir', and so comparable with the man whom no one loves. The profound emotional identification of the poet with both the *trémenn* and the fir-tree culminates in the plaintive final lines of 50:

svá er maðr	so it is with the man
sá er manngi ann;	whom no one loves;
hvat skal hann lengi lifa?	how should he live for long?

The expression of man's passionate need for companionship now modulates into a cooler, more considered reflection on excessive affection in friendship. Stanza 51 depicts a powerful infatuation— 'friðr' often has sexual connotations[45] — a false feeling which flares up 'eldr heitari' for a short while, but when the fire burns out, no friendly feelings survive the disillusionment: 'versnar allr vinskapr'. Violent emotions stirred by the ending of friendship, rather than its inception, are suggested in 121 through equally powerful imagery.

(52) 52 appears, on first reading, to share the detached, cooler tone of 51, almost to the point of seeming calculating:

Mikit eitt	Not just a big gift
skala manne gefa:	should a man give a man:
opt kaupir sér í litlo lof;	often one buys oneself praise
með hálfum hleif	with little; with half a loaf
ok með hǫllu keri	and a tilted cup
fekk ek mér félaga.	I got myself a companion.

Half a loaf and a tilted cup may seem little indeed; but if, as has been suggested,[46] they represent an exact half share of the giver's resources, then the gift is a mark of sensible generosity. Cynical calculation does not enter into the Gnomic Poem's concept of friendship: such considerations are exclusive to *Loddfáfnismál.* This verse marks the end of the friendship sequence; the effect of what has gone before shows that the intention of the giver here is not to 'kaupa lof' but rather to get a 'félagi' for his journeyings.

The Limitations of Wisdom, 53–6

The next sequence of verses, unusually, is concerned with the limitations of that wisdom which a man can gain in life.

(53) The first verse of the sequence evokes the limited nature of men's understanding — 'lítil geðs' — through the implicit comparison with 'lítilla sanda, lítilla sæva' '(of, by) small shores (of, by) small seas', an image resonant with a number of possibilities and interpretations, literal and metaphysical. Ocean and sand normally convey infinity, the boundless, open space of the sea, and the uncountable grains of sand on the beach. Yet here this infinity is paradoxically modified by 'lítill', so that the image is at once enormous and tiny. In the same way, the juxtaposition of the minds of men, 'geð guma', with 'sandar' and 'sjávar' suggests that the human mind can be boundless, ranging through time and space, and capable of a myriad thoughts, while at the same time limited by human perceptions and understanding. Like the sea and the sand, 'geð' contains infinity within itself, but yet it is confined.

On a more literal level, the qualifying — or adverbial —genitive of 'lítilla sanda, lítilla sæva' implies that the man who lives isolated in a remote, narrow fjord (a small sea with small shores), will not be as wise as other men — for all men are not 'iafnspakir':[47]

því allir men   for all men
urðot iafnspakir;   have never become equally wise;
hálf er ǫld hvar.   mankind is, overall, half wise, half not.

The last half verse is rueful in tone, admitting that we cannot expect everyone in this world to be clever, given the unequal opportunities available for developing cleverness.

The verse presents the opposite of 18 and 57; the man who is not exposed to a variety of other people is 'dœlskr', foolishly self-absorbed.[48] The mathematical precision of 'iafnspakir' and 'hálf' in the last half of the verse leads into the 'meðalsnotr' of the next stanzas, which rehearse the comfortableness of being averagely wise. From the resigned acceptance of human limitation, there is an optimistic turn of thought: it is, in some ways, an advantage to be only middling wise, rather than All-wise (Alvíss) like the eponymous hero of *Alvíssmál*.[49]

(54–6) The next three verses drive home their moral by repeating it in the first half of each verse: the averagely wise man, 'er vel mart vito' — who knows a fair amount — has the best sort of life (54), while the wise man is seldom happy (55). Stanza 56 offers a definition of what 'snotr' means in this context: contemplation of sad things:

Meðalsnotr   Averagely wise
skyli manna hverr,   should every man be,
æva til snotr sé;   never too wise;
ørlǫg sín   his fate
viti engi fyrir;   let no man know beforehand;
þeim er sorgalausastr sefi. his is the most carefree soul.

To be 'meðalsnotr', a man must deliberately rein in his curiosity, not actively try to discover his fate. Control and choice are once more at issue; but these are within the wise man's own power, not imposed by the constricting circumstances of the narrow fjord-existence.

The ostensible advocacy of a middle position between the two poles of wise man and fool is difficult to parallel, although the warning that wisdom seldom brings happiness is found in other wisdom literatures.[50] While the idea of moderation in wisdom may be seen as an extension of the theme of moderation in eating and drinking, focused on in 19–29, the recommendation of the 'meðalsnotr' man's position is only partial. The deliberately limited wisdom of the 'meðalsnotr' man is to be distinguished from that of the man who knows what common sense is, 'sá er vitandi er vits' (18[6]) or from other types of wisdom elaborated later in the poem.

(57) Breaking away from such measured weighing of the advantages and disadvantages of being wise, the verse returns to the imagery of the physical world with a striking image of flames and sparks. In the same way, a man is stimulated by others to be wise in his speech, but if he remains absorbed in himself, he becomes too 'dœlskr', too introverted. The fire image recalls the cheerful blaze of 2, promising comfort and warmth at the same time as providing a test of conversational abilities; the fickle flame of a bad friendship (51) is also to be sensed.

Stanza 57 extends the conclusions of the friendship section about the importance of companionship beyond the simple realization of 47— 'maðr er mannz gaman' — to consider the role of companionship in the acquisition of wisdom: 'maðr af manni | verðr at máli kuðr'. The value of eloquence, contrasting with the advisability of silence earlier in the poem[51] is to be restated with increasing emphasis in the last movement of the Gnomic Poem, culminating in the demonstration of its usefulness in the 'Gunnlǫð Episode'.

Energy and Preparation, 58–62

Now comes another sharp break in the development of the train of thought: the next sequence focuses on foresight and self-command, the control of that which can be controlled even when material resources are limited.

(58–9) Early rising as a key to success is the moral of 58 and 59. The first verse strikes a ferocious tone, in which the suggested purpose for the day's activities is taking one's neighbour's life or property — the vigorous man who does not linger in bed appropriately compared with the wolf, a detail which also appears in Saxo.[52] This ferocity seems to contrast with the scene in the second verse, where rising early is a practical aspect of successful farm management. Yet failure to rise early is a motif known from the sagas, where it may have deadly consequences.[53]

(60) The depiction of an organized, energetic life continues: a man can calculate the quantity of firewood and roofing materials he will need in a given season. The detail is as precise as the

minimum requirements of the smallholder in 36: we are again in the milieu of the hard-working cotter with limited resources. Line 3 'þess kann maðr miǫt' draws an implicit contrast between timber, which can be reckoned (especially given the limited amount of this commodity available in Iceland), and less quantifiable elements in life.

(61) As in 33, the man who has eaten will be in better command of himself: no one should allow limited means to lower his self-respect. The unusual sequence of first lines, 'þveginn ok mettr' (washed and fed), 'snapir ok gnapir' (snapping and stretching forward) has an energy and forcefulness which accords well with the vigorous theme of the verses.

(62) At first this verse seems to offer a swift transition to a natural image, but in fact it continues with the theme of foresight. The hungry sea-eagle is compared with the man who arrives at the Þing to find that, like the man in 25, he only has a few supporters. At a loss, he opens and shuts his mouth and cranes his neck to look for help. Just as a man does well to ensure a supply of roofing and wood for the season, so is it advisable to secure in advance supporters for a case at the Þing.

A Casual Sequence of General Observations, 63, 64, and 65

(63)   The next three verses are a relatively unstructured and disconnected series of general observations. Stanza 63 has been mentioned above in connection with 28; here the observation: 'Fróðr sá þykkiz | er fregna kann | ok segia it sama' (Wise that man seems who knows how to ask questions and likewise to answer) is rendered prescriptive.

(64–5)   To find in *Hávamál* as much as a half-verse repeated elsewhere is unusual. Stanza 64[4–6] varies a verse in *Fáfnismál*, in which Sigurðr, having just struck Fáfnir a deadly blow, counters the dragon's threats and warnings with gnomic remarks:

þá þat finnr	then he finds
er með fleirom kømr,	when he comes among the multitude,
at engi er einna hvatastr.	that no one is bravest of all.

(Fáfnismál 17[4–6])

Hávamál gives 'frœknom' — warriors instead of 'fleirom' in l. 5, but is otherwise virtually identical. Both verses concern themselves with the exercise of power: in *Fáfnismál*, the dragon speaks of his 'œgishjálm', the helm of terror with which he ruled; Sigurðr responds that such power cannot be absolute. In *Hávamál* the subject is the 'ráðsnotra' man, the man wise in counsel, advised to make only moderate use of his power, for it may not be absolute. The repeated half-verse is perhaps a tag which could be used to form a concluding half-strophe in several gnomic contexts. Stanza 65 appears to be a warning against idle talk, a variation on 29^{4-6} and 63^{4-6}.

Experiences while Journeying, 66 and 67

In contrast to the loose construction and assortment of themes in 63–5, these two verses, representing the third statement of the theme of the wayfarer, are carefully structured, recounting the experience of untimely arrival at the houses of others.

(66–7) These ironically realistic anecdotes, reinforced by the use of 'ek', contrast with the idealized experience of the stranger in the introductory verses, where food and drink were freely available to the chilled traveller. Stanza 67 is to be understood as parallel to 66: in the first verse the speaker complains that he is never in the right place at the right time, for either the ale has been drunk, or else it has not yet been brewed; with a rueful shrug he blames his bad timing on his unpopularity (he is 'leiðr'). Stanza 67 continues the theme.[54]

The Good Things of Life, 68–72

(68) The thematic use of food and drink, necessities dependent on other men's generosity, in the preceding verse leads to a third necessity, independent of human intervention: warmth, from fire or the sun.[55] A swift change of tone, from the cynical pessimism of the unpopular guest in 66–7 to an exhortation to count one's blessings, is effected. The 'blessings' are simple, the radiance of the sun, the innocence of a pure life — living without shame is posited as the fourth good, recalling the importance of reputation in 8 and 9.[56]

(69) This verse, optimistic and pragmatic, lists various kinds of benefit which even the man who lacks the good health of 68 can enjoy: kinsmen, sons, property. Family relationships are evoked for the first time, rather than the friends who have formed the main social framework hitherto.

(70) The sheer fact of being alive is the greatest good as 70

makes clear. Stanzas 9, 15, 16, and 50 have hinted delicately at the possibility of life coming to an end; 70 and the verses following abandon euphemism, speaking openly, even bluntly of death. Without life, none of the other benefits, health, family, property can be enjoyed. With the brief glimpse of the rich man by his hearth enjoying the fire for the last time, as death waits for him outside the door, the poet shows us that life is the real wealth.

(71–2) Next, people are shown coping with their disabilities and leading useful lives. Even the blind man, whose disability is perhaps the worst of all, is in a better state than the dead man who is of no use to anyone: 'nýtr manngi nás'; man is finally nothing more than carrion. Yet in 72 the corpse is once more restored to the status of human: 'genginn guma' (the departed man), an ancient euphemism is employed. The verse offers a surprising, inevitably ironic consolation for the dead man; though he can get no other joy of his posthumous child[57] he can still derive some benefit if the child erects a memorial[58] to commemorate him.

Uncertain Things: Wealth, Women, 73–89

(73–4) A sudden change in metre echoes a sharp break in theme; a sequence of brief, proverbial statements, some paralleled elsewhere,[59] generates a change in tone from the solemn, meditative stanzas which precede it, to a jerky and more cynical voice. The proverbial matter is combined in an introduction to the theme of uncertainty, a theme sounded already in the warnings against trusting 'viðhlæiendr vini' (25), and against assuming that wealth can insulate against the unpleasant fact of death (70). The treacherous nature of riches, hinted at in 70, is revealed explicitly in 75 and in 78 (auðr er . . . valtastr vina) (Wealth is . . . the most fickle of friends). Stanzas 73 and 74 are a proverbial demonstration of unreliable things: words, external appearances, and the weather. The proverbs produce a sense of vulnerability: man is once more alone, facing the world, as in 47ff., rather than controlling his own existence on a little farm (59–61). The cumulative effect of 73 and 74 is to show that only changeability is predictable, in preparation for the *málaháttr* stanzas of 81 ff.

(75) The first lines 'Veita hinn | er vætki veit' (He knows who knows nothing) echo 27[7–8], a tag which works well in context

there, but which offers some difficulties here. The lines have probably been borrowed unthinkingly as an introductory formula for the thought that wealth makes fools of men, further developed in 78 and 79. Just as a man cannot be blamed for falling in love (93, 94), nor should he be blamed for poverty.

(76–7) As the theme of mortality, hitherto submerged, is brought to light in 70–3, the focus of the Gnomic Poem widens out from the relatively superficial wisdom of the earlier sections of *Hávamál*, encompassing the everyday conduct of life, to a more philosophical consideration of ultimate truths. This movement is not sudden; rather there is a gradual deepening of the level of the poem's engagement with human existence. The poetic method of *Hávamál*: circling back to recapitulate and illuminate anew themes already established, then slowly unravelling the next strand of thought, allows a leisured yet steady progression towards the dramatic climax of 76 and 77.

Deyr fé,	Cattle die,
deyja frændr,	kinsmen die,
deyr siálfr it sama;	the self dies likewise;
en orztírr	but glory
deyr aldregi	never dies
hveim er sér góðan getr.	for him who gets himself good (fame).

In contrast to the studied reluctance to mention the fact of death in earlier verses (for example, death sketched as an unarticulated alternative to 'meðan lifir' (93)), the insistent, thudding syllables of 'deyr/deyja' in 76 and 77 are inescapable. 'Dómr' and 'orztírr' alone can outlive death; a conclusion prepared for as early as 8 and 9, where the possession of 'lof' (esteem) is equated with happiness. 'Orztírr', a good reputation perpetuated by others, is seen as the ultimate Good in *Hávamál*: the recognition of an essentially secular moral worth.[60]

(78)   Now a reprise of the theme of 75: 'valtastr vina' is a metaphorical recasting of wealth as the unreliable friend of 42–6. The juxtaposition of this verse with 76 and 77 suggests that fame outlasts both riches and life; the sons of Fitjungr, famous — perhaps proverbial — for having lost their wealth, are left only with the reputation of former prosperity and the staff of the beggar. Their 'dómr' outlasts their riches, but not in the desirable sense of 76–7.[61]

(79) Concluding the examination of the theme of riches, and the last comment on the 'ósnotr maðr' (foolish man), whose distinguishing characteristics were outlined in 23–7, 79 links the delusions of self-conceit which wealth brings to the delusions caused by sexual conquests, 'fljóðs munuð', the next major thematic preoccupation of the Gnomic Poem. Such worldly success brings an increase in the self-esteem with which the 'ósnotr maðr' regards himself: 'metnaðr',[62] but not in his common sense (manvit). The result is a steady progress into the mire of self-delusion, into which, like an unheeding animal, he sinks deeper and deeper: 'ganga driúgt í'.

(80) Now comes a sudden, unexpected break from the gnomic; a vatic utterance signalling the poet's intention to pass beyond the human and earthbound to the realm of the rune, the 'ginnregin' and 'fimbulþulr'. A link with the preceding verse is provided by the syntax, which pretends that such wisdom as in 79 is also to be elicited from the runes: (þat er þá reynt | er þú at rúnum spyrr). 'Þú' — each member of the audience, later represented by Loddfáfnir — will, it is promised, have the social wisdom of the Gnomic Poem confirmed by what can be learned from the runes. In the event, nothing more about the runes is recounted except their origins and effect upon Óðinn (138 ff.), although the Eddic poem *Sigrdrífumál* gives evidence of the relevance of runic knowledge to such ordinary human concerns as giving birth, healing, and preventing law-suits.[63] The subject of l.6 remains obscure: 'hann' (he) is perhaps a general enquirer after wisdom, for 'hann' is used most frequently in the Gnomic Poem in reference to a hypothetical foolish man 'ósnotr maðr'.

Complete transition to the mystical realm is delayed until 104 ff., where Óðinn's adventure with Gunnlǫð the winning of the mead of poetry, locates the scene of the poem's action outside the human world for the first time since 13–14. The metrical irregularity of the verse brings to an end the leisurely, discursive *ljóðaháttr* for the time being, in preparation for the ritualistic *málaháttr* and *galdralag* chant which follows.

(81–3) Anticipated by the proverbial catalogues of 73 and 74, the loose metre permits an eclectic range of observations. Although 81–3 burst forth in a torrent of single statements, each verse has a distinct character. While 81 cynically warns that unknown quantities are not to be relied upon until they have been consumed: the day, women, swords, ale, 82, incorporating another proverbial statement, 'mǫrg eru dags augu' (many are the eyes of the day), explains how to make use of other unpredictable phenomena: women, ships, weather, ice, a theme which continues into the first lines of 83, before modulating into a series of tips for the profitable rearing of horses and dogs — tips rooted in the practicality of everyday farming, and the audience's own experience, reassuring them — and us — of the validity of the other observations in these stanzas.

Foremost among the unpredictable creatures in these verses are women: out of the stream of ideas a single current begins to emerge. Apart from the reference to 'fljóðs munuð' in 79, women have been absent from *Hávamál* hitherto: the poet remedies this now with an extensive overview of the character of woman and the relations between the sexes which occupies most of the rest of the Gnomic Poem.

(84) In 81–3 woman is viewed as a freak of nature, one more uncertain factor in the management of life. Now the poet becomes aware of woman as Other, a creature which, unlike the weather, can speak and feel, and he warns of the innate deceitfulness of women: no man should trust the words of maiden nor married woman:

því at á hverfanda hvéli	for on a turning wheel
váru þeim hjǫrtu skopu	were their hearts made,
brigð í brióst um lagið.	changeableness lodged in the breast.

The 'hverfandi hvél' evokes a potter's wheel, or perhaps a turning lathe. The moon, characterized as a 'hverfandi hvél' in *Alvíssmál* 14, also underlies the image of the wheel here, for the moon's changing form is a symbol of inconstancy in many cultures, and the rhythms of its waxing and waning are those of the menstrual cycle, dictating the pattern of women's lives, as the term 'tunglmein' (menstruation) makes clear.[64]

(85–9) The characterization of women as untrustworthy gives a clue to the puzzle of the catalogue[65] which follows: a riddling list of things which clearly have something in common, since they are grouped together, but what? The answer is given in 88[2] and reiterated in 89[7–8]: 'verðit maðr svá tryggr | at þessu trúi ǫllo' (let no man be so trusting as to trust all these). Women as archetypes

of treachery are almost forgotten: only the bed-talk of women,
'brúðar beðmálom' (86[5]) recalls the starting-point of the
catalogue.

Men versus Women, 90–110

(90) Lest this long list of perils should have dissipated the impact
of the warning about women in 84, the poet returns to the
subject. Dangerous enterprises, as fraught with danger as the love
of a deceitful woman, are enumerated; one unlikely condition
piled upon another in a comic *tour de force* of exaggeration until
the very premise of the first lines is undercut by the excess:

Svá er friðr kvenna,	So is the love of women,
þeira er flátt hyggia,	those who think falsely,
sem aki ió óbryddom	like driving a horse, with
	unspiked hoofs,
á ísi hálom,	on slippery ice,
teitom, tvévetrom,	a frisky two-year-old,
ok sé tamr illa,	and badly broken-in,
eða í byr óðom,	or in a raging wind,
beiti stiórnlauso,	steering a rudderless boat,
eða skyli haltr henda	or having to catch when lame
hrein í þáfialli.	a reindeer on a thawing hillside.

It is the woman's capacity for falseness, 'flátt hyggia', which
prevents the exasperated man from controlling her; while he
attempts to direct her in one way, driving her like a horse or
steering her like a boat, she intends to go in quite a different
direction. The woman has a mind of her own, which may not be
revealed by her words: speech is a strategy by which the 'geð' is
concealed.

(91) The humour partly counterbalances the accusation of 84, —
'meyjar orð skyli manngi trúa' — and prepares for the Tiresias-
like voice of 91, where men's falsity to women is freely admitted,
an admission rare in other wisdom literatures:

Bert ek nú mæli,	Now I speak plainly,
þvíat ek bæði veit,	since I know both,
brigðr er karla hugr konom;	changeable is the mind of men
	towards women;

Once more, as in 47–9 and 66–7, 'ek' represents both the poet and Óðinn, but here Óðinn's voice sounds more strongly, for the charges of 'brigð' made against both women and men are to be substantiated by anecdotes from Óðinn's experiences with 'Billings mær' and with Gunnlǫð.

Sexual success is a matter of intelligence, of pitting 'hugr' against 'hugr', attempting to deceive the woman's 'horska hugi' by means of flattery. The strategy is outlined in 91³⁻⁶ and further developed in 92. Pretty speeches and the offer of money are put forward as methods of gaining physical love — 'ást', and access to the woman's body — 'líki . . . ens liósa mans'. The moral of the verse: 'sá fær er friár' (he who flatters, gets), cynically advocates wooing to one end only: sexual satisfaction. Nevertheless, *Hávamál* makes a categorical distinction between this type of casual encounter between men and women and the more serious relationship possible with a 'góð kona' as close confidante and adviser. Such a relationship is recommended in *Loddfáfnismál*, where Loddfáfnir is warned that promises made in order to win the woman must be kept (130⁸⁻⁹).

Most wisdom literatures tend to depict women in only two possible roles: the virtuous wife and mother, whose 'price is far above rubies', or the dangerous temptation, whose 'house is the way to hell, going down to the chambers of death'.⁶⁶ *Hávamál*'s sexual game-playing, epitomized by the sparring between Óðinn and 'Billings mær', is unique.

(93) Next comes the strikingly perceptive idea that a woman's beauty may affect the wise man where the fool fails to respond to it, a subtle and unusual observation in comparison with the cruder, misogynist perceptions of love found in other wisdom literatures.⁶⁷ Hence no one should be blamed for being ensnared by love; the condition is no more one's own fault than poverty, as 75⁴⁻⁶ show.

(94–5) Articulating a more usual tribute to the mighty powers of love, 'sá inn mátki munr', 94 suggests the alarming possibility of transformation from wise man, the ideal of the Gnomic Poem hitherto, into fool, the *bête noire* of the earlier part of the poem. Stanza 95 demonstrates how this transformation may come about: in a return to the theme of 'the mind', the wise man ensnared in the first stages of love, completely absorbed in the love object and his own condition, as delineated in 97⁴⁻⁶, can be satisfied by nothing else. Such self-absorption, comparable with 'dul' in 79, blunts the wise man's usual receptivity and lively awareness of his surroundings, so that he becomes 'heimskr', engrossed in a narrow field of perception.

Óðinn's Adventure with 'Billings mær', 96–102.

As evidence of women's fickleness, 'hugbrigð', towards men, Óðinn recounts the tale of his abortive love-tryst with 'Billings mær'. The story is scarcely told with high seriousness: we experience the gap between Óðinn's expectations, as he sits in the reeds, and his hostile reception at the woman's house, as a comic shock, a joke against the god himself.

(96) Óðinn's tone in telling the tale of his deception is rueful: reminiscent in 96[6] and 102[6-9] of the luckless traveller in 66–7. The moral of the tale of 'Billings mær', is not so much that which Óðinn draws in 102, but rather that of 66–7: 'sjaldan hittir leiðr í lið' (seldom does the unpopular man find the right time), an ego-bruising conclusion. Stanza 96 links back to the preceding sequence, 'þat ek þá reynda' (that I experienced then) referring to the subject of 95, the lover's total absorption in the love-object. As Óðinn sits in the reeds, nothing but 'Billings mær' seems of importance: 'hold ok hiarta | var mér in horska mær' (heart and flesh was the wise woman to me). The woman is radiantly beautiful, 'sólhvíta' 97[3], but the quality which seems to attract Óðinn most is her intelligence: 'horska mær' 96[5], 'it ráðspaka' 102[5], 'it horska man' 102[8]. While he craves her sexual love 'gaman' 99[6] he also covets her 'geð', her innermost liking.

(97–8) The story is briefly and allusively told, but the events are clear enough. Óðinn attempts to seduce 'Billings mær' (Billingr's wife seems the most likely translation, given the stated possibility of accusations of 'flærð' (social disgrace)).[68] His first attempt upon her, perhaps breaking into her house, since he finds her 'beðiom á', in 97, is met in 98 with a cleverly worded speech in which the woman quotes the proverbial wisdom of 82[3-4] back at Óðinn to win herself time to elude his designs:

myrkri [skal] við man spialla	in darkness should one whisper with a girl
mǫrg eru dags augo;	many are the eyes of the day;
Auk nær apni	And near evening
skaltu, Óðinn, koma,	shall you, Óðinn, come,

ef þú vilt þér mæla man;   if you want to win yourself a
                      girl with words;
                        (98[1-3])

Quick thinking and a ready, persuasive answer are a means of escape for the woman; an appeal for discretion in view of the social stigma of discovery 'slíkan lǫst'[69] convinces Óðinn, who pictures himself as a courtly wooer – 'jarl' 97[4], and he retreats. The events of 96[1-3] are best understood as occurring after this first encounter: Óðinn whiles away the afternoon among the reeds, waiting for darkness 'nær apni' and looking forward to his 'munar'; an expectation which he now realizes was never justified: 'þeygi ek hana at heldr hefik' (yet I did not have her any the more). (99–101) Now Óðinn sets off hopefully for the assignation, but is too early; the hall retainers are still awake and watching (100). In 101, Óðinn returns near morning 'nær morni', but the woman is absent. A bitch is tied on the bed, 'beðiom á' once again, not as a watch-dog, but as an insulting alternative for Óðinn's lust.

(102) Óðinn presents the moral of his experience: fickleness 'hugbrigð' specifically links the apparent deceit of the woman with the changeable women of 84:

Morg er góð mær,	Many a good maiden,
ef gǫrva kannar,	if you come to know her well,
hugbrigð við hali;	is fickle of heart towards a man

In 84, however, the implication is that women have been created changeable; it is an essential if regrettable part of their natures. In this episode, it is clear from the beginning to the audience, if not to the god, that 'Billings mær' had no intention of keeping her assignation with him. 'hugbrigð' is thus a female defence strategy, misunderstood by men, part of the same system of behaviour as women's propensity to 'flátt hyggja' in 90, a refusal to co-operate with men's attempts to control them. The true moral of the episode, together with 'sjaldan hittir leiðr í lið', as suggested above, is that of 90, that women cannot be constrained to do what they do not want to do.

'Góð' is not meant ironically here, as has been suggested;[70] the 'mær' is good, partly because she has escaped Óðinn's designs, avoiding 'lǫst' and 'flærðr', shame and deceitfulness, and partly because she is 'it ráðspaka fljóð': she has wit and a ready tongue to enable her to elude Óðinn. Remarkably, the god shows no rancour at being baulked of his desires, but rather an ungrudging respect and admiration for the ingenuity of 'Billings mær', and the episode ends good-humouredly.

(103)   A transition stanza treating the duties of the host emphasizes the importance of polished speech and ready conversation. The ideal host has a cultivated worldliness, able to talk in a dignified way about matters of note: 'oft skal góðs geta'. To be 'málugr' is indispensable: 'Billings mær' owed her escape from Óðinn to her quick thinking and persuasive speech when he first approached her; Óðinn will attribute his success with Gunnlǫð to the same skill: 'fátt gat ek þegiandi þar' (little did I get there by silence). Thus the stanza links the two adventures, one designed to illustrate women's 'hugbrigð' towards men, the second — although it has other functions — to show that men are equally changeable in their dealings with women: 'brigðr er karla hugr konom', a thematic link emphasized by the repetition of 'brigðr' and its compound.

Thematically, 103 offers a reprise of the discussion of speech and silence earlier in the poem (26–9), but the ideas held up for examination are now turned about in a different light. Silence is now no longer seen as advisable: when one is playing the role of host, it is necessary to display eloquence or be regarded as a fool. 'Fimbulfambi' (great booby) enacts the stuttering utterance of the man incapable of producing conversation. Likewise, as the two love-adventures framing the stanza imply, to be eloquent 'málugr' is vital when one has to talk one's way out of difficulties. Thus for Óðinn in his adventures at the court of Suttungr, loquacity will prove to be invaluable for the achievement of his goal, just as drunkenness was in 13–14, even though both are represented as undesirable in the Gnomic Poem.

1.4 GUNNLǪÐ AND THE MEAD OF POETRY, 104–110

The tale of Gunnlǫð functions partly as an exemplum, illustrating men's fickleness towards women (91), but it also has a structural purpose: to draw the audience into a different world from the everyday human one which has formed the backdrop for the Gnomic Poem until now. The new realm of existence is one where access to different types of knowledge is possible, knowledge which cannot be acquired through will-power or experience, unlike the wisdom with which the first movement of the poem has been concerned. Winning poetic inspiration is a difficult and dangerous business, and the lessons of the Gnomic Poem are of little assistance: facility with words, appropriately enough, is the means by which the prize is won, not the watchful silence enjoined in 6 and 15:

mǫrgom orðom	with many words
mælta ek í minn frama	I spoke to my advantage
í Suttungs sǫlom.	in Suttungr's halls.

$$(104^{4-6})$$

The didactic spirit of the Gnomic Poem is not entirely left behind, for Óðinn gives the occasional moralizing aside in a self-congratulatory tone: 'fás er fróðom vant' (107[3]: little is lacking to the wise) — a witty intrusion of the gnomic.

(104–5)   Although Snorri helps us to understand in part the events to which 104–10 refer, the tale to which Óðinn refers is in many respects quite different from Snorri's reworked and logically organized version. Óðinn narrates the stages of his adventure in swift glimpses, emphasizing different aspects of the episode from those of interest to Snorri. In 104, Óðinn is paying a social visit to Suttungr.[71] The observations about the duties of the host in 103 provide a generalizing gloss on Suttungr's role here. Óðinn's situation, making a visit to an unknown and probably dangerous hall, recalls the opening sequence of the poem: the god's experience offers a divine archetype for the initial theme of Hávamál. Gunnlǫð acting as hostess, on her golden throne 'gullnum stóli á' offers Óðinn a drink (105), the god's first taste of the precious mead.[72]

(106–7)   After the feast, Óðinn uses the augur Rati to gain access to the rest of the mead, perhaps stored in the giant's cellar. The god is anxious to stress the danger to himself: 'svá hætta ek hǫfði til' (thus I risked my head), an emphasis which distinguishes this episode from Óðinn's first appearance in the poem in 13–14. There the god was 'ǫlr . . . ok ofrǫlvi' (drunk . . . excessively drunk), the danger regarded light-heartedly. The serious intention behind the drinking-bout in 13–14 is only now revealed.

(108–9)   Óðinn escapes from Suttungr's courts, with Gunnlǫð's assistance in an Ariadne-like role. There is no elaboration of the escape; Gunnlǫð's deception is the main concern of the verse. Óðinn is next seen in his own hall: 'Háva hǫllo í', where the frost-giants, who do not seem to have identified Óðinn with Bǫlverkr as Snorri does, appear to ask for counsel, 'ráð'.

(110) The poet, speaking in his own voice, seems to deplore Óðinn's behaviour, deceiving Suttungr, making Gunnlǫð weep: 'hvat skal hans tryggðom trúa!' (how can his pledges be trusted!) His sympathy with Gunnlǫð contrasts with Óðinn's careless shrug in 105: 'ill iðgjǫld | lét ek hana eptir hafa | síns ins heila hugar' (a poor return I let her have for her whole-heartedness).

Óðinn is not 'in love' — sexually infatuated — as he was with 'Billings mær', but rather uses love to gain his own purpose, just as he used his drunkenness in 13–14; from the poet's point of view Óðinn's purpose, the winning of the mead, is wholly admirable. The cynical manipulations advocated in 92, 'sá fær er friár' (he who flatters, gets), are part of Óðinn's strategy to gain the mead, but Gunnlǫð herself is used and abandoned.

(111) Yet next the poet turns abruptly away from the girl's sorrow, for he — 'ek' — is suddenly caught up in the incantatory language which marks the incursion of the divine and mysterious into the poem:

> Mál er at þylia   It is time to recite
> þular stóli á   from the seat of the sage
> Urðar brunni at;   at the well of Urðr;

Transported to a mysterious, if confused,[73] location, the poet exults in his privileged position, emphasized by the repetition of 'ek': 'sá ek ok þagðak, | sá ek ok hugðak' (I saw, and was silent, I saw and considered) in the hall of Hávi. There he listens to 'manna mál' from which wisdom of one sort is derived, the human wisdom of *Loddfáfnismál* which follows, and to talk of runes, anticipating 138–45.

1.5 *LODDFÁFNISMÁL*

Stanza 111 signals the passing of the narrator's consciousness beyond the ordinary surroundings in which he declaims the Gnomic Poem, much like the hall of the introductory section, to a transfigured hall: that of Hávi, the High One. The hall is not clearly visualized; here sounds are more important: 'manna mál' (human speech) and talk of runes, 'of rúnar . . . dœma' come to the ears of the silent listener.

Where, after 111, we might reasonably have expected a glimpse of a divine mystery, as in 138 ff., the poet reverts to the human world once more. Stanza 112 brings the audience squarely back to everyday practicalities, an abrupt change from the mysterious, highly charged atmosphere of 111. Many of the thematic concerns of the Gnomic Poem are re-examined in *Loddfáfnismál*; only a few wholly new gnomic motifs are introduced, yet the section offers more than mere repetition or variation. *Loddfáfnismál* is distinctive both in its formulaic style and in its constant perception of the supernatural as an invisible dimension parallel with human activity, an awareness of the unseen world which is absent from the Gnomic Poem.

Whereas the inherently organic flow of thought in the Gnomic Poem makes a framework unnecessary, the formula[74] 'Ráðomk þér, Loddfáfnir . . .' (I advise you, Loddfáfnir), prefacing the precepts of *Loddfáfnismál* imposes a superficial structural unity. The device presupposes a speaker and a listener 'Loddfáfnir',[75] addressed as 'þú' (you) unlike the Gnomic Poem where pronouns are rarely used.[76] The colloquy form emphasizes that didacticism is *Loddfáfnismál*'s guiding mode; hence also the insistent use of the direct imperative, frequently prohibiting, 'rísat' (do not rise), 'skalattu' (you must not), 'teygðo þér aldregi' (never entice), contrasting with the impersonal 'skal'/'skyli' in the Gnomic Poem. (112) 111 indicates that the poet heard 'manna mál', the speech of men in the hall of the High One; the everyday human world is not yet to be abandoned, though its dimensions are extended to include the supernatural. Stanza 112 warns against going out at night, except for good reason. The implication is not, as one would have expected in the Gnomic Poem, that human enemies lurk outside to attack, but that the dark is dangerous because strange, other-world forces make the darkness their home. The nature of the danger is not specified, but we may imagine such spirits as the malevolent *dísir* in the story of Þiðrandi Síða-Hallssonr,[77] in which Þiðrandi meets his fate precisely because he ignores the warning of Þorhallr *spámaðr* against venturing outside. (113–14) The hint of the supernatural is made more explicit in the next verses, where Loddfáfnir is warned against a witch, a human conduit of the unseen menace. Her enchantments do not bring danger of themselves, but they prevent a man from attending to important public functions: the Þing or the King's business.[78] *Sigrdrífumál* 26 illuminates the relative perilousness of 112 and 113, suggesting that the danger of being out at night is preferable to risking a witch's hospitality.

(115) In counselling against forming a close attachment to the wife of another, as 'eyrarúna' (a close confidante), 115 continues to demonstrate how undesirable relationships with certain types of women may be. However, that a good woman may be an 'eyrarúna', or a provider of pleasant, private entertainment 'gamanrúnar' (130), seems to be taken for granted in *Hávamál*: just as contradictory advice is freely given about drunkenness, there is no tension between this view of woman as counsellor and friend, and the perception of women as the self-willed, fickle creatures of 84 and 90. Later verses (121–2) stress the necessity of having someone to whom the heart can be unburdened, but intimacy with another man's wife is to be eschewed (131). Again, as in the 'Billings mær' episode, emotional seduction is of more significance than physical, the appropriation of the loyalty which the woman owes rightly to her husband or lover. We may compare *Vǫluspá* 39, where those who have enticed away the 'eyrarúno' of another suffer in powerful currents 'þunga strauma' with oath-breakers and murderers.

(116) To some extent, the verse is a variation on the idea of 33, also picked up in 61, and encapsulated in brief, proverbial form in 74. The adjuration to see to the provision of food before setting out on a journey is, however, here divorced from the social implications of arriving on a visit too hungry to make conversation; the advice is simple and practical. Stanza 116 also links with the 'hungry traveller' motif of 66/67; the implication is that the traveller cannot expect food to be provided when he arrives at his lodging-place. Returning to the image of the traveller out on the mountain 'fiall', the verse sounds again for a moment the theme of the outsider from the opening verses of the Gnomic Poem (1–5).

Friendship, 117–131

(117–18) Two matched portraits of maliciousness, the 'illr maðr' (wicked man) and the 'ill kona' (wicked woman) of the next verse reopen the theme of friendship, so central to the Gnomic Poem.

Stanza 117 makes use once more of the imagery of exchange and payment — 'gjǫld' — as also in 123³. The question of how to respond to the man whom one does not trust, as in 44–6, is reopened: do not let him know if any mischance should befall you, for, far from getting the sympathy you might hope for, he may seek the opportunity to lower your fortunes still further:

illan mann	a wicked man
láttu aldregi	never let
óhǫpp at þér vita;	know of misfortune in your life;
þvíat af illom manne	for from a wicked man
fær þú aldregi	will you never get repayment
gjǫld ens góða hugar.	from a well-meaning mind.

The precision of the verse suggests that the poet has a specific incident in mind; perhaps an illustrative anecdote, such as those which constitute the 'Advice Section' of Sólarljóð.[79]

Stanza 118 continues the theme of malice: the weapons of an 'illrar kono' are slanderous words, which bite 'bíta' and cause the death 'fjǫrlagi', of an innocent man as effectively as a sword. Again the detail, and the pretence that the scene is part of the poet's own experience, 'ek sá', suggests an underlying narrative structure. We might compare the role of Þórhalla in málga in Laxdœla saga 47. Although she reports Kjartan's movements accurately enough to Bolli, she adds a slanderous remark, that Kjartan was crowing over Bolli's defeat in the matter of land-purchase from Þórarinn í Tungu. This untruth finally determines Bolli and his sons to ride against Kjartan.

(119) Reiterating the importance of frequent visits for the maintenance of friendship, first expressed in 44⁶, the verse develops the imagery of 34, a variation of the theme of 'out on the road', one of the major oppositions of the Gnomic Poem. In 34, as here, the path is envisaged both literally and metaphorically. In one of the few natural images[80] of Hávamál, 'hrísi vex | ok hávo grasi' (brushwood and tall grasses grow), the poet evokes the obstacles which can spring up between friends who do not make an effort to maintain their friendship. Emotional closeness, so highly prized in the Gnomic Poem, can be destroyed through one's own fault.

(120) Now the verb 'teygja' 'to attract' is used for the first time in a positive, rather than pejorative sense: in contrast to enticing women to shame 'flærðir' (102), or wives to be 'eyrarúnor' (115),

Loddfáfnir is advised to 'teygia' a good man as friend. The use of the verb here implies a degree of calculation, of deliberately selecting a friend for the benefits which he or she may bring, which is absent from the Gnomic Poem, where friendship grows naturally and unforcedly. This element in *Loddfáfnismál*'s understanding of friendship is also glimpsed in 123³⁻⁶. 'Góðan mann' l. 5, the simple epitome of the desirable friend, is paralleled by the 'góð kona' of 130, and both contrast with the 'illr maðr' and 'ill kona' of 117 and 118. The two portraits of the good man and woman are closely linked by vocabulary: both provide 'gamanrúnom' — a combination of enjoyable company and helpful advice. The last line employs a metaphor taken from magic: a good man as friend is a healing charm 'líknargaldr', a metaphorical counter to the supernatural — the night-terrors of 112, and the dark powers of the witch in 113–14.

(121–4) Quarrels are the subject of 121, which warns against being the first to break with a friend. Violent imagery — 'flaumslitom', 'sorg etr hiarta' — recalls the sudden flaring up of infatuation, the passionate, but ultimately shallow feelings of 51. 'Flaumslit', a *hapax legomenon*, combines a powerful, uncontrollable torrent 'flaumr'⁸¹ with 'slit', a cut or tear; a condensed metaphor for the pain of severance of friendship, while 'sorgr etr hiarta' evokes the peculiar loneliness of the man who has lost his friends through his own fault.

Stanza 122 warns against falling into conversation with fools 'ósvinna apa', while 123 justifies the admonition apparently by equating the fool and the bad man. The 'illr maðr', as in 117, will give no recompense 'laun' (cf. 'giǫld' 117¹⁰) for kindness shown to him. *Sigrdrífumál* 24 offers a parallel, warning against bandying words with a fool, for a fool in an argument may be provoked to say something irrevocable; danger may result:

þvíat ósviðr maðr	for a foolish man
lætr opt kveðin	often lets be said
verri orð en viti.	worse words than he realizes.⁸²

While *Sigrdrífumál* continues by explaining why swift retaliatory action is preferable to lengthy argument, *Loddfáfnismál* returns to its favourite contrast between the bad man and the good. Association with a good man is to be preferred, not because he will make a faithful friend, the prime requirement of the Gnomic

Poem, but, in accord with *Loddfáfnismál's* self-interested understanding of friendship, because he will do you credit and assure you of esteem ('lof'), cf. 8[3], respect in the eyes of others.

Stanza 124 draws together several observations on friendship by way of a finale for the theme: a striking metaphor for spiritual closeness 'sifiom blandat', literally mixing of kinship (cf. 44[4]), emphasizes the intimacy which results from sharing one's thoughts entirely, 'allan hug'. The image of close friendship contrasts with 121[10], where sorrow eats the heart 'sorg etr hiarta' of the man who has no one as confidant: 'allan hug' providing a verbal link. Lines 4–5 deplore the possibility that a man may be 'brigðr' in friendship. Hitherto, fickle behaviour has been a characteristic of sexual relationships (84, 91, 102); now that men and women are seen in the role of friends or enemies, rather than that of sexual opponents, the concept of fickleness is extended to friendship.

The last lines of the verse contain a corollary to ll. 2–3, the link made by the contrasting 'allan' and 'eitt':

hverr er segia ræðr	he who decides to tell
einom allan hug;	his whole mind to someone;
	(ll. 2–3)
era sá vinr ǫðrom	he is no friend to another who
er vilt eitt segir.	says only kind words.
	(l. 6)

The confidant of the man in ll. 2–3, who opens his heart, must not be a sycophant, only saying what his friend wants to hear; an answering honesty and openness is required. With this reflection on the need for spiritual reciprocity in friendship, echoing the exchange of material gifts in 41, the exploration of friendship is concluded.

(125) As if intending to amplify the theme of 122, the poet takes up the subject of disputes once more, suggesting that one should not demean oneself by arguing with an adversary who is not of one's own calibre: under these circumstances retreat is not cowardice, but wisdom (cf. 31[1–3]). This unheroic advice, contradicted in 127, where enemies are to be given no quarter, contrasts strongly with that given in *Sigrdrífumál* 25, the continuation of the verse cited above, where Sigrdrífa warns that in such quarrels, silence will be construed as cowardice or guilt. The opponent should be killed as quickly as possible.

(126) In a sharp break from the theme of disputes, 126 seems close to superstition in the arbitrary selection of shoes and spear-shafts as items which one should not make for others. On the surface the recommendation is mere common-sense, for a badly fitting, pinching shoe is likely to irritate its wearer, and in a fight lives depend on the strength and straightness of the spear shaft. One senses, however, that the meaning of the verse is not only literal. The idiom is paralleled in *Arinbjarnarkviða* 20,[83] where Egill praises Arinbjǫrn for his ability to be a friend in all circumstances:

kveðka skammt	I do not say it is a short way
meðal skatahúsa	between generous men's houses,
né auðskept	nor easy to shaft
almanna spjǫr.	the spears of people in general.

The idiom here appears to mean that people are difficult to satisfy: thus 126 suggests that one should not do favours for others, lest they rebound on one's own head. The verse echoes the overall emphasis of the Gnomic Poem on individualism and caution.

(127–8) 'bǫl' (evil) 126[9] provides a verbal link with 127. Wickedness should not be ignored, it must be named for what it is — 'kveðu þat[84] bǫlvi at' — when it is perceived. Stanza 128 reinforces the moral of 127 — evil should not be condoned by silence. 'Good' and 'Evil' as moral abstractions are employed here for the first time in *Hávamál*. The Gnomic Poem's discussion of human behaviour moves along an axis between wisdom and folly, not good and evil: the ethics of *Hávamál* hitherto have been expressed in terms of expediency and utility. Although 'good' and 'bad' have been used to categorize types: friend, woman, man, such absolutes as Good and Evil suggest orientation by a different morality from the rest of the poem. The sentiment of 128 seems to belong rather to *Sólarljóð* with its system of Christian values, than to *Hávamál*.

(129) This cryptic warning against looking up in battle[85] is a superstition more congruent with the list of battle-omens in *Reginsmál*[86] than the common-sense advice of the Gnomic Poem. While the apparent superstition of 126 has a rationale: the avoidance of blame for faulty manufacture, this verse belongs rather to the theme 'incursions of the supernatural', of increasing prominence in *Loddfáfnismál*.

(130) Now there is a sudden reversion to the concerns of the

earlier part of *Loddfáfnismál*, to the delineation of the types of the good and the bad person — an interest in moral types which is absent from the Gnomic Poem. Stanzas 117 and 118 have sketched the wicked man and woman, while 120 and 123 have depicted the good man. To complete the range of portraits, a good woman is needed. The vocabulary links the verse with 120, but 130 looks farther back, to the cynical advice of 92 on how to deal with women, and contradicts it. Promises made to a good woman should be kept, unlike those of 92, and the possibility that a man may tire even of a good woman is not admitted: 'leiðiz mange gott, ef getr'. (131) Functioning almost as an index to some of the conclusions of the Gnomic Poem, 131 glances briefly at caution, urging moderation in this, before adverting to the themes of women and alcohol.

Guests and Hospitality, 132–136

Now *Loddfáfnismál* returns to the scene of the early verses of the Gnomic Poem, the society of men in hall: precepts governing the behaviour of both host and guest are given.

(132–3) Neither invited guests nor wandering tramps — 'gest né gangandi'[87] — should be subjected to mockery. Stanzas 132–3 suppose a contrasting situation to that of the opening verses of *Hávamál*: now Loddfáfnir is already inside the hall, one of those who, in 2, look curiously at the newcomer. He does not know the identity of guests who arrive later, and may make enemies through his careless talk, as in 31[1–3]:

Veita gǫrla	he does not really know,
sá er um verði glissir,	who sneers in the feast,
þótt hann með grǫmum glami.	whether he is noisy
	among sharp-tempered foes.

Stanza 133[1–3] reiterates this uncertainty:

Opt vito ógǫrla	Often they do not really know
þeir er sitia inni fyrir,	those who already sit inside,
hvers þeir ro kyns, er koma;	of what family are those who arrive;

Stanza 31 continues with a general observation about mankind: that the mocker is not aware that he himself is not perfect — 'hann era vamma vanr'. The opposition once more of 'góðr' and 'illr' in 133 modifies the previous absolute portraits of the good and evil men and women above: no man is entirely good or entirely evil.

While 71 shows how even the deaf and the lame are good for something, fighting or riding horses, showing the Gnomic Poem's interest in what is useful, this moralizing observation offers just the type of platitude to be expected from the aged wise man 'hárr þulr' of the next verse.

(134) Recommending respect for the wisdom of the aged, a theme universal in wisdom literature,[88] the thought of 134 moves to other proverbial statements as justification:

opt er gott þat er gamlir kveða;	often what the old say is good;
opt ór skǫrpom belg	often from a shrivelled bag
skilin orð koma,	judicious words come, from
þeim er hangir með hám	one who hangs among the hides
ok skollir með skrám	and hovers among the skins
ok váfir með vilmǫgum.	and swings among the cheese-bags.

The first of these is straightforward, but the second is metaphorical. While, paradoxically, the term 'skǫrpom belg' is at first glance just such a piece of mockery that ll. 5–6: 'at hárum þul | hlæðu aldregi' (never laugh at a grey-haired sage) would eschew, the image is resonant with magical and, looking forward to 138, mythological significance. The old man is a leathery, dried-up object into which sustenance must be put to keep him alive, but out of which wise words may often come; cf. *Hamðismál* 26: 'opt úr þeim belg | bǫll ráð koma' (often out of that bag evil counsels come).[89]

The thought moves from the metaphor of the old man as bag, behind which we sense the outline of the *þulr* who hangs himself on a tree to gain wisdom,[90] to the literal picture of the dangling bags and cheese-bags[91] of a farm kitchen. The effect of the last lines is partly comic, the figure of the tottering old man is vividly realized, but also clear is the respect for the old man's knowledge, analogous to the wisdom of Óðinn.

(135–6) The host of 135 undergoes a metaphorical transformation into a fierce watch-dog:

gest þú ne geyia	don't bark at your guest,
né á grind hrækir;	nor drive him from the gate;
get þú váloðom vel.	be well-disposed to the poor.

Stanza 136 urges further the fundamental importance of hospitality: the image of the strong door-beam in the first lines is obscure, but the implication seems to be that a man must endeavour to show generosity and hospitality whenever it is asked of him, however difficult that may be.[92] The last lines warn of the likelihood of curses being called down on the stingy, looking forward to the counteracting lore of 137.

(137) A recital of healing charms brings *Loddfáfnismál* to an end. Some themes in the Gnomic Poem and *Loddfáfnismál* are touched upon again: earth is offered as a remedy for drunkenness, subject of 13–14; 'fiǫlkyngi' (magic), mentioned in 113, can be countered by 'ax' (an ear of corn); 'hýrogi' (strife in the household), exemplified in 32, requires 'hǫll' (possibly an elder-tree).[93] Finally runes are a protection against 'bǫl', anticipating the concerns of the *Rúnatal*.

The main purpose of *Loddfáfnismál* is to recapitulate and explore further the themes of the Gnomic Poem: friendship, hospitality, mockery, caution, but in addition, *Loddfáfnismál* intimates that there are phenomena which lie beyond the realm of 'manvit'. Common-sense is not enough in the face of witches, darkness, and curses: other kinds of knowledge must be sought. Stanza 137 signals the new direction with magico-medical advice; the poet of *Hávamál* now turns to kinds of wisdom which can only be won through mystical practices: runes which men do not know how to carve and spells which Óðinn will not impart.

1.6 *RÚNATAL*

The last lines of *Loddfáfnismál* have turned sharply away from the counsel, 'ráð' of the earlier verses towards a new theme: the application of arcane knowledge in the world of everyday. Although in 137 the 'rúnar' are only one remedy amongst many (a remedy against unspecified evil), runes and the power which they give are to be the subject of the next sequence of verses. The 'rúnar' hinted at in 80, and promised in 111, 'of rúnar heyrða ek dœma' (I heard talk of runes), emerge from the shadowy edges of the poem to occupy the foreground; the practical application of magical knowledge to healing in 137 gives way to a profounder vision of divine self-sacrifice. For any human to control the runes, their origin must be known and re-enacted;[94] 138–9 rehearse the ordeal by which Óðinn gained this knowledge, and thus the poet is able to persuade the audience of his own familiarity with hidden powers.

The poetry of these verses is quite different in quality from that of *Loddfáfnismál*; once again the swelling, hieratic tones of 80 and 111 are heard. The striking description of the tree (139), as 'vindga meiði' (windy tree), is of the same imaginative register as the heron of forgetfulness of 13, while the repetitions 'siálfr siálfom mér' (myself to myself), 'nam ek upp rúnar | œpandi nam' (I took up runes, shrieking I took them) and the rhythmic chant of 141$^{4-7}$ are those of ritual and incantation.

(138–9) 138–9 form a wonderfully triumphant climax to the poem, after the little climax of 111, and the sudden intrusion of the vatic voice in 80; 138 is sombre in tone; the slow development of the description of the 'vindga meiði' in the final lines of the verse, the 'tree with roots in unknown soil', evokes the nine nights 'nætr allar nío' of the god's ordeal. Nothing helps sustain Óðinn for the god is quite alone, an apotheosis of the theme of the man alone on the mountain 'á fialli'. Then from below, the runes appear and the god seizes them: 'œpandi' is both a scream of pain and a shout of victory.

(140) Now finally *Hávamál*'s purpose becomes apparent: the revelation of the many forms which wisdom takes. The mead of poetry (104–9), the runes, and the spells are structural types of one another; all are inaccessible to the human, but through his daring in the halls of Suttungr, through his endurance on the tree, and through his kinship with the chthonic, Óðinn has won knowledge for all beings.[95] Acquisition of the spells is necessary to complete the triad and to prepare for the *Ljóðatal*, while the second half of the verse reminds us of Óðinn's earlier exploit in gaining the mead, deliberately juxtaposing the three kinds of wisdom. No more is told of the origin of the spells: it is enough that they are 'fimbul' (mightily magical), and that they are learned from the giants, the first inhabitants of the world and possessors of an ancient knowledge to which the gods are not privy. For the present, runes are the poet's concern.

(141) Thus the process of thought in *Hávamál*, an accumulation of definitions and types of wisdom, builds to a crescendo of fulfilment:

> Þá nam ek frævaz   Then I began to be quickened
> ok fróðr vera   and be wise and fertile,

ok vaxa ok vel hafaz;	and grow and prosper;
orð mér af orði	one word from another
orz leita,	sought further words for me,
verk mér af verki,	one deed from another
verks leita.	sought further deeds for me. [96]

Knowledge of the runes comes from a different sphere of existence, mysterious and hidden, not the pragmatic world of the Gnomic Poem in which the magical and mystical has no part. Runic wisdom gives control over the uncertain, invisible forces which shape the everyday world, a control, however, which cannot be learned from the practical lessons of common-sense. The actual power of the runes can only be apprehended in terms of the human world: the god becomes 'fróðr', a desideratum of the Gnomic Poem, and his eloquence and powers of action increase. The runes are enabling; not in those specific areas of human activity that we find in *Sigrdrífumál* (childbirth, lawsuits, medicine),[97] but in more generally conceived terms. Rune-wisdom complements the knowledge won from human experience (cf. 80), reinforcing the human skills of speech 'orð' and action 'verk' with divine inspiration.

(142–3) In a break from Óðinn's self-exaltation, the poet asserts the necessity of familiarity with the runes, for the human needs to know how to make practical application of the gift. Stanza 143 suggests that the poet already possesses this wisdom; 'ek' in l. 5 is the poet, the *hroptr* for the race of men, who are otherwise the only class of creation missing from the verse:[98] 'ek reist siálfr sumar' (I myself cut some [runes]).

(144–5) The wisdom of the runes is thus shared by some humans, although the mocking rhetoric of 144–5, asserting the poet's superior knowledge, assumes that such knowledge can only be partial, an incompleteness of understanding reflected in the impatient movement of thought from verse to verse. Using the technical vocabulary of rune-magic,[99] and the formulaic repetition of the *galdralag* metre, the verse moves from such precise details as the carving of runes to other rituals; prayer and sacrifice. In an unexpected modulation into cautiousness, as if suddenly recalling the darker side of the magic in which he professes to be so proficient, the poet warns of the dangers of performing ritual with excessive zeal: moderation in religious practice, as with all else, is best.

The last cryptic lines of 145, seem, from the details of movement
and place — 'aptr', 'upp' (back, upwards) — to refer back to 139,
and the seizing of the runes by Óðinn (here called Þundr). Thus
the *Rúnatal* is enclosed by Óðinn's ordeal; the hanging is the
structure within which the runes are presented.

The *Rúnatal* is perhaps the most inchoate section of *Hávamál*, a
deliberate departure from the measured *ljóðaháttr* tread of the
Gnomic Poem, and the cool detachment of the 'Billings mær' and
Gunnlǫð Episodes. Yet the ecstatic mode is aesthetically apt, for
out of the chaos of form and language, the runes emerge,
controlling and enabling powers, through which the process of
ordering, in 'orð' and 'verk', is intensified. The fragmentary
allusion in 138–9 illuminates the scene only in partial flashes, as if
the structure of the verse itself were unable to contain the
awesome vision. Through the word 'œpandi' (shrieking) the poet
engages directly for the first time with naked emotion: the
triumph and agony are not now veiled in the generalizing,
distancing language of the gnomic mode.

The verses which follow 138–9 alternately emphasize the
importance of the runes, and warn of their inherent danger.
Although this sequence lacks the careful structuring of *Loddfáfnismál*, or the complex developments of thought of the Gnomic
Poem, the *Rúnatal*'s place in *Hávamál* is fundamental to the
poet's scheme; Óðinn's self-revelation on the tree is a divine
validation of the paramount importance of wisdom gained
through experience, which both endorses the poem's theme, and
forms a superbly powerful climax.

1.7 *LJÓÐATAL*

The *Ljóðatal* is a list of eighteen spells, whose contents are briefly
sketched, but whose text is never given. It is organized by
enumeration: the spells are presented in a numbered list, a
structural device common in wisdom poetry.[100] Enumeration gives
superficial unity to a sequence of disparate material; the
numbering need have no closer relation to the contents than
numerals entered in the margin of the manuscript, nor need
there be any significance in the order. Yet in the *Ljóðatal*, the poet
skilfully uses the alliterating ordinal to provide a mnemonic hook
for the key word of the spell's subject, a system which breaks down

only in 160 with the fifteenth spell. A good example of the numeral's mnemonic function is:

> þat kann ek it tíunda: I know a tenth one:
> ef ek sé túnriðor   if I see fence-riding witches
> leika lopti á,   sporting in the air,
>
> (155[1-3])

where 'tíunda' alliterates with a distinctive word of the spell, providing a prompt for the subject of the verse.

The *Ljóðatal* is no mere rigmarole of disparate spells, for an examination of the thematic areas which they encompass reveals that at least seven spells evoke, whether directly or more subtly, earlier preoccupations in the poem, while other verses look outside the poem itself to characteristics of Óðinn. For example, 159 recalls the situation of *Vafþrúðnismál* and *Grímnismál*, where the god must display his knowledge of the facts of Creation or the geography of Ásgarðr to an interlocutor, while 161 looks back to the 'Billings mær' episode, not only in subject, but with direct verbal parallels: cf. 99:

> þat kann ek it sextánda: I know a sixteenth one:
> ef ek vil ins svinna mans   if I want to possess all the wise
> hafa geð allt ok gaman   maiden's mind and love.

Stanza 162 continues this theme: once the maiden's affections have been gained, the second spell ensures that there will be no sudden change of heart on her part. Stanza 155, cited above, with its reference to shape-changing *túnriðor*, picks up the motif of the 'fjǫlkunnigri kono' (woman skilled in magic) of 113. The spell of 154 is able to counteract the uncertainty of wind and weather, images of untrustworthiness in 74, 82, and 90, while the first spell, offering protection against disputes and misery, 'sǫk' and 'sorg', accusations which destroy a man in 118, and sorrow which 'eats the heart' in 121.

The *Ljóðatal* is an index to spells, but spells which are not 'genuine', in the sense that the Old English *Charms*, or the Old High German *Merseburg Charms* are. Rather these are a literary device, consciously selected, possibly even composed, by the poet to illustrate the two concerns of the poem: different types of wisdom, and, subordinated to the first, but ultimately serving to unify its different elements, the character of Óðinn. Thus the 'spells' either echo the preoccupations of the Gnomic Poem and *Loddfáfnismál,* or else they broaden our knowledge of Óðinn's abilities.[101]

Hávamál comes to a brisk close. Loddfáfnir reappears briefly in 162, where he is teasingly told that the spells would benefit him greatly if he were to learn them, but this is not to be:

lióða þessa	of these spells
munþú, Loddfáfnir,	will you, Loddfáfnir,
lengi vanar vera;	long be in need;
þó sé þér góð ef þú getr,	though it would be good for you
nýt ef þú nemr,	if you get it, useful if you learn it,
þorf ef þú þiggr.	needful if you receive it.

The mocking tone recalls 144, but the effect here is more playful, a reminder that human capabilities are limited — 'lítilla sanda, lítilla sæva' (of small shores, of small seas). The re-introduction of Loddfáfnir serves partly to link the *Ljóðatal* with *Loddfáfnismál,* but he also represents the audience of *Hávamál,* of whom the poet-Óðinn speaker is about to take leave. By asserting the exclusivity and inaccessibility of divine wisdom to the ordinary mortal, the poet lays claim, through his familiarity with the arcane, to a similar superiority to Óðinn's.

The eighteenth spell, which will never be revealed except to Óðinn's lover or (non-existent) sister, is an unanswerable riddle, like the god's final question in *Vafþrúðnismál,* by which the giant has to admit himself beaten. It is a triumphant demonstration of Óðinn's complete mastery over wisdom; the audience of *Hávamál* must, with Vafþrúðnir, acknowledge the god's superiority:

nú ek við Óðin deildak	now I have been contending with Óðinn
mína orðspeki;	in wisdom;
þú ert æ vísastr vera!	you are always the wisest!

(*Vafþrúðnismál* 55[7-9])

The last verse of *Hávamál* declares the poem to be complete, and asserts its value to its human audience; the types of wisdom it contains are those most useful to men, 'ýta sonom', but not at all needful for giants 'iotna sonom'.[102]

Finally the poem is given its name[103] and the location of the final movement confirmed: 'Nú ero Háva mál kveðin | Háva hollo í'

(Now is the High One's speech recited in the High One's hall).
We are in Óðinn's hall, a transfiguration of the ordinary human
hall of the first stanzas of the poem, yet in this hall, as in the first,
the acquisition of knowledge is all-important. Exhortation to
digest the poem's wisdom has become increasingly insistent from
the beginning of *Loddfáfnismál*; now good luck is invoked for
those who have listened to and profited from the poem, as well as
for the poet himself, in a rousing crescendo:

Heill sá er kvað!	Luck to him who has spoken!
Heill sá er kann!	Luck to him who has known!
Níoti sá er nam!	Let he who has learned, profit!
Heilir þeirs hlýddo!	Luck to those who have listened!

1.8 CONCLUSION

Structure and Unity

Hávamál is a coherent poem. The problems which readers have
experienced in making sense of it in the past lie not in the text
itself, but in the readers' expectations of the genre. Wisdom
poetry has no prescribed form; no narrative or chronological
principle, by which the poet may order his gnomes, is inherent in
the material. Connections may be made by grouping together
gnomes which share a theme, for example 'Friendship', by verbal
links: 'Bú er betra' (36–7), or the rhymes and half-rhymes of the
first lines of 61–3.

Once expectations of a 'logical argument' have been abandoned, the reader is freed to perceive the subtler movements of
sense. *Hávamál* is not linear in its progression; rather it takes up a
theme, examines it, drops it to turn to another, then picks up the
original theme in a variation. As the Gnomic Poem develops, the
consideration of each subject becomes more profound. Metaphysical questions are raised: in 8, 'lof' (esteem) is little more
than another's good opinion, but by 76 it has become the eternal
part of man, that which survives death.

The depth of *Hávamál's* vision of mankind becomes apparent
only gradually. The earlier verses are concerned chiefly with
getting by, surviving 'þurrfiallr' (with a dry skin). But soon the
limitations of mankind's intellect are under scrutiny ('lítilla

sanda, | lítilla sæva, | lítil ero geð guma'), then the implications that the inevitability of death holds for a man's priorities in life. The perception of all things as fickle and finite leads into the sophisticated comedy of Óðinn's jilting by 'Billings mær'; yet another change of tone modulates into the pathos of Gunnlǫð's abandonment.

Just as the Gnomic Poem reiterates and re-examines its themes, so too does *Loddfáfnismál*. At the same time it begins to intimate that the human world is only one dimension of existence, that the supernatural exists beyond that which can be seen. Óðinn irrupts once more into the poem at 138, the emotional and thematic centre of the poem, where all the difficulties and dangers exposed by the Gnomic Poem are compounded into one terrifying glimpse of Óðinn's sacrifice. Finally, after the deliberate obscurities of the *Rúnatal* and *Ljóðatal*, the poem ends on a teasing note: Loddfáfnir will long be in need of the spells which have been listed. Last of all, a general blessing is called down upon the attentive.

Óðinn's role

Óðinn is the poem's patron. Not only god of wisdom, he also inhabits *Hávamál* in many guises. Archetypal wanderer, unknown guest, drunken visitor in hall, frustrated and successful wooer, all these may conceal the god. Óðinn's voice, which the poet assumes at will, unifies *Hávamál* and draws together all modes of wisdom, revealed to be aspects of the divine wisdom which Óðinn has won through his visit to Suttungr and his ordeal on the tree.

The main purpose of the great poetic synthesis of *Hávamál* is to display the range of wisdom current in the poet's culture. Social wisdom is vital, and hard enough to obtain, but divine wisdom: runic mastery, magical knowledge, poetic inspiration can only be won through extremes of courage and sacrifice. The poet himself has access to the divine knowledge of Óðinn: he knows how it was won (138-9), and how it should be used (142-5). He himself knows how to carve runes (143) and the power of his poetic inspiration is manifest in the poem of *Hávamál* itself. The vatic utterances of 80 and 111, locating the poet in Hávi's hall where he is privy to the secrets of gods and men, prepare for his enhanced stature at the poem's end. As Óðinn and the narrative voice become more closely identified, ultimately indistinguishable, we begin to believe that the poet too knows all the spells of the *Ljóðatal.*

The penetrating nature of the insights of the Gnomic Poem, for example the evocation of a shallow friendship in 51, and the subtle analysis of relations between the sexes, are unparalleled in Germanic wisdom literature. *Hávamál* is no mere collection of truisms; the precision, the psychological acuity of the observations makes each gnome sound newly minted. In general, the social wisdom of *Hávamál* is sensible, cautious, and worldly, agreeable to a twentieth-century sensibility. This secular age applauds the unheroic ethos of the Gnomic Poem, and no longer deplores the absence of reference to absolute moral values, whether pagan-heroic or Christian.[104] Such wisdom remained viable in the post-Christian era; just as the originally pagan *Disticha Catonis*, purveying a secular common-sense, were used as an educational text for fourteen hundred years, so the social wisdom of *Hávamál* would have spoken to the anxious men and women of the Sturlung Age with the same relevance as when it was first put into metrical form.

Notes

1. *Vǫluspá* 20.
2. For MS details and citations of *Hávamál* in other texts, see J. Helgason ed. *Eddadigte*, i, *Vǫluspá Hávamál* (NF Serie A; Oslo, etc.,1971), pp. ix–x.
3. G. Lindblad, *Studier i Codex Regius av Äldre Eddan*, Lundastudier i nordisk språkvetenskap 10 (Lund, 1954).
4. Lindblad, *Studier*, 263–4.
5. D. A. Seip, 'Har nordmenn skrevet opp Edda-diktningen?', *MM* 43 (1951), 3–33.
6. See e.g. S. Karlsson, 'Om norvagismer i islandske håndskrifter', *MM* (1978), 87–102; J. Benediktsson, *Sturlunga saga*, Early Icelandic Manuscripts in Facsimile, i (Copenhagen, 1958), 14–16 and J. Helgason, *MS. AM 764 A4to*, Manuscripta Islandica, iv (Copenhagen, 1957), pp. xx–xxiv.
7. *Hávamál*, ed. D. A. H. Evans (London, 1986), 13, but see also Evans's *MCS*, 129, where he is more explicit: 'the various Norwegianisms in the Gnomic Poem, both lexical and material, . . . also suggest an early date: two of them, . . . are limited to pre-Christian Norway.'
8. See C. A. Larrington, review of D. A. H. Evans ed., *Hávamál*, *SBVS* 22 (1987), 128.
9. *Hákonarmál* is discussed below at ch. 6. 1.
10. The extra-Scandinavian parallels are discussed in C. A. Larrington, '*Hávamál* and Sources outside Scandinavia', *SBVS* 23.3 (1992), 141–57. Von See's comparisons with *Disticha Catonis* are discussed below at ch. 3. 1.
11. See J. Kristjánsson, 'Stages in the Composition of Eddic Poetry', in *Poetry in the Scandinavian Middle Ages*, 7th International Saga Conference (Spoleto, 1988), 145–60.
12. H. Schneider, *Eine Uredda* (Halle, 1948).
13. K. von See, *Die Gestalt der Hávamál: Eine Studie zur eddischen Spruchdichtung* (Frankfurt-on-Main, 1972).

14. Such attempts at excision and rearrangement were made by K. Müllenhoff, *Deutsche Altertumskunde*, 5 (Berlin, 1891), 250–84; A. Heusler, 'Die zwei altnordischen Sittengedichte der *Hávamál* nach ihrer Strophefolge', *Sitzungsberichte der Preußischen Akademie der Wissenschaften phil. hist. Klasse* (1917), 105–35 (repr. *KS* II, 292–313); and I. Lindquist, *Die Urgestalt der Hávamál: Ein Versuch zur Bestimmung auf synthetischen Wege*, Lundastudier i nordisk språkvetenskap 11 (Lund, 1956).

15. E. W. Heaton, *The Hebrew Kingdoms* (Oxford, 1968).

16. Ibid. 195

17. See D. Davidson, 'Earl Hákon and his Poets', D.Phil. thesis (Oxford, 1983); M. Clunies Ross, 'An Interpretation of the Myth of Þórr's Encounter with Geirrøðr and his Daughters', in U. Dronke, G. Helgadóttir, G. W. Weber, and H. Bekker-Nielsen ed. *Speculum Norrœnum: Norse Studies in Memory of Gabriel Turville-Petre* (Odense, 1981), 370–91 and M. Clunies Ross and B. K. Martin, 'Narrative Structures and Intertextuality in *Snorra Edda*: The Example of Þórr's Encounter with Geirrøðr', in J. Lindow, L. Lönnroth, and G. W. Weber ed., *Structure and Meaning in Old Norse Literature* (Odense, 1986), 56–72. See especially 66–8 for some illuminating comparisons with *Hávamál*. The interesting speculations of Richard North in *Pagan Words and Christian Meanings*, Costerus New Series, 81, (Amsterdam and Athens, Ga., 1991) pp. 122–44 unfortunately came to my attention too late to be given consideration here.

18. T. S. Eliot, 'Little Gidding' II. *Collected Poems: 1909–1962* (London, 1974), 217.

19. As defined at ch. 1.1.

20. As most reviews of von See's *Die Gestalt* have pointed out. Typical is S. Beyschlag, 'Zur Gestalt der *Hávamál*: Zu eine Studie Klaus von Sees', *ZDA* 103 (1974), 1–19, especially 7.

21. A term borrowed from narratology: G. Genette, *Narrative Discourse: An Essay in Method*, tr. J. E. Lewin (Ithaca, NY, 1980).

22. If *Hávamál* is to be read as essentially a dramatic text, in which the poet assumes the mask of Óðinn at will, the question of how far it is to be regarded as 'Odins Rede' need no longer apply. For a similar, though not identical understanding of the voices in *Hávamál*, see Clunies Ross, 'Voice and Voices in Eddaic Poetry', *Poetry in the Scandinavian Middle Ages*, 7th International Saga Conference (Spoleto, 1988), 43–53.

23. Stanzas 29–32 suggest that enemies can be made through incautious speech while 132–3 warn that mockery of strangers can cause trouble.

24. See L. C. Gruber, 'The Rites of Passage: *Hávamál* Stanzas 1–5', *SS* 49 (1977), 330–9.

25. *Hugsvinnsmál* 73: 1–2; for the relationship between these two passages, see below at ch. 3.1.

26. *The Vision of Piers Plowman: The B-Text*, ed. A. V. C. Schmidt (London, 1978), Prologue 114–15. Schmidt comments (p. 306): 'Kynde Wit refers to natural and practical reason as opposed to speculative intellect. It is here shown as responsible for the proper ordering of society.' Cf. also R. Quirk, 'Langland's Use of *Kind Wit* and *Inwit*', *JEGP* 52 (1953), 182–9.

27. See U. Dronke, '"óminnis hegri"' in *Festskrift til Ludwig Holm-Olsen* (Øvre Ervik, 1984), 53–60.

28. Heusler, 'Die zwei altnordischen Sittengedichte' (*KS*, 200), excises 13–14 with the comment 'they are better taken as a didactic introduction to the Odinic tale'. Cf. also S-G, 87 who agree with Heusler that 12–14 are 'fragments of a third Óðinn-exemplar'.

29. Both Schneider and von See believe that the *Sammler/Redaktor* has composed 11–12 as an introduction to the Óðinn-verses. See Schneider, *Eine Uredda*, 51 and von See, *Die Gestalt*, 15.

30. This image is the subject of R. Pipping's article, '*Háv*. 21 och ett par ställen hos Seneca', *APS* 20 (1949), 371–5. His parallel with Seneca does not stand up, however; see also J. Harris, 'Eddic Poetry', Clover-Lindow, 107–8 and C. A. Larrington, '*Hávamál* and Sources from outside Scandinavia' *SBVS* 23 (1992), 141–57.

31. e.g. 'hann var svá lastvarr at hann vildi ekki vamm vita á sik' (he was so wary of blame that he did not want to know of any blemish in himself), *Stj.* 547: 27; 'Sómir sálunni í

ǫllum hlutum sik svá venja at varast vǫmmin' (It is fitting for the soul to make a habit in all things of guarding against faults), *HMS* II 356: 16.

32.   Cf. also *Sonatorrek* 24: 4: 'vammi firrða' (estranged from faults) referring to Egill himself. Egill's son, and Egill are wary of moral flaws, dishonour, cowardice, rather than free from sin in a Christian sense.

33.   See Evans, 86. If this verse is to be seen as parallel with 63, which advises discretion, then the sense 'is said about' is probably better.

34.   Cf. the behaviour of Unferð in *Buf.* 499–606.

35.   For examples of quarrels springing up at feasts, see in particular *Egils saga* ch. 44, for Egill's fight with Bárðr, and ibid. ch. 71, for his quarrel with Armóðr.

36.   This formulaic pair of opposites has a similar function in OE; *Ex. Max.* 60b–61. See also *The Seafarer* 109–12.

37.   References to weapons and fighting in *Háv.* are markedly few, in comparison with the *Exeter* and *Cotton Maxims* in OE. Such references occur in 15, 16, 38, 41, (58), 81, 82, 89, 126, 129, 148, 150, and 156. For von See's view that the relative paucity of such references implies that *Háv.* is dependent on *DC*, see below, ch. 3.1.

38.   These verses, 85–7, 89, are sometimes referred to as '*Priamel*-type'. The *Priamel* was a specifically German literary genre, 'consisting in epigrammatic improvisation, which sought to bind together a series of parallel units in a particular form into an inner unity, for an artistic purpose.' *Reallexikon der deutschen Literaturgeschichte*, ed. P. Merker and W. Stammler (Berlin, 1926–8), ii. 724.

39.   Cf. the Arab proverb 'My enemy's enemy is my friend'.

40.   Cp. Gestumblindi (the blind guest) in *Hervarar saga*, 30 ff. and other analogues in M. Schlauch, 'Widsith, Víðfǫrull, and some other Analogues', *PMLA* 46 (1931), 969–87.

41.   As in *Vafþrúðnismál.* Other Odinic appearances are listed in Schlauch, 'Widsith'.

42.   Cf. the Icelandic' Rune Poem' in B. Dickins ed., *Runic and Heroic Poems* (Cambridge, 1915), 32.

43.   See below ch. 4.1.

44.   *Trémenn* were apparently wooden idols, which had a magical or ritual significance. They could sometimes talk and move: cf. *Þorleifs þáttr jarlsskálds* (*ÍF* ix. 225 ff.), and *Ragnars saga Lóðbrókar* 20. Ibn Fadlan also encounters them among the Rus: H. M. Smyser, 'Ibn Fadlan's Account of the Rus, with some Commentary and some Allusions to *Beowulf* in J. B. Bessinger and R. P. Creed ed. *Medieval and Linguistic Studies in Honor of Francis Peabody Magoun, Jr.* (London, 1965), 92–119.

45.   See Fritzner, *Ordbog*, i. 489: 'friðr', a) Kjærlighed (love) citing this passage and *Skm.* 19. Compare also 'frjá' (to love, make love) in *Sig.sk.* 8, and 'friðill' (lover) in *Vkv.* 27.

46.   See A. Holtsmark, 'Til Hávamál str. 52', *MM* (1959), 1. She suggests that 'hǫllu' means 'sloping, tilted' to such an extent that the man to whom the cup is offered gets an exact half-share.

47.   H. Lie, 'Noen gamle tvistemål i *Hávamál*', in *Festskrift til Ludvig Holm-Olsen* (Øvre Ervik, 1984), 215–20, suggests that the point is the insignificance of man viewed against the vastness of the landscape (p. 216). In the anthropocentric world of *Háv.*, the poet is not so utterly dismissive of human capabilities however.

48.   'Dœlskr' is etymologically related to 'dul', which occurs here and in 79: 6. H. S. Falk and A. Torp ed. *Norwegisch-dänisches etymologisches Wörterbuch*, i. (Heidelberg, 1910), 177 warn that 'dølskr' (foolish) must be differentiated from 'dølskr' (living in a valley). Folk etymology may have partly conflated the homonyms, and that 'dœlskr' thus carries an echo of the limited horizons of the fjord-dweller in 53.

49.   I am indebted to Dr Paul Acker of the University of St Louis for this point.

50.   For parallels in OE *Precepts* and Ecclesiastes to the idea that wisdom does not bring happiness, see below, ch. 4.5.

51.   Silence is adjured in 6, 7, 15, 27, and 29, both in general, and specifically for the foolish man.

52. Cf. Saxo, i. bk. v, p. 145: 'Nemo stertendo victoriam cepit, nec luporum quisquam cubando cadaver invenit' (Nobody has ever won victory by drowsing, nor has any sleeping wolf found a carcase).

53. *Hrafnkels saga Freysgoða* ch. 13; *Gísla saga* ch. 9.

54. Evans, 105, records some of the difficulties which commentators have had with this strophe. D. Martin Clarke's translation, *The Hávamál* (Cambridge, 1923), 61, gives the best sense: 'Now and then I would be invited to a house when I was in no need of ood for a meal; or two hams would be hanging up in the house of an intimate friend when I had already eaten one.'

55. Contrast *Ex. Max.* 111–13 which asserts that the man who is given too little to eat will die, despite the restorative powers of the sun.

56. 'Lǫstr' is found in a Christian sense 'sin' in *Lilja* 19, *Líknarbraut* 47, *Harmsól* 4 and 15 among others. Evans interprets 'lǫstr' here as 'physical defect', following *HMS* i. 584, and similar usages in *Grágás*. This would fit with 'heillyndi' (health), but, given *Háv.*'s preoccupation with public standing, 'lof', 'dómr', etc., I prefer to take 'lǫstr' as 'social disgrace', as in Sigvatr 37.

57. See von See, '*Sonatorrek* und *Hávamál*', *ZDA* 99 (1970), 26–33, who notes that *Sonatorrek* 17 and *Háv.* 72 share the rare 'niðr' (descendant) as well as the theme of loss of family. See below, ch. 6.1.

58. The 'bautarsteinar' (memorial stones) are used by Evans, 13, 108, and in MCS, 129 to support his contention that the Gnomic Poem originated in Norway in pagan times.

59. See S. Singer, *Sprichwörter des Mittelalters*, i. (Bern, 1944), 149–50 gives the MHG 'zwene sint eines her' (*Iwein* 4329), and a Latin example from the *Ysengrimus*, composed in twelfth-century Holland: 'Duo sunt exercitus uni' (Two are as good as an army to a single opponent) B 12. 311. The phrase 'tunga huwudhbani' (tongue slayer of the head) occurs in the *Old Swedish Laws* (*SGL* iii. 275 n.100.) And 74: 3 recurs in *Málsháttakvæði* 12.

60. According to von See, *Die Gestalt* 47 'orztírr' is (despite its appearance in *Hǫ fuðlausn*) another late, Christian word, and 'dómr' is to be understood in a Christian sense also. For a refutation of these claims, see MCS, 135–7 and cf. *The Seafarer* 72–80b.

61. The sons of Fitjungr are unknown from other sources, like the similarly representative, often evocatively named figures in *Sólarjóð*. They may have been made up, or they may represent a series of 'narrative precipitates' — in F. Amory's phrase ('Kenning' in P. Pulsiano et al. ed., *Medieval Scandinavia: An Encyclopedia* (New York, 1992)) — tales so well-known that the names of the characters alone wereallusion enough. Despite Evans's note, *Hávamál*, 112–13, the derivation of the name 'Fitjungr' from 'feitr' (fat) seems a good one. Cf. 'rífa'(to tear); 'reifa' (vb); 'rifja' (vb)and 'rifjungr' (sword): see *Altnordisches Etymologisches Wörterbuch*, s.v. 'rífa'.

62. See below ch. 3.1 for von See's observations about 'metnaðr' and the possible relationship with *Hugsvinnsmál.*

63. See below ch. 2.3.

64. See K. Albertsson, 'Hverfanda Hvel', *Skírnir* 151 (1977), 57–8, and Singer, *Sprichwörter*, 9

65. See n. 38 above for the term *Priamel*, often applied to these verses by German scholars.

66. Proverbs 30: 10 and Proverbs 7: 27

67. Compare anti-woman sentiments in Irish wisdom poetry: K. Meyer ed., *Instructions of Cormac*, Todd Lecture Series (Royal Irish Academy), 15 (Dublin: 1909), ll. 115–20. See also Prov. 7: 27, 9: 1, 21: 9, 19, 27; 15, 30: 20, 23; *Laws of Manu* ii. 213, 214.

68. See S. Nordal, '"Billings mær"' in *Bidrag till nordisk filologi tillägnade Emil Olson* (Lund, 1936), 288–95.

69. 'Lǫstr' again means 'social shame', as in 68: 6. See note 56 above.

70. Evans, *Hávamál*, 101.

71. Suttungr is pictured as the host, Gunnlǫð the hostess offering refreshment, and Óðinn the deceitful guest; the account is quite dissimilar to Snorri's narrative (*Skáldskaparmál* ch. 6).

72. See S. Jakobsdóttir, 'Gunnlöð og hinn dýri mjöður', *Skírnir*, 162 (1988), 215–45, and *Gunnlaðarsaga* (Reykjavik, 1987). She argues that the drink offered to Óðinn is a 'sovereignty-drink', and Óðinn a candidate for kingship. The context in *Háv.* suggests thatÓðinn is guilty of a breach of hospitality, his behaviour that of the bad guest, rather than disruption of ritual.

73. Several traditions: the well of Urðr, known from *Voluspá* 19, the '(røk)stólar'(judgment thrones) of the gods in*Voluspá* 23, and the 'sal' (hall) in the Hauksbók and *Snorra Edda* versions of *Voluspá* 20, situated 'und þolli' (under the tree) (Yggdrasill), seem to have influenced this surreal hall.

74. See de Vries, 'Om Eddaens Visdomsdigtning', *ANF* 50 (1934), 24–5 for analysis of the construction of the *Loddfáfnismál* stanzas.

75. The etymology of 'Lodd-fáfnir' remains obscure. Lindquist, *Die Urgestalt der Hávamál*, 150 compares the mocking use of 'laf-Hamðir' in *Hemings þáttr* as an epithet for Haraldr *harðræði*, and connects 'lodd' with Modern Icelandic 'loddast' — nachschleppen' (to wander about).

76. The pronoun 'þú' occurs in the Gnomic Poem only at 19: 6, 44, 45, and 46.

77. *Þið randa þáttr ok þórhalls*, in *Íslendinga sögur*, 10, ed. G. Jónsson (Reykjavik, 1947), ch. 3.

78. Cf. Haraldr *hárfagri*'s distraction from his royal duties by the Lapp woman Snæfríðr who enthrals him through her father's magic powers. *Haralds saga ins hárfagri*, ch. 25.

79. On *Sólarjóð*see my thesis: 'Old Icelandic and Old English Wisdom Poetry', 276–83.

80. The cattle of 21 and the eagle of 62 are the main examples of images drawn from nature. The landscape is a backdrop for human activity: travelling over the mountain, walking over the open plain. In contrast to OE wisdom verse, nature has no significance unless it is inhabited by human figures. See below ch. 5.

81. Fritzner, *Ordbog* i. 427 gives the simplex 'flaumr' — Flom, voldsom strøm (river, violent current), only in *Bp.* ii. 510, but the figurative compound 'flaumsemi' (f.) Tilbøieliged til at fare voldsomt frem (inclination to rush violently forward): 'flaumsemi tungunnar' (headlong rush of the tongue), *Mar.* 1692

82. See below ch. 2.3.

83. *Egils saga*, ch. 78 (ÍF 3, 265).

84. See Evans, *Hávamál*, 127: the abbreviationin the manuscript may be expanded to 'þat' or 'þér'.

85. See E. Ó. Sveinsson, 'Vísa í *Hávamálum* og írsk saga', *Skírnir*, 126 (1952), 168–77, in which he relates 'gialti' to an Irish phenomenon of panic in battle, noted also in *Konungs skuggsjá*. The prohibition against looking up in battle could also have had a practical explanation: to gaze upwards wouldput one in danger of being shot in the face.

86. See below ch. 2.1.

87. 'Gestr ok gangandi' is a common formula: cf. Fritzner, *Ordbog*, i. 555 'ala gest ok ganganda með góðum hug til gúðs þakka' (nourisha guest and a wanderer with a good heart in gratitude to God) *Hom.* 123:6.

88. See e.g. Ecclus. 8: 9; 25: 6. Cf. also *Precepts* 11–14 (see below ch. 4.5).

89. Cf. also *Gull-þóris saga*, ch. 18: 'hafa skal góð ráð, þó þat ór refsbelg koma' ([one] shall have good advice, even though it comes out of a fox-skin bag)See U. Dronke, *PE*, 237 for further parallels.

90. See J. Fleck, 'Óðinn's Self-Sacrifice, a New Re-interpretation. I: The Ritual Inversion', *SS* 43 (1971), 119–42.

91. Raw skins and hides ('hám' 'skrám') are hanging up to dry in the farm kitchen, together with 'vilmogum'. One persuasive suggestion, first made by E. Magnússon, '[on *Háv.* st. 4, 8, 13, 19, and 134]', *PCPhS* 16 (1887), 5–18 and 'Vilmogum or vilmogum?', *ANF* 15 (1899), 319–20, is that 'vil' is 'rennet' and 'mogum' is from 'magi', 'stomach': the stomach of beasts is used as a bag to contain fermenting rennet and milk.

92. See Evans's note on this difficult verse, 130–1.

93. See Evans, *Hávamál*, 132.

94. Cf. M. Eliade, *Myth of the Eternal Return*, tr. W. Trask (Paris, 1949), 5 and 84.
95. Cf. 107: 4–6. Thus the mead is brought to Miðgarðr, the home of men. See also *Sigrdrífumál* 18, where the sacred mead is sent 'á víða vega' (on wide ways) among the Æsir, Elves, Vanir and 'mennskir men' (human beings).
96. 'Verk' has the double sense of 'deed' and, in the context of 'orð' and Óðinn's acquisition of the mead of poetry, 'poetic composition'. Cf. the verb 'yrkja' (to compose). Von See (CS 141) claims that the appearance of 'orð' and 'verk' together here is evidence of Christian missionary vocabulary. However, the formula appears many times in OE in contexts which are not *markedly* Christian: *Bwf.* 289, 1100, 1833, for example. See MCS 134, and von See's reiteration of his position in 'Duplik', *Skandinavistik*, 19 (1989), 142–8, especially 143–4.
97. See below, ch. 2. 3.
98. 'mennskir menn' (human beings) are included in the distribution of runic knowledge in *Sigrdrífumál* 18, however.
99. Lindquist, *Die Urgestalt*, 160–3 notes the occurrence of 'ráða' (to interpret) and 'fá' (to colour) in runic inscriptions on the stone at Sparlösa in Västergotland and the Fyrunga and Tose I stones respectively. See also Evans, *Hávamál*, 135–6.
100. Numbered lists occur in the OE poem *Precepts*, Proverbs 6; 16; 30; 15; Ecclus. 25: 1 for example.
101. Since we know that Snorri was acquainted with part of *Háv.*, citing the first verse in *Gylfaginning*, it seems probable that *Ynglinga saga* has drawn upon the *Ljóðatal* for its information about Óðinn's powers.
102. The manuscript has 'ýta' (of men); 'iǫtna' (of giants) is a later correction in the margin.
103. The naming of a poem in its final stanza seems to have been traditional in Norse wisdom poems: cf. *Hugsvinnsmál* 148; *Sólarljóð* 81.
104. B. Guðnason, 'Þankar um siðfræði Íslendingasagna', *Skírnir*, 139 (1965), 65–82 notes that 'heroic' and 'social' values cannot be mapped exactly on to 'heathen' and 'Christian'; there existed an 'almenn, hagnýt lífsvizka, sem ekki er bundin einu siðakerfi fremur en öðru'(general, useful wisdom for life, which is not related to one religion any more than another) (p. 72). See also G. Karlsson, 'Dyggðir og lestir í þjóðfélagi Íslendingasagna', *TMM* 46 (1985), 9–19, and id. 'The Ethics of the Icelandic Saga Authors and their Contemporaries: A Comment on Hermann Pálsson's Theories on the Subject', *Workshop Papers, 6th International Saga Conference*, i. (Copenhagen, 1985), 381–400.

2 WISDOM AND THE EDUCATION
OF THE HERO: THE POEMS
OF SIGURÐR'S YOUTH

2.1 INTRODUCTION

Just as *Hávamál* brings together different modes of wisdom in its desire to encompass all kinds of knowledge, so the poems of Sigurðr's youth, *Grípisspá, Reginsmál, Fáfnismál,* and *Sigrdrífumál,* show how Sigurðr acquires different types of knowledge from various sources. Broadly speaking, these are, in *Reginsmál,* fortunate omens, in *Fáfnismál,* mythological wisdom, and in *Sigrdrífumál,* runic lore and social wisdom. Each poem complements the others: there is no overlap between the different types of wisdom imparted. The wisdom in *Fáfnismál* is employed for an exceptional purpose, having not only an instructive function, but also a dramatic one.

The traditional hero learns in one of two ways. Either he is educated according to a learned, literary tradition: the type of education embodied in the instruction-text, or he gains his training through experience, learning from several teachers as he travels, the method most typical of folk-tale and oral tradition.

The instruction of the prince (*speculum regale*) is an ancient literary form: one of the earliest examples is the work commonly known as *Advice to a Prince,*[1] a Babylonian text dated between 1000 and 700 BC. The genre persisted in most Western cultures[2] until the end of the medieval period; the chief Scandinavian speculum, *Konungs skuggsjá,* is dated to around 1250.[3] The *speculum regale* characteristically concerns itself with such problems as the administration of justice, fair taxation, proper enactment of ritual, and other activities specifically the duty of the ruler.[4] Related to the *speculum* in purpose, but distinct in theme and form, are the traditions of the apprenticeship of the hero. Typically he must go on a journey, often studying with several teachers before his initiation is complete. The hero's instructors tend to be less concerned with the duties of kingship and the arts of peace; it is more necessary for him to acquire skill in battle and to master a range of weapons.[5] The Irish hero Cúchu-

lainn graduates from one teacher, Domnall, who teaches him tricks
of warfare, to study with Scáthach who completes his training, ar-
ranges for his sexual initiation, and prophesies his future. Among
other skills, he learns from Scáthach: 'the feats of the sword-edge
and the sloped shield; the feats of the javelin and rope; the body-
feat; the feat of Cat and the heroic salmon-leap; the pole-throw and
the leap over a poisoned stroke'.[6]

Analysis of the kinds of wisdom which constitute Sigurðr's
education must then distinguish between two layers of tradition
which the figure has attracted, corresponding to the two patterns
identified above. The layer which I would regard as older,
substantially the material in *Reginsmál* and *Sigrdrífumál*, depicts
the hero journeying from one instructor-figure to another, from
Reginn, to Fáfnir, to Sigrdrífa, gaining knowledge of runes,
spells, battle-omens: an apprenticeship in magic and supernatural knowledge for the hero alone. The more recent material
is found in the prose accounts of Sigurðr's life: *Vǫlsunga saga* and
Norna-Gests Þáttr.[7] their conception of the education of the young
man is rather different from that of the older traditions, closer to
the contemporary ideals of education for kingship, as exemplified in *Konungs skuggsjá*. I shall consider the prose sources
first.

2.2 PROSE TRADITIONS

Vǫlsunga saga envisages the instruction of the young Sigurðr as
similar to that of other young aristocrats: he learns various
íþróttir,[8] both practical skills and athletic feats. His first teacher is
Reginn the smith, his foster-father, who teaches him all the skills
fitting for a king's son: 'Hann kenndi honum íþróttir, tafl ok
rúnar ok tungur margar at mæla, sem þá var títt konunga sonum,
ok margra hluti aðra' (He taught him skills, chequers,[9] runes, and
to speak many languages, as was then customary for the sons of
kings, and many other things).[10]

Similar tallies of accomplishments are given in *Rígsþula* 35 and
42, but it is rune-wisdom, arcane knowledge, of divine origin,
which lifts the emerging hero, Konr, above the level of his other
brothers, and marks him out as chosen for kingship.[11]

Norna-Gests þáttr depicts Sigurðr as fully conscious of the re-
sponsibilities which he will have as a future king. Meeting Hnikarr

(Óðinn), who offers to give him some counsel ('ráð'), Sigurðr accepts enthusiastically:

Hann spurði ef Sigurðr vildi nokkut ráð af honum þiggja. Sigurðr kveðst vilja, sagst at ætla, at hann mundi verða ráðdrjúgr ef hann vildi mönnum gagn gera.

He asked if Sigurðr wanted to receive some counsel from him. Sigurðr said that he would, said that he thought that he ought to become a man of much counsel if he wanted to be of help to men.[12]

The prose accounts thus conceive of Sigurðr's instruction as the acquisition of *íþróttir*, the standard education of the young nobleman in Norse sources, in preparation for kingship.

2.3 *GRÍPISSPÁ*

Grípisspá is a later poem than *Reginsmál*, *Fáfnismál*, and *Sigrdrífumál*.[13] Although it draws substantially upon the poems which follow it in the cycle, in its understanding of Sigurðr's education, *Grípisspá* is more akin to the prose tradition. Already upon his arrival at his uncle's court, Sigurðr is characterized as 'wise', almost Grípir's equal. Grípir prophesies that Sigurðr will learn the runes — and foreign languages — from Sigrdrífa (17). The runes will mark Sigurðr as pre-eminent among warriors as Konr was among his brothers.

Grípir skims over the subject matter of *Reginsmál* in one verse, strangely omitting any mention of Sigurðr's meeting with Óðinn, a meeting significant not only for the omens in which Sigurðr is instructed, but also because it represents the sole encounter in the *Poetic Edda* between the hero and the patron of his clan.[14] *Grípisspá* is purged of mythological reference in order to increase the human realism of the story, the drama of personalities in which Sigurðr will become embroiled at the court of the Gjúkungar.

Nor does Sigurðr in fact learn languages from Sigrdrífa — 'mæla á mannz tungo hveria': it seems clear that the poet of *Grípisspá* interpreted 'mál' in *Sigrdrífumál* 4 and 'málrúnar' in *Sigrdrífumál* 12 as ability in foreign languages, a concern of *Konungs skuggsjá*,[15] rather than eloquence in one's own tongue, a gift with which *Hávamál* is especially concerned.[16]

The prose accounts and *Grípisspá* assume that Sigurðr has had the basic education of the contemporary nobleman before he sets out. The older poetry of the Codex Regius gives us no information about his early education. Sigurðr is a *tabula rasa* — with an inherited courage and ferocity — upon whom the three instructors, Óðinn, Fáfnir, and Sigrdrífa write their wisdom.

2.4 *REGINSMÁL*

Óðinn appears to Sigurðr in the midst of a storm. Hailing Sigurðr's ship from the top of a cliff, he asks for passage; when this is granted to him he boards the ship, and the storm abates.[17] Clearly the stranger, who calls himself Hnikarr, has extraordinary powers. Recognizing this, Sigurðr requires Hnikarr to instruct him in good omens for the warrior going into battle (19).

Since Sigurðr has just embarked on his first military venture, avenging his father, Óðinn's advice is most opportune. The verses which follow, (20–5), giving both battle-omens and practical fighting techniques, have a dramatic, as well as informational function. Sigurðr's battle against the sons of Hunding is briskly passed over in a prose insert and a single stanza describing the cutting of the blood-eagle on an enemy. Stanzas 20–5 prefigure the battle to come, anticipating the fight with the sons of Hunding in a swift, impressionistic evocation of the ebb and flow of battle, just as *Fáfnismál* dramatizes the physical battle between Sigurðr and Fáfnir into a battle of words.

Óðinn specifies three good omens, one bad, and two pieces of advice, adding to the two possible outcomes of fortune advice which may help the young fighter tip the balance. The good omens of stanzas 20 and 22 are provided by a raven and a wolf — beasts of battle and Odinic animals.[18] A fighter is to be considered lucky if he is followed by a raven, or to hear the howling of a wolf, as he sets out for battle, for the animals are prescient; they know instinctively that a feast will be provided for them by the victorious warrior. Ravens as omens of good fortune are frequent in the sagas and *Heimskringla*: after his enforced baptism, Hákon jarl sacrifices to Óðinn and sees two ravens, indicating that the day was auspicious for battle (*Óláfs saga Tryggvasonar*, ch. 27).

21 predicts a fortunate outcome if, on leaving the house, two warriors 'hróðrfúsa' — eager for fame — are seen standing on

either side of the threshold. The appearance of two such figures may have a supernatural significance,[19] or simply be a superstitious recognition that to set eyes first of all upon something connected with one's enterprise is lucky. More prosaically, to have two brave men ready to accompany a warrior to battle is bound to increase his chances of success.

Stanza 23 combines a common-sense observation with an allusion to a type of battle-formation ('hamalt fylkia') particularly associated with Óðinn's protégés.[20] The man who fights facing the afternoon sun is likely to become dazzled, and so lose the advantage; a fact of which the good commander, a man who would know how to 'hamalt fylkia', would be aware.[21]

Stanza 24 warns of the danger of stumbling when setting out for battle, a widely held superstition, attested in some sagas.[22] Stumbling puts the warrior into the power of the *dísir*, malevolent female spirits who intend an evil outcome to the enterprise.[23]

The advice, 'ráð' of 25:

Kembðr ok þveginn	Combed and washed
skal kœnna hverr	should every sensible man be
ok at morni mettr	and fed in the morning

is similar in phrasing and vocabulary to *Hávamál* 61:

þveginn ok mettr	Washed and fed ought
ríði maðr þingi at,	a man to ride to the Þing,
þótt hann sét væddr til vel;	though he be not clothed too well;

$$(61^{1-3})$$

A man should be ready, washed, and well-fed to face the day. In *Hávamál* 61, the protagonist is on his way to the Þing; that he is clean and fresh should increase his self-respect, even though his means are limited. The gnome in *Reginsmál* is given a pointed relevance by the use of 'kœnna' (sensible, thoughtful). The wise fighter will take time to make himself ready for what the day may bring, for he does not know where he will come by nightfall:

þvíat ósýnt er,	for it is not forseeable,
hvar at apni kømr;	where he will come in the evening;
ilt er fyr heill at hrapa.	it is bad to rush headlong before your fortune.

The gnome is skilfully shaped to fit the dramatic context: the reference to nightfall, in the context of battle, suggests that by evening 'at apni', a warrior may well find himself in Valhǫll.

The last line of the verse in *Reginsmál* warns against rushing ahead without proper preparation or consideration. Undue haste will cause the rash man to trip and fall, both literally and metaphorically. Stanza 24 has suggested that a stumble puts one in the power of the *dísir*; 25 gives a practical gloss: without calm, solemn preparation in the morning, a man risks making mistakes through carelessness. '[I]lt er fyr heill at hrapa' also serves as a concluding comment on the whole sequence: it is ill-advised to rush into an expedition without taking the opportunity to determine what the omens foretell, a danger which Sigurðr has avoided.

This list of battle-omens is unique in Old Norse poetry; practical advice 'ráð' on military matters is also rare. Omens predicting the outcome of fighting in the sagas are a frequent motif, however; protagonists are usually forewarned of impending strife in dreams rather than in waking visions.[24]

Battle-omens and 'ráð' — strategies for fighting, a combination of superstition and common-sense, are an essential part of the hero's education; these, placed in the mouth of the god of war, must have been of particular value, for the laconic prose report of Sigurðr's battle against the sons of Hunding which follows suggests that the young man put what he learned from Óðinn to good use. Interest in battle-omens and strategy must have been enduring, for *Norna-Gests þáttr*, which recounts the famous battles in which Norna-Gestr took part, dwells longer on this part of the Sigurðr cycle than on any other episode in the hero's career, citing these *Reginsmál* verses in full.

2.5 *FÁFNISMÁL*

Fáfnismál differs from *Sigrdrífumál* in that it is not a wisdom poem *per se*; its main purpose is not to show the further instruction of Sigurðr, but to depict the events subsequent to Sigurðr's attack on Fáfnir.

When the main poem begins, the action is already over: Sigurðr has struck Fáfnir's death-blow. The antagonists now embark upon a long conversation, unparalleled in Germanic analogues to the dragon-fight,[25] during which Sigurðr uses riddles and gnomes to avoid answering the dragon's questions. First Fáfnir demands to know who this unknown boy might be, who — astonishingly — has succeeded in overcoming him. Sigurðr tries to conceal his name and lineage, answering Fáfnir with a riddling mystification of his origins: 'Gǫfugt dýr ek heiti' (Precious animal I am called)[26] (2¹). Fáfnir acknowledges the riddle genre, employing a variant of a phrase familiar from Old Norse and Old English riddles 'hvat er þat undr' (what is that wonder),[27] but the purpose of the riddle is reversed: Fáfnir is seeking information rather than trying to bewilder his opponent (3):

Veiztu, ef fǫður ne áttat	Do you know, if you had no father
sem fira synir,	as the sons of men do,
af hverio vartu	from what wonder
undri alinn?	were you born?

Surprisingly, Sigurðr admits his name and parentage in the next verse: 'Sigurðr ek heiti | — Sigmundr hét minn faðir' (Sigurðr is my name — my father was called Sigmundr); the attempt at concealment is one of the poem's many blind motifs.[28] Fáfnir then wishes to know who has incited Sigurðr to attack him (5). Unwilling to let Reginn's role be known, Sigurðr claims with aristocratic pride that it was a deed of daring: 'hugr mik hvatti' (my spirit spurred me), and tries to divert Fáfnir with a gnome: only the bold, promising youth — like Sigurðr himself — will grow into a courageous man:

fár er hvatr,	few are brave,
er hrøðaz tekr,	when they become old,
ef í barnœsku er blauðr.	if they are cowardly in childhood.[29]

(6⁴⁻⁶)

With this exchange of hostilities, the dialogue abandons the style of the riddle contest and becomes a modified flyting in which Fáfnir tries to prick the bubble of the young man's self-esteem. Sigurðr's confident prediction of future prowess draws from Fáfnir the admission that the young man may become a good fighter in time,[30] but the revelation of Sigurðr's name and descent has given Fáfnir a weapon to use against him. The young man is not the noble prince which 6 suggests; rather he is an ignoble captive of war (his mother was 'hernumin' while carrying him), and the proverb-like last line of 7 asserts that the bound man is always trembling with cowardice.[31] Sigurðr denies the charge; he may once have been taken captive, but, with a paradoxical twist to the image of the bound prisoner in 7[6], he asserts that this bound man is free to act, as Fáfnir has found to his cost: 'þú fant at ek lauss lifi!' (You found that I live free!) (8). Fáfnir responds with a prophecy of Sigurðr's future which differs from the boy's vision of his own maturity in 6[4–6]: the gold will be Sigurðr's death (9). The hero shrugs off the threat with another gnome:

Fé ráða	Power over his property
skal fyrða hverr	shall every man have
æ til ins eina dags,	always until the last day,
þvíat eino sinni	for on one occasion only
skal alda hverr	shall every man
fara til heliar heðan.	depart from here to hell.

(10)

The generalizing terms 'fyrða hverr', 'alda hverr', distance the terror of the dragon's prophecy; every man must die, and that but once – in the mean time Sigurðr intends to enjoy the treasure he has won.

Seeing that Sigurðr is unafraid of his intimations of doom, Fáfnir invokes a higher, inescapable power: that of the Norns. Sigurðr cannot escape their judgment which will be his fate — 'dómr' is used in a double sense, 'fate' and 'judgment'.

Norna dóm	The judgment of the Norns
þú munt fyr nesiom hafa	you will have before the headlands
ok ósvinnz apa	and the fate of a fool;

(11[1–3])

Skilled though Sigurðr may be in bandying proverbs, mere cleverness will not save him. Fáfnir seems to envisage Sigurðr returning to the Viking life, for death by drowning is the fate which he prophesies; even if Sigurðr sets out in a propitious breeze, 'ef í vindi rœr',[32] he cannot escape. This prophecy is not fulfilled; possibly it belongs to an earlier stratum of the story. Fáfnir's prediction of Reginn's treachery is pre-empted by Sigurðr's slaying of his foster-father: a result which Fáfnir probably intended in order to revenge himself upon his brother, whom he correctly identifies as the instigator of the attack. While in *Vǫlsunga saga* Fáfnir's curse is not seen as instrumental in Sigurðr's fate, it may be that the poems in the *Poetic Edda* lacuna linked the curse and Sigurðr's downfall, giving the motif a structural function.

The reference to the Norns provokes a change of subject and of genre: the structure is no longer that of a dramatic interchange. Objective, apparently unattached wisdom obtrudes into the poem; the pace becomes leisurely, even conversational after the swift interchanges of 1–11. Stanzas 12–15 are closer to *Vafþrúðnismál* in style than to the preceding verses: a similarity signalled by the question-formula with which Sigurðr asks for further information:

Segðu mér, Fáfnir,	Tell me, Fáfnir,
allz þik fróðan kveða	you are said to be wise in all things
ok vel mart vita:	and to know a great deal:
hveriar ro þær nornir	which are those Norns
er nauðgǫnglar ro	who go to those in need and
ok kiósa mœðr frá mǫgom?	help mothers in childbirth?

(12)

This question, and that of 14, interrupts the development of the exchange between Sigurðr and Fáfnir. The allusion to the Norns in 11 seems to have triggered an automatic addition of further information about the Norns, irrespective of its relevance. However, the questions and answers are not irrelevant, for even while the main subject is apparently neutral — Fáfnir's response to Sigurðr's request for information — the theme of impending disaster is heard in a minor key. As Kragerud[33] has shown, Fáfnir's answers carry a subtextual warning: no one can escape Fate. Even when the gods think that they have achieved victory on the field of Óskópnir, Bifrǫst breaks and they are doomed. Innocuous information — the name of the battlefield — encodes a hidden warning to Sigurðr, that he cannot thwart his destiny (15).

Sigurðr chooses this moment to question Fáfnir about the most profound secrets of the cosmos: the nature of the fates and the death of the gods, because the dragon is dying. It is a widely-attested folk-belief that those on the point of dying have access to an arcane knowledge not accessible to those occupied with the concerns of ordinary life.[34] The dying Christ teaches healing herb-wisdom from the Cross in Old English;[35] Óðinn gains knowledge of the runes only *in extremis* (*Hávamál* 138 ff.). Moreover, Fáfnir is possessed of a special wisdom, for as an anthropomorphic being transformed into a dragon, he might be thought especially potent in supernatural knowledge: gnomic observations about dragons in Old English characterize them as ancient in wisdom.[36] Sigurðr thus takes the opportunity to learn what he can from Fáfnir before he dies.

Within the immediate context of the poem, the purpose of these questions and answers is to extend Sigurðr's education. He has already been instructed in battle-omens by Óðinn (*Reginsmál* 20–5), and will learn runes and maxims from Sigrdrífa, and spells and charms from the 'minnis veig' (memory drink) which she gives him. The only type of traditional wisdom which Sigurðr is not depicted as acquiring elsewhere in this cycle is the type in *Vafþrúðnismál* and *Grímnismál*: mythological information. Such knowledge may be a prerequisite of kingship,[37] as Fleck has suggested: in any case, Sigurðr is eager to gain it.

Until 12 the conversation between Sigurðr and Fáfnir is hostile: Fáfnir attacks, Sigurðr parries; the questions and answers have a dramatic function, imitating the ebb and flow of the battle which has just taken place. The dramatic qualities of the poem, mimetic of attack and parry, seem to represent a fight more similar to the description of Sigmund's battle with the dragon in *Beowulf* 884b–897, rather than the ambush described in the prose introduction to the poem and *Vǫlsunga saga* ch. 18. The original identity of the dragon-fights of father and son was suggested by G. Neckel in 1920,[38] with the method of attack — open battle or ambush from a pit — a variable in the account. Although the Sigmund fight in *Beowulf* retains the older form, by the tenth century the pit-motif had become firmly attached to the Sigurðr-tale, as evidenced by the representations on Viking crosses in the Isle of Man (Malew Church, Jurby 93).[39] The content, as opposed to the structure, of *Fáfnismál* confirms the tradition of the carvings. Fáfnir's accusations of cowardice and grudging admission that Sigurðr may yet prove a good fighter (7) fit better with an ambush than a fair fight.

Fáfnir tries every possible stratagem to pierce Sigurðr's self-confidence, while Sigurðr parries with evasions and gener-alizations: the gnome is transformed from a vehicle of instruction into a means of dissimulation and defence. However, at 12 the verbal sparring modulates into a lull in the hostilities, for Sigurðr's desire for knowledge draws him closer to Fáfnir. The tone of 12–15 is that of a friendly conversation between wise men, a *rapprochement* between the two. After the mythological interlude, Fáfnir sounds a nostalgic note: once he bore the *Œgishjálmr* over men. Just as the gods will — mistakenly — believe themselves invincible, so he thought that he was the strongest of all (16). Sigurðr comments that no one can be always pre-eminent (17).[40] Fáfnir offers Sigurðr a final warning: the gold will be his death:

Ræð ek þér nú, Sigurðr,	Now I advise you, Sigurðr,
en þú ráð nemir	and you take that advice
ok ríð heim heðan!	and ride home from here!
it gialla gull	the resounding gold and
ok it glóðrauða fé	the glowing-red treasure
þér verða þeir baugar	those rings will be your slayers!
at bana!	

(20)

The use of 'ráða' and 'ráð', exhorting the listener to take to heart what is said, locates the advice within the same instruction-tradition as the *Loddfáfnismál*. The tone of the warning is almost friendly; Fáfnir reverts to the instructor-role of 12 and 14 in a last attempt to impress Sigurðr with the fatal curse on the hoard. Sigurðr violently rejects the warning, now without gnomes or evasions; the struggle is over and Sigurðr dispatches Fáfnir to his doom with a curse, his brutal words re-enacting the death-blow:

en þú, Fáfnir, ligg	and you, Fáfnir, lie
í fiǫrbrotom,	in life-fragments,
þar er þik Hel hafi!	there where Hell may have you!

(21[4–6])

Fáfnir's last words are a prophecy that Reginn will prove as treacherous to Sigurðr as he has to his brother – a prophecy which is not fulfilled.

When Reginn returns with flattering words for Sigurðr: 'þik kveð ek óblauðastan alinn' (I say you have been brought up the least cowardly) (cf. 6), Sigurðr turns aside his praise, just as he turned aside Fáfnir's threats and curses, with another gnome:

þat er óvíst at vita,	There is no knowing for certain
þá er komom allir saman,	when all are come together,

sigtíva synir,	the sons of the glorious gods,
hverr óblauðastr er alinn;	who is brought up the least cowardly;
margr er sá hvatr	many a man is bold
er hiǫr ne ryfr	who does not redden his sword
annars brióstom í.	in another's breast.

(24)

Sigurðr dissimulates his distrust of Reginn with an indirect taunt: Reginn has not had to bloody his sword. The next verse, in a wonderfully observed range of tones, shows Reginn trying to avert Sigurðr's bad temper with a forced cheerfulness, reminding him of the role that the sword Reginn forged for Sigurðr played in the battle. The tone changes swiftly to a relishing satisfaction at the death of his brother (ll. 4–5); finally, in an attempt to appropriate some of the credit for the victory, Reginn observes 'ok veld ek þó siálfr sumo' (and yet I have caused some of it myself). Sigurðr acknowledges that he would have left the dragon alone, if Reginn had not challenged his courage: 'nema þú frýðir mér hvaz hugar'.[41] In 28 Sigurðr returns to the attack with an open accusation: while he was fighting Fáfnir, Reginn was hiding at a distance in the heather: 'meðan þú í lyngvi látt'. Reginn defends himself by arguing that without the sword which he forged for Sigurðr, the dragon would still be alive. Sigurðr parries with further gnomes (30–1). The gnomic structure 'X er betra en Y' is found several times in *Hávamál*,[42] but the heroic sentiments expressed here are unlike anything in that poem:

Hugr er betri	Courage is better
en sé hiǫrs megin,	than the edge of a sword,
hvars <v>reiðir skolo vega,	where angry men have to fight,
þvíat hvatan mann	for a brave man
ek sé har<ð>liga vega	I see fighting strongly
með slævo sverði sigr.	conquers with a blunt sword.

(30)

The relative importance of Sigurðr's courage and Reginn's sword is perfectly expressed in the gnome; similarly, a contrast, implicit here, is expressed in more general terms in 31, where bravery and cheerfulness, cf. 'glaðr ertu nú, Sigurðr' (now you are cheerful, Sigurðr) (25[1]) are contrasted with cowardice and panting with fear. As Reginn falls asleep after devouring the dragon's heart, the gnomic exchanges come to an end. Yet the poem's interest in wisdom is not exhausted; the nuthatches intervene in the narrative to discuss Sigurðr's choices. The first nuthatch recommends eating Fáfnir's heart as a wise course of action: this would enable Sigurðr to understand the birds' advice. The other nuthatches agree (35–7) that for Sigurðr, wisdom resides in killing Reginn and having sole control of the treasure.

The earlier poems in the cycle, corroborated by *Vǫlsunga saga*, have shown Sigurðr struggling to exert his own will in the face of his foster-father's urgings to attack Fáfnir. *Reginsmál* 15 gives Sigurðr's response to Reginn's first attempts at persuasion: Sigurðr retorts that to ignore the obligation of revenge for his father in favour of winning the dragon's treasure would be viewed as cowardly by the sons of Hunding. After the mission of vengeance is accomplished, Sigurðr acquiesces in Reginn's plans for Fáfnir; the ambush set for the dragon is the idea of the cunning dwarf, not of Sigurðr himself.

Fáfnir's warnings about Reginn's treachery plant the seeds of suspicion in Sigurðr's mind, suspicions deepened by the chatter of the nuthatches. Despite the flattering words with which he greets Sigurðr, Reginn continues to treat the young hero as his apprentice, ordering him to cook the dragon's heart while he takes a nap. Only when he is able to understand the conversation of the nuthatches[43] does Sigurðr realize that he has won the right to act independently of Reginn: his apprenticeship is over. By taking their 'ástráð' (affectionate advice) (35[3]), Sigurðr avoids the accusation of being insufficiently wise 'horskr' (36[1]), and 'ósviðr' (37[1]). Ridding himself of the foster-father whom he has now out-grown, he rides off in search of further 'ástráð' from Sigrdrífa. The hero has proved his courage in attacking the dragon; by acting on the nuthatches' advice, he proves his wisdom.

The gnomes which Sigurðr deploys against Fáfnir and Reginn are heroic maxims; their subject is the warrior's conduct. As such they are almost unique in Old Norse verse, the closest parallel being *Sigrdrífumál* 36. Even *Hávamál* 64[4–6,] which uses a variant of *Fáfnismál* 17[4–6,] seems to refer to political power rather than martial strength. For the closest parallels in Germanic literature, we must turn to *Beowulf;* see below chapter 7.

The poet of *Fáfnismál* employs the techniques of wisdom verse with a high degree of sophistication. The riddle, the flyting, the instruction-poem, and the basic structure of the wisdom dialogue, are used not to illuminate, but to obfuscate. Thus the point of the dialogue is not what is being said, but what is being concealed. The subtle subtextual messages of threat and defiance which Fáfnir and Sigurðr, and to a lesser extent Sigurðr and Reginn, send to one another through the gnomic interchanges contrast with the deceptively simple language of the poem, and the traditional nature of Sigurðr's gnomes. The poem dramatically re-enacts the battle between Sigurðr and Fáfnir, creating a powerful impression of deceit, mistrust, and foreboding, unparalleled in the other poems of the cycle.

2.6 *SÍGRDRÍFUMÁL*

Sigrdrífumál is the most straightforwardly 'instructional' of the poems recounting the youth of Sigurðr; unlike *Fáfnismál* or *Reginsmál*, it has no other intentions. Like *Hávamál*, it depicts the combination of different types of wisdom, rune-knowledge and maxims governing social behaviour.

A prose introduction explains how, after killing the dragon Fáfnir, Sigurðr rides up to the mountain Hindarfjall where he finds the valkyrie Sigrdrífa asleep in a 'skjaldborg' — a rampart of shields. Sigurðr awakens her and she asks his name (1^1–1^4). Sigurðr identifies himself (1^5–1^8). Sigrdrífa then gives him a 'minnisveig', literally a 'memory-drink'. The phrase is paralleled in prose in *Göngu-Hrólfs saga*, ch. 25, while in verse the similar 'minnis ǫl' is found in *Hyndluljóð* 45. Since the function of these two drinks is to enhance or to restore the power of memory, we may assume that one role of the 'minnis veig' of *Sigrdrífumál* is to enable Sigurðr to keep in mind Sigrdrífa's instruction.

In an impressively dramatic invocation of the cosmic powers: day, night, and their descendants, the Æsir and Ásynior, and the richness of earth,[44] Sigrdrífa asks for blessing upon herself and the warrior, and for three particular gifts: 'mál', 'manvit', and 'læknishendr' (eloquence, native wit, and healing hands). The wisdom which the valkyrie will impart to Sigurðr thus derives from all the powers of nature as well as from divine beings; the only invocation of such powers found in the *Poetic Edda*.

Stanza 5 describes the magical drink, a potent liquid compounded of almost every conceivable magical device, endowing the recipient with all kinds of power, physical and spiritual. 'Magn' suggests that the liquid gives the drinker magically enhanced power;[45] 'megintír',[46] a *hapax legomenon*, 'mighty glory', perhaps ensures that the hero's fame will endure. Of the other ingredients 'ljóð' (spells) are encountered in the *Ljóðatal* of *Hávamál*, while 'galdrar' (charms) are paralleled in *Grógaldr* and *Oddrúnargrátr*. The other two constituents, 'líknstafir' and 'gamanrúnar' are elsewhere found only in *Hávamál*, where they appear with figurative meanings in a more prosaic context. Since *Sigrdrífumál* focuses on runes in the verses which follow, the 'líknstafir' and 'gamanrunar' in 5 should be interpreted literally as runic symbols ensuring, in the first instance, that others should be disposed to show one 'líkn' (favour), in the second, that one should secure 'gaman' (sexual favours).[47]

The 'minnisveig' resembles the mead of poetry, for both are liquids which give access to mysterious knowledge. Thus in partaking of the 'veig', Sigurðr imitates the original action of Óðinn: as the god drank, so too does the hero. While the mead is an archaic symbol, a sacrificial drink found in varying guises throughout Indo-European cultures,[48] one among several methods by which Óðinn acquires his wisdom, the 'biórr', as a probably later reflex of the mead, synthesizes all possible forms of wisdom, providing them in one swift gulp. After the solemn ritual of the opening, the exclusivity and value of Sigrdrífa's wisdom has now been established. Next the poet concentrates on two specific types of wisdom; rune-knowledge in 6–19, and counsel 'ráð' in 22–37.

Rune-Wisdom

Stanzas 6–13 detail kinds of runes, comprehensive in their range of functions: a magical system facilitating all types of human activity. Each verse names a type of rune, indicates a situation where the rune is to be applied, and a surface on which the rune should be inscribed. In Eddic tradition there is some overlap in the functions of runes and spells: *Hávamál* 54 knows a 'ljóð' (spell) with the same effects as the 'brimrúnar' (sea-runes) of *Sigrdrífumál* 10, while in *Oddrúnargrátr* 7, 'galdrar' (chants) perform the same function as 'bjargrúnar' (birth-runes) in *Sigrdrífumál* 9. The runes of *Hávamál* have their origins in a mysterious Other World,[49] and manifest themselves among the gods, giants, and dwarfs. The 'hugrúnar' (thought-runes) of

Sigrdrífumál 13 also have a mysterious origin, but while the runes
of *Hávamál* function as an element in religious and ritual practice
(*Hávamál* 142–5), those of *Sigrdrífumál* operate in the human
world: the carving of the runes gives visible results, as do the 'ljóð'
of the *Ljóðatal. Sigrdrífumál,* like the *Ljóðatal,* gives insufficient
detail for the runes to be of practical use to the auditor; both
poems are an index of magical possibilities rather than a guide.
The 'human world' to which the poems refer is a literary
construct, bearing only a tangential relation to the reality of the
audience's experience. (It should be noted that the literary
notion of practical applications for runes cannot be connected
with their historical uses as evidenced by surviving rune inscriptions.)

In the order in which they are listed in *Sigrdrífumál,* the runes
progress from those most useful to a hero, 'sigrúnar' promising
victory in battle, through other runes with practical applications
for any man, to a more abstract kind of rune. The 'málrúnar' give
eloquence, and perhaps prevent malignant speech on the part of
others 'ef þú vilt at mangi þér | heiptom gialdi harm' (if you wish
that no one repays you harm with malice); while the 'hugrúnar'
increase intellectual powers. Stanzas 12 and 13, in a departure
from the structure of the other verses, do not specify places where
the runes can be carved; 12 states that 'málrúnar'[50] should be
woven:

á því þingi	at that meeting
er þióðir skolo	where people must
í fulla dóma fara.[51]	go to fully constituted courts.
	(127–9)

The scene seems to be laid at a Þing; Sigurðr is imagined to be
taking part in a law-suit, in which the 'málrúnar' will somehow
protect him from his opponents. Thus 'mál' punningly refers
both to the legal case, in which the runes will ensure the user's
success, and the gift of eloquence.

The 'hugrúnar', endowing the man who knows them with
greater wisdom than other men, mark the end of the catalogue of
different types of rune; now the poet's concern is to re-enact the
origin of the 'hugrúnar', the subject of the verses which follow
(14–18) and the only runes in the poem directly associated with
Óðinn — Hroptr. In language recalling the technical terminology

of *Hávamál* 144: 'Veiztu hvé rísta skal? | Veiztu hvé ráða skal?' (Do you know how they must be cut? Do you know how they must be interpreted?) (144¹⁻²), stanza 13 recounts Óðinn's acquisition of the 'hugrúnar' while the elliptical first lines of 14 suggest that there was some narrative — now lost — attached to the inform-ation of 13, explaining how Mímr's head was stimulated into speech. Mímr's utterance (14⁴⁻⁶) tells where the runes were cut (15–17), and how they were disseminated among the different orders of beings (18), scraped off into the holy mead, they swirl out on wide ways 'á víða vega':

þær ro með ásom,	they are with the Æsir,
þær ro með álfom,	they are with the Elves,
sumar með vísom vǫnom,	some with the wise Vanir,
sumar hafa menzkir menn.	some humans have.

(18⁵⁻⁸)

This account of the origin of the runes differs considerably from that of *Hávamál* 138–9; as with most mythological themes, more than one variant tradition about the origin of the runes must have been current.[52] We cannot tell whether the origin-tale preserved in *Hávamál* was also known to the *Sigrdrífumál*-poet, but, with the 'bíórr' of 5, his emphasis on a tradition in which liquid aspects predominate, 'leki' and 'helgi mioð', results in a finely har-monious conception.

Ráð (Counsel)

Sigrdrífa links her digression on the origin of runes to her earlier exposition of their uses with a summarizing verse (19), adjuring Sigurðr to take to heart the knowledge offered in a phrase echoing *Hávamál*: 'nióttu ef þú namt' (it will be useful to you if you take it) (19⁸) and offering, in elliptical terms, further instruction (20). The choices offered to Sigurðr are ambiguous: whether he is to decide if he himself will speak or remain silent, alternatives frequently presented in *Hávamál*, or whether he is asked to assent to further speech from Sigrdrífa, despite the last line's hint that the warrior's future is inauspicious — a warning which perhaps looks forward to the ominous last line of 37.

Sigrdrífa's forebodings — that Sigurðr's fate is decreed already, and that malevolent forces are shaping his destiny — form a curious introduction to the series of maxims which follow. There

are among the maxims certain motifs which recur elsewhere in
the cycle: the warning against oath-breaking in 23, for example,
anticipates the emphasis on oaths in *Brot* and *Sigurðarkviða in
skamma*,[53] while the image of the enemy's son as a young wolf
ironically recurs as Brynhildr urges Gunnarr to kill both Sigurðr
and his son, but the prophetic tone of 20[6] promises more than is
finally delivered. Prophecy and wisdom poetry are not normally
compatible, for while gnomic poetry may sometimes conclude
that fate is inescapable,[54] its fundamental premise is that man has
some freedom of choice, that good advice can influence him to
behave in a certain way. The logic of the genre dictates that
mankind's lot can be improved; fate need not be eternally fixed.
The impulse of gnomic verse is thus towards open-ended
possibilities, rather than the ineluctable conclusions towards
which the prophecy looks.

   Sigrdrífa now presents a numbered series of eleven maxims.[55]
The Codex Regius breaks off at 29[2], the beginning of the sixth
maxim; the nine concluding verses (29–37) are taken from paper
manuscripts.[56] The verses predicate a typical warrior existence:
fighting, feasting, and maintaining one's honour. These maxims,
like those of the *Loddfáfnismál*, are to teach Sigurðr how to
conduct himself in human society.

   Considerations of personal honour are of paramount importance to the warrior, both during his lifetime and after death:
according to 22, slowness to take revenge against kindred is a
course approved by society: 'þat kveða dauðom duga' (that is said
to succour the dead man) (22[6]).

   The implication seems to be — in the light of *Hávamál* 76–7 —
that since the only thing which remains after death is the 'orztírr'
or 'dómr' (reputation, the judgment of posterity, of the
departed), a reputation for patience with kindred will enhance
the dead man's fame.

   Stanzas 24 and 25 are concerned with a particular social situation: a quarrel with a foolish man. The scene is realized with
some detail: the quarrel takes place in public, 'á þingi'. The
incensed fool may say something irrevocable; if this should
happen, reprisals will be necessary to restore one's standing,
otherwise, the verse points out with an acuity worthy of *Hávamál*,
either the accusation will be believed, or else one will be
considered a coward. The peace of the þing must not be

shattered by public brawling: revenge must be taken on another occasion, 'annars dags'.

Stanza 27 represents a restatement of two omens from the *Reginsmál*: the fighter needs 'forniósnar[57] augo' eyes which see far ahead ('kunna sjá' (know how to look) *Reginsmál* 23[6]), in order to see malevolent women (*Reginsmál* 24[4–6]) who will blunt his sword. Further practical advice for the warrior comes in 31: it is better to fight outside in the open than be burned inside the house – the bleak alternatives Skarpheðinn recognizes in *Njáls saga* 128.[58] Showing respect for the bodies of the dead and ensuring a fitting burial for them is also part of the warrior's code (33–4).

Other dangers are encountered in the hall rather than on the battlefield. As in *Hávamál* 15–17, 'óvist er at vita | hvar óvinir sitja á fleti fyrir' (there is no knowing where enemies sit in the hall ahead), the society of one's fellows is as uncertain as the road outside. In 29–30 ale is singled out as cause of hostility and fighting amongst warriors;[59] as in 24 where the dispute is at the Þing, one should remain aloof from such quarrels in hall:

Sǫngr[60] ok ǫl	Singing and ale
hefir seggium verit	have been for many men
mǫrgum <at> móðtrega,	a grief at heart,
sumom at bana,	slayers to some,
sumom at bǫlstǫfum;	to some cause of evil;
fiǫlð er þat er tregr fira.	manifold is that which grieves men.

(30)

The consideration of drink in *Sigrdrífumál* is not as nuanced as in *Hávamál*, where the guest is urged not to eschew the cup entirely (19[1]), and ale-drinking in moderation is permissible. *Hávamál* deprecates the springing up of quarrels at feasts, but does not blame drunkenness in particular, observing philosophically that such bad feeling is unavoidable:

aldar róg	strife amongst men
þat mun æ vera,	there will always be,
órir gestr við gest.	guest shows hostility to guest.

(30[4–6])

Nor does *Sigrdrífumál* allow that association with women can bring any benefit; all women are as dangerous to the warrior's peace of mind as the witch in *Hávamál* 113–14. Apart from the witch, the women in *Sigrdrífumál* are neither sinister nor scheming. They are pictured in a courtly setting, dressed in their best, yet they are still a dangerous distraction to the warrior:

þóttu fagrar sér	though you see fair
brúðir bekkiom á,	ladies on the benches,
sifia silfr	silver-decked women
látaðu þínom svefni ráða,	do not let them disturb your sleep,
teygiatu þér at kossi konor.	nor entice women to you to kiss.

(28)

All women are to be avoided: 32 makes clear that neither maidens nor wives are to be seduced, a strong contrast to *Hávamál*'s assertion that no one should be blamed for falling in love (93), and to the outspoken counsels for the most effective method of winning women's hearts (92).

Although they are often presented within a specifically realized setting, the maxims of *Sigrdrífumál* tend to be sweepingly general in their application: all drink brings sorrow to men, all women are to be eschewed. There are none of the subtle distinctions between excess and moderation which *Hávamál* brings to bear upon the pleasure of drink and the company of women.

The final maxim of the poem[61] seems once again to prophesy the hero's future; if this is the last stanza of the original sequence, the poet seems to return to the threatening theme sounded in 20: 'ǫll ero mein of metin' (all harms are measured out). However, the text offers several difficulties:[62]

þat ræð ek þér ellipta,	That I advise you eleventhly,
þat þú við illu sér	that you beware
hvern veg at vegi;	in every direction on your path;
langt líf	a long life
þikkiumsk ek lofðungs vita;	I think the prince will have;
rǫm eru róg of risin.	stern quarrels are sprung up.

As the text stands, the first half-verse urges caution, the last line is also ominous, yet ll. 4–5 predict a long life for Sigurðr. If 'þikkiumsk ek' is emended to 'þikkiumkak' (I do not think), 37 would form a fitting close to the poem: despite the advice, Sigurðr will have to exercise much vigilance if he is to overcome the forces arrayed against him. The author of *Vǫlsunga saga*, ch. 21 is of little use here, for his prose seems to paraphrase a different verse.

The two types of wisdom of *Sigrdrífumál* have a single function: the completion of Sigurðr's education, for 'vits ok vápna | vant er iǫfri at fá' (common-sense and weapons are needful for the prince to acquire) (36⁴⁻⁶). The reference to weapons here, when Sigurðr is already in possession of the sword Gramr, forged for him by Reginn, suggests the influence of the belief that the patron valkyrie gave her protegé a sword as in *Helgakviða Hiǫrvarðssonar* 8–9.

Sigurðr's acquisition of rune-wisdom emphasizes his relationship — and that of his clan — with Óðinn, the culture-hero, first finder of the runes, as opposed to Óðinn, god of war, as in *Reginsmál*. The counsel, 'ráð' — augmenting the young man's 'vit' — offers maxims for the hero in everyday situations: how to deal with kin, friends, fools, drunkards, and women.

Sigurðr has now completed his education, in both arcane matters and practical common-sense: emerging from the fabulous world of his youth, he is ready to hold his own in the dangerous world of human society. Sigurðr still retains his natural attributes of courage and ferocity, but these may not be enough — as 37 suggests — in the complex system of loyalties and jealousies which await him at the Gjúkungar court.

Notes

1. For the text of *Advice to a Prince*, see *Babylonian Wisdom Literature*, ed. W. G. Lambert (Oxford, 1960), 110.

2. Other notable examples of the *speculum* include Dhuoda, *Manuel pour mon fils*, ed. P. Riché, Sources chrétiennes, 225 (Paris, 1975), a Latin instruction written 841–3 by a mother for her son; John of Salisbury's *Policraticus* and King James I's *Basilikon Doron or His Maiesties Instruction to his Dearest Sonne Henry the Prince* (London, 1603). See W. Kleineke, *Englischen Fürstenspiegel vom Policraticus Johanns von Salisbury bis zum Basilikon Doron König Jakobs I*, Studien zur englischen Philologie, 90 (Halle, 1937).

3. *Konungs skuggsjá*, ed. L. Holm-Olsen (Oslo, 1983).

4. Cf. the Indian *Laws of Manu*, dating from the second century BC, ed. G. Bühler Sacred Books of the East, 25 (Oxford, 1886), in particular the section entitled *Advice to a King*, bk vii, 46 ff, as well as *Advice to a Prince*.

5. I have been unable to find much material pertaining to the training of the hero for the feats he later performs. J. Campbell, *The Hero with a Thousand Faces*, 2nd edn. (New York, 1968), 69–73, briefly discusses the instructor-figure. One further parallel to Sigurðr and Cúchulainn, although later and closer to courtly traditions is Parzival. Wolfram von Eschenbach, *Parzival*, tr. A. T. Hatto (London, 1980).

6. *The Táin*, tr. T. Kinsella (Oxford, 1969), 34.

7. See *Vǫlsunga saga* and *Norna-Gests þáttr*, in *Fornaldar sögur Norðurlanda*, i, ed. G. Jónsson and B. Vilhjálmsson (Reykjavik, 1943). The earliest manuscript of *Vǫlsunga saga* is dated at 1400, while the saga's composition is normally put in the last half of the fourteenth century. The Flateyjarbók manuscript containing *Norna-Gests þáttr* is also dated to *c.*1400.

8. See G. R. Russom, 'A Germanic Concept of Nobility in *The Gifts of Men* and *Beowulf*, *Speculum*, 53 (1978), 1–15.

9. For an account of *tafl*, see *KLNM* ii. 223 ff.

10. *Vǫlsunga saga*, ch. 13, p. 29.

11. Cf. *Grímnismál*; although here the arcane knowledge which marks Agnarr out as future king is the mythological information which Óðinn recites in the poem. See J. Fleck, 'Konr-Ottar-Geirrødr: A Knowledge-Criterion for Succession to the Germanic Sacred Kingship', *SS* 42 (1970), 39–49.

12. *Norna-Gests þáttr*, ch. 6, p.176.

13. See J. de Vries, *Altnordische Literaturgeschichte*, ii. (Berlin, 1967), 155, and T. Andersson, *The Legend of Brynhild*, Islandica, 43 (Ithaca, NY, and London, 1980), 103–4.

14. Contrast the frequent appearances of Óðinn to Sigurðr in *Vǫlsunga saga*.

15. *Konungs skuggsjá* 5 stresses the importance of foreign languages: 'æf þu villt vær fullkomenn í froðleic. þa næm allar mallyzkur en alra hælzt latinu oc valsku. þviat þær tungur ganga viðazt' (if you want to be perfect in wisdom, then you should learn all languages, and especially Latin and French, for those tongues are most widely known).

16. Cf. especially *Háv.* 103, emphasizing the value of eloquence for the cultivated host. Other references to eloquence are found in *Háv.* 28, 63, and 92.

17. Cf. the appearance of Sigrún to Helgi in a storm in *Helgakviða Hundingsbana* II, in the prose between vv. 18 and 19.

18. The raven and wolf are Odinic animals: cf. *Grímnismál* 19, 20; *Njáls saga* ch. 79, *Íslendinga saga* I, 512; and *Haraldskvæði* 4. The howling of a wolf is sometimes interpeted as hunger, or as singing: see B–S, ix. 727, 763 for a wolf as a good omen.

19. 'Hróðrfúss' is a *hapax legomenon*. See S–G, ii. 179. Possibly the two men are spirits, since they are encountered on the threshold, the boundary between inside and out, where supernatural influences make themselves felt: see A. van Gennep, *Les Rites de passage* (Paris, 1909), 22, and B–S, x. 151 ff.

20. Saxo, bk i. p. 31 tells how King Hadding of the Danes is sailing along the Norwegian coast when he is hailed by an old man from the cliff-top. The old man introduces him to the 'hamalt' battle-formation, and the 'svínfylking'.

21. S–G, ii. 180 think that west is the direction of misfortune, citing the account in Paulus Diaconus, *Historia Langobardum* I[8], of Frigg's advice to the Winila to look to the east, to the rising sun to gain Óðinn's favour.

22. *Njáls saga*, ch. 75, and in *Grænlendinga saga*, ch. 2. In *Eiríks saga rauða*, ch. 5, the stumble is rationalized into a fall from the horse which injures Eiríkr sufficiently to prevent him from undertaking the journey. See also B–S, viii. 492–6.

23. Cf. the maleficent influence of the *dísir* in *Hamðismál* 15, 28.

24. For numerous prophetic dreams in ON literature, see I. M. Boberg, *Motif-Index of Early Icelandic Literature* (Copenhagen, 1966), 84. Entry D 1812.3.3.

25. See E. Ploss, *Siegfried-Sigurd der Drachenkampfer* (Cologne, 1966). Ploss suggests that, while the basic components of the dragon-fight variants: warrior/dragon/maiden, or warrior/dragon/hoard remain constant, details vary (p. 12). The conversation between Sigurðr and Fáfnir may be regarded as one such topos. (For talking dragons, see n. 36 below.)

26. For an ingenious attempt at solving the riddle Sigurðr poses here, see O. M. Ólafson, 'Sigurðr duldi nafns síns', *Andvari*, ns 12 (1970), 182–9.

27. *Hervarar saga ok Heiðreks*, ed. E. O. G. Turville-Petre (London, 1956), 39–41 and 48. An Old English reflex is found in *Solomon and Saturn II* 103 (see below, ch. 4.6). 'Wundor' or 'wundorlic' are used frequently in the *Exeter Book Riddles*: Riddles 20, 24, 25, 29, 69, 84, 87, and 181.

28. *Vǫlsunga saga* explains Sigurðr's concealment of his identity by suggesting that he feared the dying dragon's curse. The motif is swiftly abandoned however.

29. Stanzas 4–6 are also found in *Sverris saga* where the king is upbraiding some of his men

for fleeing in battle; see *Eddadigte*, ed. J. Helgason, 3rd edn. (Copenhagen, 1971), iii. pp. xvi–ii and 79.

30. The two halves of the verse are not an exact fit: in the first half Fáfnir admits the possibility that Sigurðr may be a good fighter, in the second he accuses him of cowardice. The conflict may be explained by the nature of Sigurðr's attack; from the dragon's viewpoint, Sigurðr's failure to attack him openly could be construed as cowardice.

31. The charge of being a captive is not found in other flytings, although accusations of cowardice are common: *Harbarðzlióð* 26; *Lokasenna* 13. The closest parallel to the proverb is perhaps the incident involving Hialli in *Atlakviða* 22 where the cowardice of Hialli is shown by the quivering of his excised heart. See Dronke's note, *PE*, 60.

32. Cf. *Hávamál* 82[2], '(í) veðri (skal) á sjó róa' (in a breeze should one row on the sea).

33. A. Kragerud, 'De mytologiske spørsmål i *Fåvnesmål*', *ANF* 96 (1981), 9–48.

34. See F. Ström, *Den döendes makt och Odin i trädet*, Göteborgs högskolas årskrift 53 (1947) for a broad-ranging account of this belief.

35. See the 'Lay of the Nine Twigs of Woden', Charm LXXX, in J. H. G. Grattan and C. Singer, *Anglo-Saxon Magic and Medicine* (Oxford, 1952), 153–4.

36. See *Cotton Maxims* 26a–27b (below ch. 4.2), and *Bwf.* 2275b–227 (below ch. 5). Talking dragons are not evidenced anywhere else in Germanic literature; the closest parallel may be the dragon Gorynchishche in the Russian *bylina* - folk epic *Dobrynya i zmei* (*Dobrynya and the dragon*), one of the oldest poems in the so-called 'Kievan Cycle'. See D. P. Costello and I. P. Foote ed. *Russian Folk Literature* (Oxford, 1967), 97–103.

37. J. Fleck, 'The Knowledge-Criterion in the *Grímnismál*: The Case against Shamanism', *ANF* 86 (1971), 49–65.

38. G. Neckel, 'Sigmunds Drachenkampf', *Edda*, 13 (1920), 122–40 and 204–29; see especially 216–17.

39. For further treatment of the pictorial evidence, see Ploss, *Siegfried-Sigurd*, 84 ff.

40. Paralleled at *Háv.* 64[4–6].

41. See *Vǫlsunga saga* chs. 13 and 18.

42. Examples are: *Háv.* 36, 37, 'Bú er betra' (where the corollary: than no farm at all is left unexpressed), 70, 71, and 72.

43. The nuthatches' urging of Sigurðr to kill Reginn and follow his fate to Sígrdrífa are paralleled by the wise crow in *Rígspula* 47. Birds are frequently to be found in pictorial representations of the dragon-slaying — e.g. the eleventh-century Ramsundberg stone, from Södermanland, Sweden in H. Ellis Davidson, *Scandinavian Mythology* (London, 1969), 107.

44. Stanza 4 is the closest equivalent to a hymn to be found in ON poetry. The address to the earth recalls the OE charm 'Æcer-bot', in which Earth — mother of men — is invoked. See G. Storms, *Anglo-Saxon Magic* (The Hague, 1948), 172–86.

45. 'Magn' should not be simply taken as a synonym for 'megin', power, strength: see Fritzner, *Ordbog*, ii. 619: 'magna' (vb.) 'styrke, gjøre stærkere, i Prosa kun om at sætte i Besiddelse af overnaturlige Kræfter ved Hjælp af Trolddom' (strengthen, make stronger, in prose only found in the context of supernatural power with the help of magic). Cf. *Grettis saga* chs. 177, 181. The implication here is that 'magn' refers rather to a supernatural strength than ordinary physical strength.

46. 'Megintírr' is a hapax legomenon: Fritzner, *Ordbog*, ii. 670 'stor Ære', LP, 399 'hoved hæder', 'megenhæder' (great glory, honour).

47. 'Líknstafr' and 'gamanrúnar' seem to be figurative in meaning in *Hávamál*: 'Líknstafr' (favourable statement, esteem, warm regard) 8[3]; 'gamanrúnar' (pleasant private intercourse, relationship (secret love?)), 120[6], 130[6]. See the glosses in A. Faulkes, *Hávamál: Glossary and Index to D. A. H. Evans's Edition* (London, 1987); I. Lindquist, 'Ordstudier och tolkningar i *Hávamál*', *SNF* 9 (1917), 11, suggests that these terms originally signified runes or letters, the carving of which would bring about the desired result: gaining 'líkn' or 'gaman' from another, for example, the runes in *Skírnismál* 36.

48. For the reflexes of the mead of poetry in other Indo-European traditions, see R. Doht, *Der Rauschtrank im germanischen Mythos* (Vienna, 1974), 18–34 and 67–88.

49. For the tradition of the origin of the runes in *Hávamál*, see above ch. 1.6.

50. Cf. *Darraðarljóð* for images of weaving in connection with magic. *Njáls saga, ÍF* xii. (Reykjavik, 1954), 454–8.

51. For a definition of the term 'fullr dómr' (vollbesetzte gericht; fully constituted court) (S–G) see *Grágás* 138.

52. An attempt to reconcile the conflicting traditions concerning the origin of runes through the construction of a 'ritual landscape', accomodating both the tree of *Hávamál* and the liquid of *Sigrdrífumál* can be found in Fleck, 'Óðinn's Self-Sacrifice — A New Interpretation. II: The Ritual Landscape', *SS* 43 (1971), 385–413.

53. See *Brot* 2, 5 and *Sig. sk* 1, 17, 20 for oaths and oath-breaking, and *Sig. sk* 12 for the comparison of Sigurðr's son to a young wolf.

54. e.g. *Hamðismál* 30.

55. The OE poem *Precepts* offers the closest parallel to the numbering of individual maxims. It is probable here that the unnumbered stanzas represent later expansions of the original numbered maxims.

56. See J. Helgason, *Eddadigte* iii. pp. xviii–xix for details of the paper manuscripts in which the remaining verses of *Sigrdrífumál* are found. These verses seem to correspond in content to the prose paraphrase given in *Vǫlsunga saga*, ch. 21; thus there is a strong possibility that they may have formed part of the 'original' *Sigrdrífumál*.

57. 'Fornjósnar' is a *hapax legomenon*. *LP*, 147–8 gives 'udspejden i forvejen, seen sig for' (to spy out the way ahead, look ahead).

58. See *Njáls saga*, ch. 128.

59. Cf. the OE *Fortunes of Men*, 48–50.

60. In the margin of AM 738, 4to (Helgason's P1) Arni Magnusson glosses 'søngr' with 'malo sennur' ('I suppose: quarrels'), which seems more logical than 'søngr' (singing) in the context.

61. This may not be the last maxim in the series, but *Vǫlsunga saga* knows no further verses.

62. Bugge suggest emending 'vegi' l. 3 to 'vini', Grundtvig to 'vinum' in order to bring the meaning closer to the *Vǫlsunga saga* paraphrase. Other early editors, G. Magnæus and T. Møbius wanted to emend 'þikkiumsk ek' in l. 5 to 'þykkiumzka' and 'þikkiumkak', preferring a negative statement here since the tone of l. 6 is so ominous.

3 CHRISTIAN WISDOM POETRY: *HUGSVINNSMÁL*

3.1 *HÁVAMÁL, HUGSVINNSMÁL* AND *DISTICHA CATONIS*: A PROBLEM OF RELATIONSHIPS

In '*Disticha Catonis* und *Hávamál*,[1] K. von See suggests that *Hávamál* shows the influence both of *Hugsvinnsmál*,[2] normally thought to be considerably later than *Hávamál*, and the fourth-century collection of Latin gnomic hexameter couplets known as the *Disticha Catonis*.[3] The *Disticha* were widely known and used as an educational text throughout the Western medieval world; there is evidence that they were used in Irish monastery schools in the seventh century, and there is an Anglo-Saxon translation dated to the end of the tenth century.[4]

The essence of von See's position is that, wherever the resemblance between *Hávamál* and *Hugsvinnsmál* is particularly close, and the vocabulary of *Hávamál* shows 'auffällig junge Züge' (strikingly recent features), there the relationship must be such that *Hugsvinnsmál* is the source for *Hávamál*. He cites two examples in particular of 'recent features' in *Hávamál*, which are also to be found in *Hugsvinnsmál*. The first of these resemblances is: 'at hyggiandi sinni | skylit maðr hrœsinn vera' *Hávamál* 6[1-2]) and: 'af hyggjandi sinni | skylit maðr hrœsinn vera' (*Hugsvinnsmál* 73[1-2]): One should not be arrogant about one's intelligence). Von See points out that the phrase is used nowhere else in *Hávamál*, and that other instances in the Edda occur only in *Sigurðarkviða in skamma* and in *Hamðismál*.

The second example concerns 'metnaðr' (pride) in *Hávamál* 79, a stanza which von See believes is, like *Hugsvinnsmál* 74, a translation of *Disticha Catonis* II[19]:

Fégirni rangri	From wrongful avarice
skalt firra þik	you should distance yourself
ljót er líkams munuð;	the love of the flesh is hateful;
orðstír hæra	a higher glory
getr maðr aldrigi	can a man never obtain

en við syndum sjá.   than to make provision against sin.

                                      (*Hugsvinnsmál* 74)

Ósnotr maðr   A foolish man
er eignaz getr   who manages to get
fé eða flióðs munuð,   property or a woman's love,
metnaðr hánom þróaz   his pride prospers,
en manvit aldregi;   but not his common-sense;
fram gengr hann driúgt í dul.   forward he goes deep in delusion.

                                      (*Hávamál* 79)

Luxuriam fugito, simul et vitare memento
crimen avaritiae; nam sunt contrariae famae.

Flee lust, and at the same time remember to avoid the crime of
avarice; these are are contrary to good reputation.

                                      (*Disticha Catonis* II 19).

Von See finds a similarity of vocabulary between the Latin series
'luxuria . . . avaritia . . . fama' in *Disticha Catonis*, and 'flióðs munuð
. . . fé . . . metnaðr' in *Hávamál*. The 'strikingly recent feature' is
'metnaðr', which von See thinks is borrowed from *Hugsvinnsmál* 30.
'Metnaðr' is found nowhere else in the Edda; while 'dugnaðr',
formed on the same type of ending, is found in *Hugsvinnsmál* 27,
31, and 85. The similarity of content, combined with 'recent features
of vocabulary' is the basis of von See's argument for the priority of
Hugsvinnsmál over *Hávamál*. He adduces other similarities in
thought and wording in other parts of *Hávamál*, but these lack the
'recent vocabulary' element, and therefore can only be significant if
the priority of *Hugsvinnsmál* over *Hávamál* has already been
satisfactorily established.[5]

In addition to arguing for the influence of *Hugsvinnsmál* on
Hávamál, von See also finds evidence that *Hávamál* is, in places,
directly dependent on the *Disticha Catonis*, without the mediation
of *Hugsvinnsmál*. The following reasons are adduced:

(*a*) There are certain places where *Hávamál* seems to come closer
to the thought of *Disticha Catonis* than the *Hugsvinnsmál*
translation does (35–6).

(*b*) There is a strong general agreement in content between
Hávamál and the *Disticha* (38–9).

(*c*) The form of the Latin hexameter has suggested the *ljóðaháttr*
as a suitable metrical form to the Norse *Redaktor* (42).

However, detailed consideration of von See's premisses shows that the priority of *Hugsvinnsmál* cannot be established.

'Recent Vocabulary Features'

at/af hygg(i/j)andi sinni

The word *hyggiandi* (intelligence) is, as von See states, only found in *Sigurðarkviða in skamma* and in *Hamðismál* in Eddic poetry. In *Hamðismál*, von See argues that the word belongs to the 'sapientia-et-fortitudo' theme, which he believes to be borrowed from Latin romance.[6] However, since *Hamðismál* contains archaic folk-tale elements as well as verse which may be more recently composed, it is not safe to argue that hyggjandi must, of necessity, be recent. The word also occurs in the *Snorra Edda* (I 544[10]), in a verse which seems to be part of *Haraldskvæði*. If authentic, this would date from *c*.900.[7] Von See states that the *-indi/-andi* ending is one which became productive only relatively late in the Old Norse period. While it is true that a large number of *-indi/-andi* formations are evidenced only in modern Icelandic, the ending is in fact an ancient Germanic one, similar formations being found in cognate languages well before the year 1000. The ending was productive in earlier Icelandic too: cf. *ørendi* (errand) in *Atlakviða* 38; *Skírnismál* 38; and *Þrymskviða* 10, 11; *tiðindi* (news) in *Þrymskviða* 10; and *þiggjandi* (receiving) in *Hlǫðskviða* 14. *-indi/-andi* words are extremely common in prose; *líkindi* (likelihood) and *þarfindi* (necessities) are both found in the *Frostaþingslǫg*. Although *hyggjandi*, perhaps because of its meaning, is not widely evidenced in Eddic verse, given the above examples of early occurrence, it is not proven as a recent formation.

metnaðr, dugnaðr

Again the words *metnaðr* (pride) and *dugnaðr* (abilty) are found only in later poetry: *metnaðr* in *Lilja* and *Merlinússpá* for example; *dugnaðr* in *Maríuvísur* and the verses of Einarr Gílsson. Both words are attested in prose, however, *metnaðr* in *Njáls saga* and *Egils saga*, among others, and *dugnaðr* in *Fornmanna sǫgur* and *Íslendinga Þjóðssaga*. Other *-aðr* formations are, however, found both in the Edda, if rarely, and in early skaldic poetry; of particular significance, since, like *metnaðr* and *dugnaðr*, they are abstract in meaning, are: *hagnaðr* (advantage) in *Vellekla* 25, *snúnaðr* (windfall) in *Vellekla* 14 and *vǫrnuðr* (warning) in Sigvatr's *Lausavísur* 11, 13, and *Atlakviða* 8. Such formations, far from being recent, as von See claims,[8] were evidently present in Norse during the pagan period; thus the presence of *metnaðr* in *Hávamál* is not conclusive evidence of the priority of *Hugsvinnsmál*.

Christian and Pagan Vocabulary Elements

The vocabulary of *Hugsvinnsmál* shows unmistakable Christian elements which are absent from *Hávamál*. Such words as *heiðinn* (heathen), *lærifaðir* (learned father), *syndugr* (sinful), *himneskr* (heavenly), *sællífi* (eternal life) *reykelsi* (incense), and *jarðliga* (earthly) are typical of the poem's diction, but are not found in *Hávamál*. Certain other key words in *Hugsvinnsmál*, not found in *Hávamál*, are typical of later — specifically Christian — poetry or prose; they are not found in the Edda or early skaldic verse. Examples are: *íþróttir* (skills) in *Merlinusspá*, *Gráfeldardrápa*, *Orms Þáttr*, *gæzku* (grace) in *Harmsól*, *Líknarbraut* (though also in *Atlamál*), and *heilsa* (to save) in *Konungs skuggsjá*, *Háttatal* and *Sólarljóð*.

In comparison, *Hávamál* shows a number of words of archaic origin, for example, *gamanrúnar* in the sense of 'close confidante', found only in *Hávamál* and *Sigrdrífumál* 5[8]. The simplex *gaman* is found in several other Eddic poems, for example, *Guðrúnarkviða II*, *Harbarðsljóð*, and *Skírnismál*: the cognates in other Germanic languages testify to its age. *Vǫmm*, used three times in *Hugsvinnsmál* and once in *Hávamál* is found in *Lokasenna*, *Sigrdrífumál*, and *Sonatorrek*, where it has a distinct pre-Christian sense of 'shame' or 'wrong-doing', as opposed to 'sin'. *Geð*[9] (intellect) is found extensively in the prose, and also in later Christian writing, but equally in Eddic and early skaldic verse: *Lokasenna* 20, and *Sonatorrek* 24. Interestingly, *geð* is not found as a simplex in later poetry, except for its occurrence twice in *Hugsvinnsmál*, perhaps influenced by its extensive use in *Hávamál*. Compounds with *geð* are common, however. *Œði* (mind) is found in *Vafþrúðnismál* and in the poetry of Hallfreðr *vandræðaskald*, and in *Arinbjarnarkviða*. *Sefi*, another word closely related in meaning to *geð* and *œði* in *Hávamál* — mind, spirit, intellectual qualities — is very common in Eddic verse: for example, *Sigrdrífumál* 27, *Rígsþula* 44, but is relatively rare in verse outside the Edda. It does not occur in *Hugsvinnsmál*.

Although Alexander takes the view that Icelandic suffers from a paucity of abstract vocabulary with which to translate the abstractions of the *Disticha*,[10] a brief glance through vocabulary items appearing several times in *Hávamál* or *Hugsvinnsmál* serves to confirm that an extensive abstract vocabulary for wisdom poetry did exist, of which several words: *afli, vamm, lǫst, ráð, duga, flærð*, and *svik* (might, shame, fault, counsel, to avail, deceit, betrayal) had definite pre-Christian meanings. *Afli* is found in *Harbarðsljóð, Sonatorrek*, and *Arinbjarnarkviða*; *horskr* (wise) (a key word in *Hávamál*) is found in *Rígspula, Fáfnismál*, and *Eiríksmál*; while *mein* (harm) is found in *Guðrúnarkviða II, Húsdrápa*, and in the poetry of Sigvatr Þórðarson. Although these words are also very common in Christian poetry, they must originally have been part of a pagan vocabulary for abstract qualities.

Hugsvinnsmál tends toward a more 'poetic' vocabulary than *Hávamál*, perhaps an indication of the increasing influence of skaldic techniques, with their emphasis on variation and elaboration. In *Hávamál*, the preferred terms for 'man' are overwhelmingly *maðr* and *gumi*, with the occasional use of *ǫld, fyrðar*, and *þegn*. The formulas *synir ýta, alda synir*, and *hǫlða sono* (all meaning 'sons of men'), are used sparingly, while the words *jarl* (nobleman), *karl*, and *rekkr* appear once each, in each instance with a particular specialized meaning in context. *Karl* in 91 is contrasted with *kona*, hence the implication is 'male', while in 49, *rekkr* is best translated 'champion', 'fine fellow'. *Hugsvinnsmál*, on the other hand, has a bewildering variety of synonyms for 'man', used indiscriminately and with almost equal frequency: *greppr, gumi, seggr, ǫld, bragr, kind*, and others.

Many further examples of specifically Christian vocabulary in *Hugsvinnsmál*, which does not appear in *Hávamál*, could be cited. These show that, if the *Hávamál Redaktor* were familiar with *Hugsvinnsmál*, he has deliberately purged his borrowings of all their Christian vocabulary. A Christian antiquarian, trying to collect together disparate pieces of gnomic verse, might construct a collection such as we find in *Hávamál*, but it would not be among his aims to try to reconstruct a coherent pagan world-view. In the *Prose Edda*, Snorri is at pains to emphasize that the Æsir were not gods at all, but refugees from Troy, and shows how belief in their powers had been superseded by Christianity.[11] There is nothing comparable in *Hávamál*; the very quality of the description of Óðinn's self-sacrifice militates against the view that Óðinn is to be regarded as nothing more than a former king. A Christian compiler of *Hávamál* who was using *Hugsvinnsmál* as a source would scarcely take the phrase 'opt sá fægrt mæli' (often he may speak fairly) from *Hugsvinnsmál*, warning against flatterers, and turn it around in *Hávamál*, so that the use of flattery is positively advocated in order to win the hearts of women, as in *Hávamál* 92 : 'sá fær er friár' (he who flatters, gets).[12]

Use in Hugsvinnsmál *of traditional Norse poetic techniques*

Alexander shows how the translator of the *Disticha Catonis* both uses the Latin material provided in the prose introduction to the couplets for his framework of a father addressing his son,[13] and incorporates the traditional call for attention of Germanic poetry (1[1-8]):[14]

Heyri seggir	Listen men
er vilja sið nema	who wish to acquire moral
ok góð verk gera	teaching and do good deeds

We may compare this stanza with the opening of *Vǫluspá*, *Hrafnsmál*, and *Háleygjatal*, but the phrase 'góð verk' indicates that this traditional opening has been recast with a Christian slant. *Hávamál* lends itself to quotation; the discrete maxims are easily detached from the poem. It is not surprising then to find the *Hugsvinnsmál* poet using *Hávamál* as a source too, since he also uses proverbial material, and, in addition, quotes from *Sonatorrek*. Given this propensity to use material from outside his source, the most probable explanation of the identical phrases 'at /af hyggjandi sinni | skylit maðr hrœsinn vera' in the two poems is that the *Hugsvinnsmál* translator, familiar with the older Gnomic Poem, recognized that *Hávamál* 6[1-2] fitted well with the distich he was translating on the theme of the concealment of wisdom, and accordingly borrowed it. The sense of these two lines is not to be found in the Latin: 'Insipiens esto, cum tempus postulat aut res | stultitiam simulare loco, prudentia summa est'. (Be foolish when the occasion demands it; pretending stupidity may be the most prudent course to take) (*Disticha Catonis* II[18]). I suggest it represents a taking-over — in an incomplete form — from already known verse. Von See[15] feels that the lines seem out of place in

Hávamál. His interpretation of these lines — as a warning against self-conceit — is valid for *Hugsvinnsmál,* but in *Hávamál* the continuation 'heldr gætinn at geði' (rather cautious in one's intelligence) clearly shows the line of thought which the *Hávamál-* poet is pursuing — advice not to trust in one's wits alone, but to observe caution at all times — a piece of practical advice to which the first lines of the stanza are perfectly suited. The moral warning of *Hugsvinnsmál* is generated by the context, not by a significance inherent in the lines themselves.

R. Köhne[16] has recently pointed out that, in an alternative *Hugsvinnsmál* manuscript (AM 624), the scribe has corrected 73^{1-2} to 'af hygiandi þinne vertu óhræsin' (do not be arrogant about your intelligence). The change from the third to the second person is thus away from the *Hávamál* pattern, which had attracted the original translator away from his exemplar, back towards the *Disticha Catonis* formulation. von See answers the point in 'Common Sense und *Hávamál',*[17] claiming that the alternation between second and third persons occurs in other *Hugsvinnsmál* verse where there is no question of influence from *Hávamál.* Nevertheless, the existence of the *Hávamál* verse is likely to have encouraged the switch from second to third person.

The *Disticha* close smartly with a brief reference to their hexameter form; there is no admonition to take the advice to heart, nor further mention of the son who appears in the prose introduction. In *Hugsvinnsmál,* as in *Hávamál,* there is a recommendation to use the advice given, and, significantly, the poem is given its title: 'Hugsvinnsmál | hefi ek fyr hǫldum kveðin' (Hugsvinnsmál I have recited before men), just as in *Hávamál* 164: 'Nú ero Háva mál kveðin | Háva hǫllo í' (Now Hávamál has been recited in the High One's hall).

The *Hugsvinnsmál-*poet has found a model for the framework of his poem in *Hávamál.* The giving of the poem's title and the admonition to use the advice which has been heard, in addition to the use of *ljóð* in the line 'hér er nú ljóðum lokit' (here is the song now finished), may have been suggested by the *Ljóðatal* of *Hávamál.* All these borrowings indicate that *Hávamál* was the model and *Hugsvinnsmál* the imitation.

Use of ljóðaháttr

The *Hávamál Redaktor* would be most unlikely to need a foreign model for the metre of his gnomic verse if *ljóðaháttr* were already in use for wisdom material in such – apparently – archaic wisdom poems as *Vafþrúðnismál* and *Grímnismál*.[18] Would he have recast the ancient fragments of lore from which much of *Hávamál* was 'compiled' into *ljóðaháttr* form? If so, in what form did these fragments exist before? Von See admits[19] that parts of *Hávamál* are undoubtedly older than *Hugsvinnsmál*: could these have been composed in a metre derived from a foreign poem, unkown in Iceland until after the Conversion? More plausibly, the *Hugsvinnsmál*-poet would have looked to *Hávamál* as an exemplar for gnomic metre when he came to translate the *Disticha*. The unevenness of some of the metre in the gnomic sections of *Hávamál*, particularly the prose-like syntax of such lines as:

en elli gefr	but old age will give
hánom engi friðr	him no quarter
þótt hánom geirar gefi.	even if spears will.

(*Hávamál* 164–6)

does not suggest that the poem could have been modelled on the workmanlike, but often mechanical verse of *Hugsvinnsmál*. *Hávamál* is, as we have seen, characterized by the variety of tones, ranging from the portentous to the colloquial and intimate, which the flexibility of *ljóðaháttr* permits. We find no equivalent variety in either *Hugsvinnsmál* or the *Disticha*.

Thematic Similarities in Hávamál *and the* Disticha

Von See contends that the similarities in thematic areas between the *Disticha Catonis* and *Hávamál* stem from the familiarity of the *Hávamál*-poet with the *Disticha*. Wider comparative examination of other gnomic literature — Old English, Old Welsh, Ancient Greek, for example — shows that the preoccupations of a pre-industrial society are largely similar, whether in the Mediterranean basin or in Northern Europe: friendship, social decorum, a theme particularly stressed in Hesiod's *Works and Days*, wealth and possessions, women, and so on. Hence it is scarcely surprising that wisdom literature tends to deal with a limited number of themes. That the literature of one society has influenced another cannot be argued from mere thematic similarity, as M. West points out in the introduction to his edition of *Works and Days*:

Many of Hesiod's principles and sentiments can be paralleled in oriental texts. This may be evidence not so much of interaction between one literature and another as of basic similarities in their moral outlook, and, to some extent, in their forms of expression . . . in some cases a shared idiom or concept may suggest a more significant relationship, but one to be accounted for from general cultural diffusion rather than from the influence of any particular type of literature.[20]

Von See observes that certain themes — feud, murder, revenge — are absent from both *Hávamál* and the *Disticha Catonis*.[21] Admittedly, there is nothing in *Hávamál* about feuds and revenge *per se*, but there is a constant sense of menace and danger from 'óvinir' in the hall at the opening of the poem; in 38 a warning is given never to move far away from one's weapons, an admonition also found in *Beowulf* 1246b–1250b, as Grendel's mother approaches. This feeling of menace from unseen enemies is quite absent from the *Disticha*, which portray an affluent urban society with law courts, schools, market-places, and temples, where the main enemy is Fortuna, who may snatch away the wealth of the *petit bourgeois* at any moment. There is a security and a complacency in the *Disticha* which contrasts strongly with the shifting uncertainties of *Hávamál*, where nothing is secure or reliable: neither woman nor sword, ice, nor ale (*Hávamál* 81). The world of the *Disticha* has no need of weapons, so long as the machinery of the state is functioning:

Breve Sententiae:

Ad praetorium stato	Maintain your position at the praetorium
In iudicio adesto	Be present at the law courts
Magistratum metue	Honour a magistrate
Rem tuam custodi	Guard your property.

In *Hávamál* the uncertain note is sounded in the first stanza:

þvíat óvist er at vita	for there is no knowing for certain
hvar óvinir	where enemies are
sitia á fleti fyrir.	sitting ahead in the hall.

(*Hávamál* 14–6)

No material goods can endure for ever:

Deyr fé	Cattle die

deyia frændr   kinsmen die
deyr siálfr it sama;   the self itself must die.

(*Hávamál* 76/7[1–3])

Von See's statement that the 'Gnomic Poem' lacks any sense of
religious feeling ignores the framework in which the gnomic
material finds itself.[22] *Hávamál* lacks the (Christian) injunctions
to fear God which we find in *Hugsvinnsmál* (for example v. 3), but
the juxtaposition of the gnomic material of *Hávamál* with the
magico-religious ritual of 138–9 shows that contempt and
scepticism towards the divine are alien to the *Hávamál Redaktor*.

In fact, *Hávamál* contains much which directly contradicts advice
given in the *Disticha*, particularly that found in Book III. *DC* III[2]
suggests that no heed should be paid to gossip, *Hávamál* 118
warns that a man can be brought low by evil talk. *DC* III[10] advises
that the counsel of slaves, if good, should be heeded. *Hávamál* 87
warns against the 'siálfræða þræli' (independent-minded slave).
DC III[24] speaks of the son's duty to his parents, and there is much
in Book III about the anger, and the deceiving tears of women.
Hávamál takes a cynical view of the worth of sons; they are apt to
turn out badly, and their only useful purpose is to erect memorial
stones (88[3], 72). The 'misogyny' that von See finds in *Hávamál*,
and which, following Singer, he believes 'originates in church
circles', is balanced by Óðinn's rueful admiration for the re-
sourcefulness of 'Billings mær', while in *Hávamál* 91 men are
seen to be just as inconstant as women. The *Disticha* see woman
only as wife or *meretrix* (whore), scheming, untrustworthy creatures who, wanting only their own way, are incapable of displaying
individuality or intelligence. In contrast, *Hávamál* 130 knows the
value of a 'góðo kono' (good woman).

Thus it cannot be argued that, because *Hávamál* has many areas
in common with the *Disticha*, it has been directly influenced by
them, for it also contradicts them on a number of points, and
ignores some of the themes of the *Disticha* entirely — for
example, *Hávamál* has no interest in advising economic caution.
We cannot then say, as von See does, that *Hávamál* has been
influenced in its thematic concerns by the *Disticha*, any more than
by Hesiod or the Old English *Maxims* or Egyptian Instruction
poems. *Hávamál*'s approach to the primary questions of human
existence differs both from *Hugsvinnsmál* and from the *Disticha*

Catonis in too many respects for influence from either text to be a serious consideration.

Von See points to three verses of *Hávamál* in particular where he feels that the *Disticha* have influenced the poem directly. These verses are *Hávamál* 42, echoing *DC* I[26]; *Hávamál* 52, echoing *DC* I[35]; *Hávamál* 40, and *DC* II[5]. The first two instances show similarities of wording: 'gialda giǫf við gjǫf' (repay gift with gift) and 'sic ars deluditur arte' (thus cunning deceives cunning); 'mikill . . . lítill' (great . . . small) and 'magna . . . parva' (great . . . small). The third instance shows a vague similarity of thought. These verses have been examined in some detail by Köhne,[23] who finds none of the supposed echoes convincing. Nevertheless, in his most recent writing about *Hávamál*, von See still adheres to his original position, although no new evidence is adduced.[24]

In summary then, von See's contention that *Hávamál* is partly based on *Hugsvinnsmál*, and partly on the *Disticha Catonis* seems untenable. It is not possible to designate certain items of vocabulary as 'recent' merely because they appear in *Hávamál* and *Hugsvinnsmál*, but not elsewhere in the Edda, without taking into account the fact that heroic and mythological poetry will require a rather different vocabulary from that used in gnomic verse. For a vocabulary for mental and spiritual attributes, early skaldic verse and praise-poems, for example, *Arinbjarnarkviða*, may provide a better basis for comparison. One should also consider the fact that, just as *Hávamál* shows a tendency towards prose syntax, to the extent of metrical irregularity, for example, *Hávamál* 16, so gnomic verse may tend to show a closer affinity to prose vocabulary.

While there are certainly echoes of the one poem in the other, without evidence of 'recent' vocabulary in *Hávamál*, it cannot be shown that *Hugsvinnsmál* is earlier than *Hávamál*. *Hugsvinnsmál* is Christian in thought and vocabulary, while *Hávamál* has many ancient and pagan words. It is inconceivable that a *Hávamál* *Redaktor* could have borrowed freely from *Hugsvinnsmál* whilst purging his borrowings of Christian thought and vocabulary, even perverting the morality of *Hugsvinnsmál* to the amorality of the 'offene Realpolitiker' (blatant pragmatist), as Heusler characterizes the poet responsible for '*Hávamál* I', the 'Gnomic Poem'.[25]

Moreover, it is apparent that the closing stanzas of *Hugsvinnsmál* have been modelled on those of *Hávamál*; it is inherently unlikely that the *ljóðaháttr* metre is based on the hexameter; nor does *Hávamál*'s apparent sharing of themes and preoccupations with the *Disticha* entail a direct literary influence from the one to the other.

Thus it is unnecessary to depart from the hitherto accepted view that *Hugsvinnsmál* is considerably more recent than *Hávamál*. Nor is it probable that *Hávamál* has been directly influenced by the *Disticha*. While the poems have some themes in common, the subtle range of tones which *Hávamál* encompasses is far from the pedestrian moralizing of the *Disticha* and there is much in *Hávamál* in direct contradiction to the gnomes of the Latin poem. *Hávamál* is the independent distillation of pagan wisdom, deeply rooted in the society and tradition which produced it, and it owes nothing to the *Disticha*, either in the original Latin or in the vernacular rendition of *Hugsvinnsmál*.

3.2 THE ADAPTATION OF PAGAN MATERIAL TO A CHRISTIAN EDUCATION

In making his translation of the *Disticha*, the poet faced a twofold task. On the one hand, he had to adapt a pagan text, originally written for a pre-Christian urban Roman society, for a Christian culture; on the other he had to assimilate the foreign material to the flourishing native traditions of wisdom poetry. How he achieved this, and with what degree of success, will be the subject of this section.

Christianizing the *Disticha* was less difficult than might be expected. The Latin text seems generally to suppose a mono-theistic belief; God, 'deus' is scarcely mentioned: only in I[1], II[12], and IV[34]; the gods, 'di' appear in II[2], a reference which is easily replaced with a singular by the translator. The author of the *Disticha* was little concerned with heavenly matters: his first distich even permits the possibility that God may not exist: 'Si deus est animus, nobis ut carmina dicunt, | hic tibi praecipue sit pura mente colendus' (If God is a spirit, as poems tell us, you should always praise him with a pure heart) (*DC* I[1]).

The Icelandic translator develops the sentiment of the second line alone when he renders the couplet in *Hugsvinnsmál* 17, so that the verse is an admonition to purity of heart in worship:

með hreinu hjarta	with a pure heart
skalt þú á hann trúa	you ought to believe in him
ok elska af ǫllum hug.	and love him with all your mind.

$$(17^{4-6})$$

An apparent reference to Janus in II[27], the god who looks both ways, is easily recast, with the help of *Hávamál* 1 'um skoðaz skyli | um skygnaz skyli' (one should scrutinize, one should spy out), as a warning to be always on one's guard:

Um at lítaz	A man should always look round
þarf maðr alla vega	in all directions
ok við víti varaz,	and guard against punishment,
glǫggþekkinn	able to distinguish clearly
skyldi gumna hverr,	ought every man to be,
fróðr ok forsjáll vera.	wise and gifted with foresight.

$$(82)$$

The image of Janus provides both a literal injunction to keep one's eyes open and an admonition to cultivate foresight: a metaphorical looking ahead. Other distichs (IV[14], IV[38]) concerned with religious practices argue the folly of sacrificing animals; a sentiment with which the *Hugsvinnsmál*-poet readily concurs (118, 138). *Fortuna*, who makes an appearance in II[23] and IV[19], is removed in the translation, which goes on to give a general warning about the uncertainty of existence.

Hugsvinnsmál is not a slavish translation. Where the poet departs from his source, it is usually with good reason: because the Latin is obscure or repetitive, or because the idea of the couplet is in some way 'unIcelandic'. References to Roman literature and advice to play with hoops and shun the dice (*Breve Sententiae* 36–7), for example, are left untranslated. *DC* II[26], dealing with the classical notion of grasping Opportunity, *Occasio*, by the forelock, has been completely recast in *Hugsvinnsmál* 81, where sudden loss of wealth is equated with sudden loss of hair:

Hársiðan mann	A man with luxuriant hair
sák í hǫlda liði,	I saw among a company of men,
þó var honum skalli skapaðr,	though he was fated to be bald,
svá er sá maðr	so is that man
er mart á fjár	who owns lots of property
ok verðr um síðir snauðr.	and afterwards becomes bereft.

Interestingly, the translator of the Old English *Cato*[26] seems to
have misunderstood II[26], for he makes the maxim into a warning
against relying on one's natural endowments: 'Monig mon hæfð
micel feax on foranhēafde and wyrd þēah færlice calu' (Many a
man has a great deal of hair on the front part of his head and yet
suddenly becomes bald).

The *Disticha* were widely used as a school text in a large number
of countries throughout the medieval period,[27] precisely because
they are not integrated into a systematic religous interpretation of
the world, but, like much of the wisdom in *Hávamál*, they stand
aloof from ideas of absolute Good and Evil.[28] The persistent use
of the second person and imperative mood suggests that a
particular course of action will benefit the individual, either in
relation to others, or, increasingly in *Hugsvinnsmál*, in relation to
God:[29] the wider concerns of society, or of the Church on Earth[30]
are not under consideration.

The *Hugsvinnsmál*-poet was highly familiar with the vernacular
conventions of wisdom poetry: here he found his model for the
use of *ljóðaháttr* for gnomic sentiments. It may be worth while
asking why the translator-poet chose to use verse, not prose as his
medium. Why should he not simply have made a prose rendition
of the sentiments of the Latin couplets, as did the translator of
the Old English *Dicts of Cato?*

The model which the *Hugsvinnsmál*-poet had before him in the
Disticha was of course largely metrical, with the exception of the
Breva Sententiae, — a list of brief, epigrammatic maxims at the
beginning of the text. The Old English translator, working within
the flourishing Old English prose tradition, eschewed verse, yet
the *Hugsvinnsmál*-poet took the trouble to expand the Latin
couplets into the more leisurely *ljóðaháttr* metre, the traditional
metre of wisdom poetry. He also versifies the *Breva Sententiae*
which the Old English translator omits altogether.

By the mid-twelfth century when *Hugsvinnsmál* was probably
composed,[31] a vernacular prose tradition had already begun to
develop, both for historical and didactic writing: the *Fyrsta
málfræðiritgerðin*[32] is dated to the mid-twelfth century, while
Íslendingabók was probably written in the early twelfth century.
Had he wished to, the translator might easily have made use of
prose. The value of verse, however, lies in its efficiency as a
mnemonic aid: the regularity of the metre, in conjunction with

the alliteration, whereby the key idea of each half-line is stressed, helps the mind to retain both the wording and the idea expressed. This may be demonstrated by a comparison of *Hugsvinnsmál* 123 with the corresponding dict in Old English:

Málum hlýðir	To the speech of men
er með mǫrgum kemr,	when he is in a crowd,
hǫlda hygginn maðr;	the wise man listens;
því at af orðum	for from their words
kynnaz ýta hugir	the thoughts of men are discerned
þokka hylr sá er þegir.	he who is silent hides his thoughts.

Ne bēo þū tō ofersprǣce, ac hlyst ǣlces monnes worda swiðe georne: for þām þā word geopenigað ǣlces monnes willan and his þēawas, þeah hē hēo hwīlum behelian.[33]

Do not talk too much, but listen very carefully to what each man says, for words reveal the intentions of each man, and his virtues, although at times he conceal them.

It is easy to see which version of the same Latin *sententia* would be retained in the memory longer. In *Hugsvinnsmál*, the alliteration falls squarely on the key ideas 'málum . . . morgum', 'hǫlda . . . hygginn', 'orðum . . . ýta', 'þokka . . . þegir'; a social occasion is clearly envisaged ('er með mǫrgum kemr') and a balance made in the first and second halves of the strophe between the idea of listening to others and keeping silent oneself. The subject of the maxim is the 'hygginn maðr', who listens quietly to what is said, and remains silent himself: 'sá er þegir', wisely hiding his own thoughts. The first half of the strophe give a piece of general advice, the next two lines (4–5) a justification 'því at', while the last line gives a complementary epigram in a terse and memorable form — perhaps proverbial.[34]

In contrast, the Old English version has no significant alliteration — although it is found in certain of the other Old English dicts — and the syntax is straggling and uncontrolled: 'Ne . . . ac . . . for þām þe . . .'. The *sententia* shifts its focus from 'þū' to 'ǣlces mon'; 'and his þeawas' seems attached to the third clause almost as an afterthought. The logical development of thought in the maxim is much less easy to trace than in the Norse. The translator writes as he thinks, using the type of colloquial paratactic syntax we find in Ælfred's *Preface to the Cura Pastoralis*;[35]

simple conjunctions, 'ac', 'for þæm þe', 'þeah' link the clauses together. The *Hugsvinnsmál*-poet is able to keep the attention of the strophe focused upon the 'hygginn maðr', while contrasting the patent thoughts of the men who speak freely with the hidden thoughts of 'sá er þegir', because he has an underlying formal structure on which to build, a pattern which helps to organize his content for him in dictating the strophe's metrical form. The Old English translator's version sprawls into several clauses; the Norse poet is constrained by, yet in control of, his poetic form.

Thus we can see the advantages of using verse for gnomic material: first it enhances the mnemonic qualities of the subject, and second, the exigencies of the form impose an ordering and clarity upon the content, an ordering which is particularly valuable for non-narrative material where no beginning, middle, or end is provided by chronology. Looking beyond the individual gnome, the effect of a series of euphonious verses, even where there is no thematic development, nor logical nor grammatical link between one strophe and the next, such as we find in *Hávamál*, is to give the impression of a unified body of wisdom, that each strophe contributes to an organic whole. The metrical form, and the dramatic framework at the beginning and end of the poem provide the unity of *Hugsvinnsmál*, and save it from appearing the rag-bag of disparate thoughts which the Old English *Cato* seems to be.

To signal the beginning of the poem, the poet uses the traditional call for attention in 1: 'Heyri seggir!' (Listen men!).[36] The poem is also given its name in the closing stanzas: 'Hugsvinnsmál I hefi ek fyr hǫldum kveðin'; (Hugsvinnsmál I have recited before men) (148[1-2]). A conscious effort is thus made to link the poem with existing vernacular traditions; the use of 'kveðin' invokes a traditional Germanic oral recitation, even though the poet was making a translation of a literary work.[37]

Next comes a particularized address to the poet's son (2). The son is also to be found in the Latin source,[38] where he is addressed as 'fili karissime' (dearest son), but it is the Norse poet who characterizes him as an only son, the only person to whom the wisdom is being handed on, suggesting a special and intimate relationship. We should not, however, assume that the son has any autobiographical significance; he is not a historical person,[39] but a literary invention, part of the dramatic framework which gives shape to the gnomic material. While the anonymous author of the *Disticha* embarks upon a father–son framework at the start of the work which is forgotten by the poem's end,[40] the poet of *Hugsvinnsmál*, ever the craftsman, ends his work with a return to the 'einkason' (only son) of 2. A shaping and organizing intelligence is clearly at work.

In addition to the numerous borrowings from *Hávamál*,[41] *Hugsvinnsmál* also makes use of material from other texts, notably *Sonatorrek*. Stanza 51 is a transformation of *Sonatorrek* 24:

af gæzku þeiri	from your magnanimity towards them
mátt þú gera þér	you can make for yourself
vísa fjándr at vinum.	certain enemies into friends.
	(*Hugsvinnsmál* 51[1-3]).

ok þat geð	and such a spirit
es ek gerða mér	that I made for myself
vísa fjandr	certain enemies
af vélǫndum. [ms. at][42]	out of secret deceivers.
	(*Sonatorrek* 24[5-8]).

In order to allude to *Sonatorrek*, the poet has departed considerably from the Latin exemplar: 'Quem superare potes interdum vince ferendo | maxima enim est hominum semper patientia virtus' (Sometimes do not triumph over him you could conquer, for patience is always the greatest of human virtues) (*DC* I[38]). The *Disticha* couplet does not refer to 'patent enemies', equal in might to the protagonist, but rather to the irritations caused by lesser men, whom one might easily crush if one chose. Patience is to be advised in such cases. *Hugsvinnsmál* speaks plainly of 'enemies', 'vísa fjandr', who can be won over by 'gæzku' (magnanimity) and thus made into friends. Perhaps the allusion is ironic, for Egill is scarcely an example of a man who offers 'gæzku' to his enemies. One suspects that 'vélǫndum' in *Sonatorrek* is a corruption — we would wish for a word such as 'velviljǫndum' (well-wisher), which would fit the alliteration equally well. Perhaps there is an allusion to Egill's last encounter with Eiríkr *blóðöx* where his poetic talent, 'íþrótt', and intelligence, 'geð', turned an implacable foe into — not perhaps a well-wisher — but certainly one inclined to show kingly 'gæzku' (magnanimity) to the poet who had fallen into his power.

Further evidence of the *Hugsvinnsmál*-poet's familiarity with

native tradition is provided by his use of proverbial material to
expand the couplets into the longer *ljóðaháttr* strophe. 'Kaldráð
kona' (cold counsels of women) in 104 alludes to the proverb
'kǫld eru kvenna ráð' known to Flosi in *Njáls saga* 116.[43] The
observation in 47: 'brigð er utlendra orð' (untrustworthy are the
words of foreigners) is probably proverbial too, since it represents
an addition to the Latin.

One of the characteristics of diction which the *Hugsvinnsmál*-
poet has inherited from the vernacular is the pairing of two
adjectives[44] joined by 'ok': 'þarflátr ok þakklátr' (humble and
grateful) 31; 'ráðhollr ok réttdœmr' (sound of advice and
judicious) 131; 'slægr ok langþǫgull' (crafty and silent) 133[5]. Such
paired words are often found in the first line of a verse, providing
an arresting opening. *Hávamál* also makes occasional use of the
pattern: 'þagalt ok hugalt' (silent and thoughtful) in 15; 'þveginn
ok mettr' (washed and fed) in 61. Where the paired words are
adjectival, they are rarely synonymous, but rather complementary
in meaning. 'Þarflátr' (humble) suggests that one is in a state of
awareness of one's deficiencies (*þǫrf*), while 'þakklátr' means
'grateful' — having had those deficiencies remedied. The phrase
is an expansion of the straightforward Latin 'Deo supplica' (Pray
to God). In 13, 'ráðhollr' (loyal in counsel) suggests the ability to
give good, reliable advice, while 'réttdœmr' (judicious) shows the
man who is able to assess a situation correctly and fairly before
giving his 'ráð'. Here the phrase expands 'Aequum iudica' (Judge
fairly). Such elaborations of the Latin demonstrate the flexibility
of the vernacular as a language of translation. *Hugsvinnsmál*, like
Hávamál, occasionally has internal rhyme, effective in emphasizing the main idea of the stanza, but more common are half-
rhyme and assonance.[45] It might be suggested that in *Hugsvinnsmál* these devices reflect the spread of skaldic conventions
into other verse, but *Hávamál* shares them, notably in the
'vatz/vitz' (water/wits) link between 4 and 5. Such devices bring
the important words of a verse to the listener's attention, perhaps
more subtly than alliteration, in addition to contributing to the
smoothness and euphony of the verse.

Allied to the use of alliteration to mark out key ideas is the use of
polyptoton (the use of words deriving from the same root in
different grammatical forms), a rhetorical device found in both
Hugsvinnsmál and *Hávamál*. Although the modern reader often

finds this device stylistically clumsy, it is used in *Hugsvinnsmál* to give both emphasis and unity to the poem's thought. The 'dugnaðr/duga/dyggr' (ability/to avail/effective) complex recurs frequently in *Hugsvinnsmál*, as does 'ráð' (counsel) and morphologically related words, and 'tryggðr/trúa' (trusty/to trust), vocabulary elements which plot the main concerns of the poem.

Hugsvinnsmál is an assured piece of translation, smoothly and competently crafted. It cannot hope to compete with *Hávamál* in range of tones, constrained as it is by the Latin exemplar, nor does it employ the variety of imagery and vivid exemplification which distinguish *Hávamál*. The imagery of *Hávamál* is used thoughtfully and consistently, as one of the methods by which the *Redaktor* is able to unify his gnomic material. The images spring directly out of human experience: the four major necessities of fire, clothing, food, and drink, the requirements of all human beings. The gnomic precepts of the first part of the poem thus become as vital (in its root sense) as the objects which provide the imagery pattern with which they are associated. The imagery of *Hugsvinnsmál*, in contrast, is limited in its reference only to the stanza in which it occurs (although arguably 63 and 133 share the same watery theme). But the images of *Hugsvinnsmál* set up no echoes in other parts of the poem, nor do they reinforce one another, or unify the poem as do those of *Hávamál*.

The most immediate impression with which *Hugsvinnsmál* leaves the reader is of the abstract and generalized nature of its moral precepts. Adjectives are few, and those which are used generally refer to particular mental or spiritual attributes. There is little advice for specific social occasions or situations, and we gain no clear picture of the outer world or of the society for which the poem was intended. In the Latin original we are strongly aware of the urban bourgeois background to the poem's observations, the forum, the law courts, magistrates, and temple. These references have been removed by the translator, but no equivalent Scandinavian apparatus has replaced them. There is not even a mention of the 'Þing', which appears twice in *Hávamál*, nor do we find any of the specific examples or expansions which make *Hávamál* the more vivid and memorable poem. Where *Hugsvinnsmál* refers to 'auðr', 'fé', and 'aurar' — all general terms for wealth, *Hávamál* 36 exemplifies a minimum standard of living. The precision of the two goats evokes a tiny farmstead with a few beasts in the yard, where *Hugsvinnsmál* offers only abstractions. Where *Hugsvinnsmál* advises moderation in eating and drinking:

Áts ok drykkju	Food and drink
neyt aldri svá	never consume in such a way
at þitt minkiz megin;	that your strength is diminished;
	(83)

Hávamál makes actual for us the boor whose only interest in food, and who contributes nothing to the social occasion:

sitr ok snópir,	he sits and gobbles,
lætr sem sólginn sé	behaves as if he is starving
ok kann fregna at fá.	and can make little conversation.
	(*Hávamál* 33[4-6])

Typically, the *Hávamál* verse leaves us in doubt as to whether the boor is really extremely hungry, or whether he says nothing and gorges himself in order to escape being tested out in conversation. Probably both meanings are encompassed.

In *Hávamál* we intuit in the background a whole world, the deceptively cosy-seeming hall, the dark, wet mountains, the changeable sea, men and women engaged in all sorts of everyday activities. *Hugsvinnsmál* gives none of this detail, but, it seems deliberately, holds itself aloof from the society which the poet knew, depicting only the aspects of life which someone from any culture would recognize and share in. Only in one stanza do we feel that the *Hugsvinnsmál*-poet speaks with his own voice, the voice of a poet who is proud of his craft and estimates highly its value in his own culture. He must directly contradict his source, in order to assert the worth of poetry:[46] 'Multa legas facito, perlectis neglige multa | nam miranda canunt, sed non credenda poetae' (Read much, but having read, discount much, admire what poets sing, but do not believe them) (*DC* III[18]).

Gamansamlig ljóð	Entertaining songs
skalt af greppum nema	you should learn from men
ok mǫrg fræði muna;	and remember much wisdom;
ágætlig minni	splendid recollections
bera fyr ýta lið	before the company of men
skáld til skemtunar.	poets compose for entertainment.
	(102)

There is a marked difference in poetic quality between *Hávamál* and *Hugsvinnsmál*. *Hávamál* is always vibrating with other possibilities, resonances set up from one part of the poem in another, with contradictions which can ultimately be resolved within the logic of the poem, and with ambiguities which cannot, and need not, be resolved. *Hugsvinnsmál* is competent, even skilful verse, the work of a poet who knows his native verse tradition well and subordinates the poetic techniques at his disposal to an end which is primarily didactic. *Hugsvinnsmál* essentially presents the thoughts of an unknown fourth-century Latin author cast in an Icelandic verse measure, with a surprising degree of success — it is certainly more successful than the artless Old English translation — but it is not organic to the rich native tradition where poetry is a gift of the gods, and which is never far away from the mythological domain, the tradition which gave birth to *Hávamál*.

Notes

1. K. von See, 'Disticha Catonis und Hávamál', BGDSL(T) 94 (1972), 1–18. (repr. in *Edda*, 27–44.

2. Text cited from *Den norske-islandske Skjaldedigtning*, ed. F. Jónsson (Copenhagen, 1912–15).

3. Text ed. J. Wight and A. M. Duff, Loeb Classical Library (London, 1934).

4. R. S. Cox, 'The Old English *Dicts of Cato*', *Anglia*, 90 (1972), 1–42.

5. e.g. *Háv.* 6[7–9] and *Hug.* 19[4–6], which have the phrase 'fær maðr aldrigi' (a man never gets) in common, or *Háv.* 91 and *Hug.* 91 which share the opposition 'fagr mæla/flátt hyggja' (speaking fairly/thinking falsely).

6. Von See, 'Die Sage von Hamdir und Sorli', in *Festschrift Gottfried Weber zu seinem 70-Geburtstag berreicht von Frankfurter Kollegen und Schülern*, ed. H. O. Burger and K. von See, Frankfurter Beiträge zur Germanistik, 1 (Bad Homburg, 1967). (repr. in *Edda*, 224–49).

7. J. Harris, in Clover-Lindow, *ON-IL*, 110–11 notices also the occurrence of *hyggiandi* in *Haraldskvæði* 11, and one in Rǫgnvaldr kali's verse, dated in the mid-twelfth century.

8. Von See, 'Disticha Catonis', 33.

9. For 'giedd' and its relationship to ON 'geð', see J. R. J. North, 'Words and Contexts: An Investigation into the Meanings of Early English Words by Comparison of Vocabulary and Narrative Themes in Old English and Old Norse Poetry', Ph.D. thesis (Cambridge, 1987), 30–7.

10. G. Alexander, 'Studien über den *Hugsvinnsmál*', *ZDA* 68 (1931), 120.

11. Snorri Sturluson, *Prologue to the Snorra Edda*, ed. A. Faulkes (Oxford, 1982; repr. London, 1988), 3–6.

12. Von See, 'Disticha Catonis', 35, cites the opposition of 'fagrt mæla/flátt hyggja' in *Háv.* 91 as most probably borrowed from *Hug.* 91.

13. See E. T. Hansen, 'Hroðgar's "Sermon" in *Beowulf* as Parental Wisdom', *ASE* 10 (1982), 53–67.

14. See Alexander, 'Studien über den *Hugsvinnsmál*', 121.

15. Von See, 'Disticha Catonis', 31–2.
16. R. Köhne, 'Zur Mittelalterlichkeit der eddischen Spruchdichtung', *BDGSL*(T) 105 (1983), 382.
17. CS, 143.
18. Harris, Clover-Lindow, *ON-IL*, 110, makes similar points about the age of *ljóðaháttr* as a metre for wisdom verse.
19. Von See, 'Disticha Catonis', 31.
20. Hesiod, *Works and Days*, ed. M. L. West, (Oxford, 1978; repr. 1980), 27
21. Von See, 'Disticha Catonis', 39, reiterated in CS, 142–3.
22. Von See, 'Disticha Catonis', 39.
23. Köhne, 'Zur Mittelalterlichkeit', 382–7.
24. The question is readdressed by von See in CS, 143–4 and by Evans in MCS, 132, who points out that if *DC* is a source for *Háv.* 62, 'one of the most notorious cruces in *Hávamál* . . . it is curious that to know their source throws no light on the puzzle'.
25. A. Heusler, 'Die zwei altnordischen Sittengedichte der *Hávamál* nach ihrer Strophefolge', *Sitzungsberichte der Preußischen Akademie der Wissenschaften phil. hist. Klass* (1917), 133.
26. Cox, 'Dicts of Cato', dict 40, 10.
27. The first citation from the *Disticha* in Icelandic is in the *First Grammatical Treatise;* Alcuin cites from the work in the late eighth century in England. In 'Áhrif *Hugsvinnsmála* á aðrar fornbókmenntir', *Studia Islandica*, 43 (Reykjavik, 1985), 12, Hermann Pálsson records that the *Disticha* were a text for the teaching of Latin in Scotland until the Second World War.
28. See above ch. 1.5.
29. God is introduced into *Hug.* 19, 39, 69, and 138, where no reference to the Deity is to be found in the Latin.
30. We may contrast the ethical concerns of *Piers Plowman*, where the themes of the relationship and duties of the individual to the community and to the Church are constantly restated throughout the poem.
31. See Pálsson, 'Áhrif *Hugsvinnsmála*', 23.
32. *First Grammatical Treatise*, ed. E. Haugen, Linguistic Society of America Mongraph 25, (1950; repr. London, 1972), 4.
33. Cox, 'Dicts of Cato', dict 57, 12.
34. This structural pattern is repeated frequently in *Hugsvinnsmál:* ll. 1–3 give the advice, 4–5 an explanation or justification, and 6, in a proverb-like epigram, sums up the thought of the stanza.
35. See 'Preface to Cura Pastoralis' in B. Mitchell and F. C. Robinson ed., *A Guide to Old English*, 4th edn. (Oxford, 1986).
36. See above ch. 3.1 and cf. *Vǫluspá, Hrafnsmál, Háleygjatal.*
37. Like Cædmon in Bede's account, the poet may have been making an oral translation, only subsequently taken down by a scribe.
38. Also in a large number of other instruction texts; see Hansen, *SC*, 41–4.
39. We may contrast Dhuoda's *Manuel pour mon fils*, ed. P. Riché, Sources chrétiennes, 225. This is a Latin work, written in the 840s, by a mother, Dhuoda, for her son William, then aged sixteen. The work has an autobiographical character which is absent from most examples of the *speculum* genre.
40. As is the framework of the OE *Ex. Max.*; see below ch. 4.1.
41. Mainly examined above, ch. 3.1, but see Pálsson for an exhaustive list of parallels between the two poems; it must, however, be noted that his study does not determine which texts have priority.
42. The MS of *Sonatorrek* has 'at' in l. 8, in the same position as the *Hugsvinnsmál* verse. 'At' with the meaning 'into' gives good sense in the context of *Hugsvinnsmál*, but not in *Sonatorrek*, if we accept the usual interpretation of the verse, that Egill had the capacity to

provoke his hidden enemies 'vélǫndom' into open acts of malice, so their real hostility would become clear, hence the usual emendation to 'af'.

43. See above, Introduction n. 11 for other parallels to this proverb.

44. A stylistic device common in OE also; see Ælfric, 'The Life of King Edmund' in *Sweet's Anglo-Saxon Primer*, rev. N. Davis (Oxford, 1978) and the translator of the Old English 'Bede' in Mitchell and Robinson, *A Guide to Old English*.

45. Examples of half-rhyme and assonance in *Hávamál*: 'hrœsinn/gætinn' (proud/cautious) *Háv.* 6; 'fregna/segja' (ask/answer) *Háv.* 28; 'þagalt ok hugalt' (silent and thoughtful) *Háv.* 15, etc.

46. Cf. the admiring portraits of the minstrel and harper in *Fortunes of Men*, 77–84, discussed below, ch. 4.3.

4 OLD ENGLISH WISDOM POETRY: ITS RANGE AND THEMES

Some predominant themes of Old Norse wisdom poetry, the mastering of magical knowledge and the mysteries of the beginning of the world, and of *Ragnarǫk*, are not met with in the Old English texts, for these subjects are inseparable from paganism. Nevertheless, the content of the Old English poems ranges widely, encompassing strongly Christian material, in, for example, *Precepts*, which takes the Decalogue as its structural model. Other poems are less overtly moralistic, seeking to describe and categorize the range of Created beings, or to explore the different possibilities of human existence. Although tracing the sequence of ideas in such poems as the *Exeter* and *Cotton Maxims* is no more straightforward than analysing the development of thought in *Hávamál*, these poems do have a marked unity, reinforced by a similarity of tone and subject, or by means of syntactical devices. The poems are all Christian in conception; although there may be outcrops of archaic wisdom in the poems,[1] it is fruitless to attempt to analyse the poetry into 'old pagan' and 'later interpolated' material, as early scholars attempted to do.[2]

In this chapter I consider only those Old English poems which are primarily concerned with imparting wisdom and use the gnome as a structural unit: the *Exeter* and *Cotton Maxims*, *Fortunes of Men*, or which are presented within the kind of framework familiar from other literatures: the *Rune Poem*, *Precepts*, and *Solomon and Saturn II*. Space does not permit examination of poems specifically concerned with Christian morality, such as *An Exhortation to Christian Living* and *Instructions for Christians*; these have recently been profitably analysed by E. T. Hansen in *The Solomon Complex*, while T. Shippey's *Poems of Wisdom and Learning in Old English* comments on doctrinal poems such as *Soul and Body I* and *Judgment Day I*.

4.1 *EXETER MAXIMS*

The *Exeter Maxims*[3] is the Old English poem perhaps most directly comparable with *Hávamál* in the apparent lack of organization and variety of its contents. Like *Hávamál*, the *Exeter Maxims* have been divided into constituent poems where major breaks in sense occur, and where there is capitalization in the manuscript. The poem is usually edited as consisting in parts A, B, and C; divisions which I use in the discussion which follows. Again like *Hávamál*, the *Exeter Maxims* have been subjected to a number of attempts to trace a 'logical' development of thought — either by verbal or by associational links.[4] Such analyses have generally succeeded in showing only that the internal structure is loose and unorganized, as Dawson remarks of the loose associations of the gnomic style:

> It is a process that may be observed in our casual conversation. The result is the same — a rambling style which covers a great deal of ground; yet never reaches any particular goal.[5]

Since each gnome exists as an independent unit, a number of gnomes combined together will not achieve any overall unity, unless they are related in theme, as in parts of *Hávamál*, or connected by parallel grammatical constructions, as in the *Cotton Maxims*. Since a gnomic poem has no inherent order imposed by the demands of chronology or narrative logic, it must draw its coherence from outside the gnomes themselves, either from some kind of framework or by a series of meaningful juxtapositions, of similar or contrasting objects.[6] Nigel Barley lucidly summarizes:

> It (*Cotton Maxims*) employs parallelism, antithesis and metaphor to establish relations. It is inherently structural . . . Its basic technique is the use of the rich and paradigmatic associations of words and ideas to link disparate fields of experience.[7]

Are the *Exeter Maxims* congenial to this mode of reading?

Part A

The opening frame of the *Exeter Maxims* is briefly sketched:[8]

> Frige mec frōdum wordum.   Ne lǣt þīnne ferð onhǣlne,
> dēgol þæt þū dēopost cunne.   Nelle ic þē mīn dyrne gesecgan
> gif þū mē þīnne hygecræft hylest ond þīne heortan geþohtas.
> Glēawe men sceolon gieddum wrixlan.
>
> (1–4[a])

Question me with wise words. Do not let your spirit be hidden, secret that which you know most deeply. Nor do I wish to tell you my secret knowledge if you hide from me the strength of your mind and the thoughts of your heart. Wise men ought to exchange sayings.

This is the last we hear of 'ic' and 'þū': the colloquy structure is swiftly abandoned. However, by sketching two 'glēawe menn' who seem to be about to embark upon a contest, the poet implies that the maxims he is about to present are a distillation of the sayings of two wise men, figures of authority and wisdom, comparable with the sages cited in *Vainglory* and *Order of the World*.

The *Maxims* proper commence with an adjuration to praise God, a natural starting-point, for he is the highest authority of all. Creation is the first theme; the poem itself begins with the archetypal Beginning, celebrating the act of Creation in language reminiscent of *Cædmon's Hymn* and the praise-song of the *scop* in *Beowulf*:[9]

> God sceal mon ǣrest hergan,
> fægre, fæder ūserne, forþon þe hē ūs æt frymþe getēode
> līf ond lǣnne willan.
>
> (4b–6a)

First God should be praised, fittingly, our Father, for he established for us at the beginning life and transient joy.

At the Creation, God brought forth a multiplicity of creatures, 'feorhcynna fela' (14a), and many nations of men. The theme of nations is now temporarily laid aside, while the poet returns to that of discussion between wise men, but these two strands of thought will be reunited later in the poem at 57–9a. Wise men settling matters peaceably together, as in the introductory lines, are now held up as an ideal (18a–21), contrasted with the troublemakers who tear peace asunder. Part A of the *Maxims* returns several times to the theme of reconciliation, but the conclusion of Part C, effectively that to the whole poem, is gloomier; it tells of unending strife for mankind after the archetypal quarrel of Cain and Abel. The earnest discussion of the role of the wise man is a justification of the genre itself,[10] akin to *Hugsvinnsmál*'s evaluation of the function of the poet. Such self-consciousness is alien to *Hávamál*.

From the Creation of the universe, the thought moves to consideration of the creation of a single new individual in 23bff. The arrival of the child is juxtaposed with the image of a tree which loses its leaves: a perennial cycle of growth and decay. The identification of tree and human seems to be an ancient one (the figure is elaborated more fully below in 4.3, while Norse parallels are discussed in 6.2). The grief of the parents who lose a child prematurely is gracefully transferred to the tree, maintaining the objectivity and impersonality of the gnomic mode.

At l. 35 there is a change of direction, loosely linked to the previous lines by the theme of death. The foolish man is contrasted both with the wise men who are cautious about the welfare of their souls, and the wise men as defined earlier in the poem. His folly is demonstrated by his ignorance of God, not, as in *Hávamál*, by his social behaviour. In the gnomes which follow, unity is provided by the similarity of grammatical structure, a formulation which occurs also in the concluding lines of *The Wanderer* and *The Seafarer*. The next lines oppose the happy man, 'eadig', with the wretched man betrayed by his friends, a theme developed at some length in the vignette of the lonely traveller in part C. The pattern is repeated in 39; the 'bliþe' man is contrasted with the blind man, the first extended description in the poem:

> Blind sceal his ēagna þolian.
> Oftigen biþ him torhtre gesihþe,   ne magon hī ne tunglu bewitian,
> swegltorht, sunnan ne mōnan.   Þæt him biþ sār in his mōde,
> onge þonne hē hit āna wāt,   ne wēneð þæt him þæs edhwyrft cyme.
> Waldend him þæt wīte tēode,   sē him mæg wyrpe syllan,
> hǣlo of hēofodgimme,   gif hē wāt heortan clǣne.
>
> (39b–44)

A blind man must suffer in his eyes. Deprived is he of clear sight, nor may they (sc. the eyes) perceive the stars, the glorious bright one, sun nor moon. That grieves him in his heart, pain[11] that he alone knows, nor does he expect that a change will come to him in this. The Ruler established that torment for him, he can grant him recovery, a cure for the head-jewel, if he knows his heart to be pure.

The plight of the blind man is treated sympathetically: we may contrast the brisk pragmatism of *Hávamál*: 'blindr er betri en brendr sé' (it is better to be blind than burnt). The description is radiant with the light of which the blind man is deprived: each of the heavenly bodies is named, and their brightness emphasized by

'torht' and 'swegltorht' (sun-bright), while the eyes are 'heafod-
gimme' (gleaming jewels of the head) which would reflect back
the brilliance of the sun and the moon, were they only healthy.
The blind man feels pain both in his eyes, and in his heart;
isolated by his disability, he despairs (ne wēneð) of any change in
his condition. Line 43 puzzles over the problem of suffering;
paradoxically, it is the Lord who has caused the man's blindness,
yet it is the Lord who can cure him — if he knows his heart to be
pure.[12]

The theme of healing leads to the next half-line: 'the sick man
needs a doctor', then modulates through an unexpressed middle
term 'things people need' into an extended description of the
nurturing of a young man (45–8). There is an implied comparison between the young man and a young animal who must be
tamed, but the tone is light and affectionate. He is to be
encouraged and rewarded with food and clothing during the
period of his education, just as the young hawk in *The Fortunes of
Men* is handled, fed, and given 'garments', varvels and jesses, until
he is ready to come to the hand. Both the young, naturally wild
creatures must be trained in the right way, with food and clothing
until they are ready to perform their proper functions: 'Hafuc
sceal on glōfe I wilde gewunian' (a hawk shall be on a glove, the
wild creature remain there), as the *Cotton Maxims* tell us, and
'Trēow sceal on eorle I wīsdōm on were' (Belief must be in a
warrior, wisdom in a man).

Just as the young man possesses a powerful natural energy which
must be channelled, so a mature temperament must be controlled. The observation: 'stȳran sceal mon strongum mōde' leads
to an extended metaphor of a furious ocean, a rage finally resolved in the treaties made between formerly warring nations. A
portrait of a rather unidealized king follows: 'Cyning bið
anwealdes georn; I lāð sē þe londes monað lēof sē þe māre
bēodeð' (59b–60: A king is eager for authority; hateful is he who
denies him land, dear is he who offers more). This king is
unattractive in his avidity; unlike the king of the first line of the
Cotton Maxims, whose duty is to guard his kingdom (healdan rīce),
this king appears to be interested only in territorial acquisition.
Next comes an impressionistic description of an Anglo-Saxon
court where things are not always as they seem; implications of
treachery seem to lurk behind the realizations of typical behaviour:

'Sceomiande man sceal in sceade hweorfan, scīr in leohte gerīseð'
(68: A man who is ashamed shall move in the shadows, it is fitting
for bright things to be in the light).

The hissing sibilant, repeated four times in the line, suggest a
sinister, serpent-like deceit in the man skulking in the shadows.
He, and the woman who gads about to the detriment of her
reputation, are placed in the context of a noble court by the
description of a gold-giving ceremony. The ritual of giving and
receiving, symbolizing the reciprocal relationship between lord
and retainer described in, for example, *The Wanderer* 41b–44 or in
Beowulf, is soured by our apprehension of the real feelings of the
participants. We have been told that kings dislike giving land away;
here the recipient of the gold is characterized as 'gifre' (avid), a
word of generally negative connotations in Old English.[13]

Part B

The next sequence of gnomes, sometimes edited as a separate
poem, so sharp is the break in subject-matter,[14] seems to present a
new beginning with a series of lyrical nature gnomes.[15] These
observations are immanent natural truths: 'Forst sceal frēosan, fȳr
wudu meltan, | eorþe grōwan, īs brycgian' (71–2: Frost must
freeze, fire consume wood, the earth put forth growth, ice form a
bridge). They function as a kind of touchstone by which the truth
of other maxims about human behaviour and society can be
measured.[16] As Jill Mann writes:

> even if it is a particular system of thought or belief that throws up
> an axiom or exhortation in the first place, its proverbial form
> assumes its enfranchisement from such a system, its transfer to a
> realm where its only support is the speaker's willingness to match it
> with experience and find justification for its use.

The demonstrable truth of the nature observations allows them to
be matched with other less demonstrably 'true' maxims. The
credibility of the natural gnomes is transferred to the maxims
concerning humans.

The gnomes which follow, both textually corrupt and obscure,[17]
epitomize the difficulties which readers seeking a continuous
thread of meaning through the poem must try to solve. The
underlying notion would seem to be that of death and funeral
customs:

Sund unstille,
dēop dēada wǣg   dyrne biȝ lengest.
Holen sceal inǣled,   yrfe gedǣled
dēades monnes.   Dōm biþ sēlast.
(77ᵇ–80)

The restless sea, deep path of the dead, is longest secret. Holly must be
kindled, the inheritance of the dead man shared out. Fame is best.

Why the sea is described as the 'deep path of the dead' is
unclear: perhaps the reference is to ship-funerals (*Beowulf* 26–52).
Holly is the wood for the funeral pyre, as Krapp and Dobbie
suggest.[18] After the obsequies, an implicit contrast is drawn
between the 'yrfe', the inheritance shared among the heirs, and
'dōm' (reputation) all that the dead man can retain:

ek veit einn	I know one thing
at aldri deyr:	which never dies:
dómr um dauðan hvern.	the reputation of each dead man.

(*Hávamál* 77⁴⁻⁶).

This meditation on death is followed by an extended discussion of
the role of a nobleman's wife (84ᵃ–92), a picture of the ideal
aristocratic lady, balanced by the lowlier domestic scene with the
Frisian's wife. Both portraits share the theme of co-operation
between husband and wife. The noblewoman performs her
duties; well aware of all the etiquette associated with mead-
drinking, she shares responsibility with her husband for maintaining the bonds between lord and retainer by gift-giving, just as
Wealhþeow in *Beowulf* gives the hero gifts of horses and necklaces
in her own right. The two compounds 'lēohtmōd' and 'rūmheort'
render the portrait particularly vivid. 'Rūmheort' implies, not
only 'generous' in a material sense, but also 'magnanimous',
possessing the ample reserves of spirit which enable her to keep
counsel and give good advice to her husband. We may compare
Beowulf 278 'þurh rūmne sefan' (through a magnanimous spirit).
Likewise, 'lēohtmōd' suggests not only light-heartedness, but an
inner radiance which imparts itself to the warriors among whom
she moves, a source of cheerfulness in others.

Although the Frisian sailor is the provider 'ǣtgeofa', it is his wife
who clothes and feeds him, performing her duties joyfully, so glad is

she to have her man home (94ᵇ–97ª). The loving wife is contrasted with the woman who is unfaithful to her absent husband; a final description of the seafarer in 103–10 rounds off the theme.

At line 111, the poem once again changes direction; first with a brief description of the man who starves to death, a contrast to the provident 'cēapēadig' merchant who obtains wood, water, and food for his men when he comes to land.

Part C

After this portrait, Part C opens with another sharp change of style, comparable with the change from *ljóðaháttr* to *málaháttr* at *Hávamál* 73 and 81 ff., a series of brief, epigrammatic, and disparate gnomes follows. Some are distinguished by rhyme or word-play (118ᵇ–21):

> Rǣd bið nyttost,
> yfel unnyttost;   þæt unlǣd nimeð.
> Gōd bið genge   ond wiþ god lenge.
> Hyge sceal gehealden,   hond gewealden

Good advice is most useful, evil least useful; that a wretched man adopts. Good prevails and is lasting before God. The mind must be restrained, the hand controlled.

Such links are necessitated by the varied nature of the contents. The section concludes with a contrast between Óðinn and God: 'Wōden worhte wēos, wuldor alwālda, | rūme roderas' (132–3ª: Woden made idols, the Almighty the heaven, the spacious skies). The only explicit reference to Woden in Old English poetry,[19] these lines celebrate the achievement of God in creating the heaven (with a pun on 'wuldor' (glory)). God is all-powerful, just as Óðinn in Norse is All-father, 'Alfǫður,' but in contrast to the Almighty, Woden can only create false idols.[20] The praise of God the Creator returns to the theme of the opening lines.

Highly disparate in content, the connections between one thought and the next in the final movement of *Exeter Maxims* are virtually impossible to trace. Possibly the uneven nature of the material indicates an older stratum of verse. Of note is the ironic description of the friendless traveller who avoids towns where he has no friends; wolves become his only travelling-companions, with horrifying consequences:

Ful oft hine sē gefēra slīteð,
Gryre sceal for grēggum,   græf dēadum men.
Hungre hēofeð,   nales þæt hēafe bewindeð,
ne hūru wæl wēpeð   wulf sē grǣga,
morþorcwealm mæcga,   ac hit ā māre wille.
(147^b–151)

Very often his companion tears him. The grey beast must be feared, a
grave provided for the dead man. He howls for hunger, in no way does
he circle the head, nor indeed does the grey wolf bemoan the slaughter,
the murderous slaughter of the men, but it always wants more.

The wolf is a companion, but, in a riddle-like inversion of
expected behaviour, one with murderous intentions. When the
man is dead, the wolf's behaviour parodies that of the mourner;[21]
although he howls in anguish, he is impelled by very different
motives from the lamenting human, for his only regret is that
there is nothing left to eat. The macabre description recalls that
of the man falling to his death in *The Fortunes of Men*; there is a
blackly ironic insistence on the horror of the fates which the
luckless men meet.

Next comes a list of things that need other things to complete
them: bow and arrow, a scholar and his book. Once more it
becomes difficult to find any pattern in the arrangement of the
gnomes; in one instance a pun on *treo* and *treow* (159) provides the
link; another line (158) sounds proverbial. At 167, the poet returns
to the theme of different nations and different mores, last met with
in 15^b–18^a. The reprise introduces a section dealing primarily with
human sociablity: a man with musical ability will never be alone,
while the man without friends or kin is lonely: 'Earm biþ sē þe
sceal āna lifgan, I wineleas wunian hafaþ him wyrd getēod' (172–3:
Wretched is he who must live alone; fate has decreed for him that
he must dwell without friends). There is no suggestion here, as
there was for the blind man above, that 'edhwyrft' (reversal) can
come for the friendless man. While the blind man's case offers an
opportunity for the demonstration of divine grace, a possibility of
dynamic intervention, the plight of the friendless man is more akin
to that of the protagonist of *The Wanderer*. Meditation, and the acquisition of wisdom show the Wanderer the meaning of his suffering,
and open for him the way to divine grace, but for the friendless man
here there is no hope of change: 'hafaþ him wyrd getēod'.

The theme of men together is treated in the rest of the section; this in turn modulates into a discussion of violence, prepared for by the accusations and insults which typically accompany dice-play in 181–2; 187–90. The closing movement introduces Cain and Abel, progenitors of strife, with a horrified recognition of the cosmic importance of the crime. The poem concludes with a list of men and weapons. Nothing signals that the work is drawing to a close; there is no return to the themes of the beginning, or a final, summarizing maxim.

How are we to read the *Exeter Maxims*? First, as far as the charge of incoherence is concerned, it is clear that, at least in the first two sections, 1–70 and 71–137, it is possible to trace the movement of the thought: there is generally an associational link between one subject and the next, either of similarity or of contrast. It is less easy to detect a logical ordering in the final section: this may have been added as an appendix to the first two movements, to add to the range of the shorter poem. Hansen addresses the question of whether the *Exeter Maxims* are to be read as one poem or three with the observation that:

> the ambiguous integrity of A, B, and C might suggest the open-ended nature of wisdom . . . Perhaps we are invited by the problematic status of the Exeter Book gnomic poem(s) to take the experience of one section or poem as complete and hence meaningful in its own right, and also to consider that, as the opening lines of A suggest, the wise can and will generate a continuing series of such artefacts . . .[22]

To pose questions of unity and coherence may be to make the wrong sort of demands of the *Exeter Maxims*. In particular, the absence of any sense of closure (unlike *Hávamál*, or as we shall see, the other Old English wisdom poems considered in this chapter), suggests that the idea of open-endedness, of infinite extension, is crucial to a reading of the *Exeter Maxims*.

The *Exeter Maxims* are distinguished by the many striking vignettes of people engaged in different, typical activities: a development of the brief descriptions of the 'catalogue poems', such as *The Fortunes of Men*. One of the charms of the poem is the ordinariness of these pictures, the Frisian's wife giving her husband clean clothes, the briefly glimpsed picture of two brothers fighting a bear, words hurled across a game of tables.

Like the natural observations of the second section, these have an authenticity which reinforces the authority of the briefer gnomes.

While the *Exeter Maxims* lack the penetrating psychological perceptions of *Hávamál*, they offer a description of Anglo-Saxon society, in which each level of the social hierarchy performs the functions expected of it, a reassuring picture of social order, complemented by the natural order which is the theme of the *Cotton Maxims*.

4.2 THE *COTTON MAXIMS*

Cyning sceal rīce healdan. Ceastra bēoð feorran gesȳne,
orðanc enta geweorc, þā þe on þysse eorðan syndon,
wrǣtlic weallstāna geweorc. Wind byð on lyfte swiftust

(1–3)

A king shall maintain his kingdom. Cities are visible from afar, the skilful work of giants, those which are on this earth, splendid stone-walled constructions. Wind is swiftest in the air.[23]

With 'Cyning sceal rīce healdan', the theme of man's social structures is taken up at once with an observation about the king, the linchpin of Anglo-Saxon society.[24] The king is at the top of the earthly hierarchy, just as God is the highest in the order of the universe. The *Exeter Maxims* took God as its first topic, but since, as I shall show, the movement of thought in the *Cotton Maxims* is from the earthly to the divine, more specifically from earthly cities to the Divine City,[25] it is appropriate that this poem should begin with the king.

1[b] visualizes a city of the sort described in decay in *The Ruin*, a stone-built Roman settlement — hence the Latin loan-word 'ceaster'. 'Þā þe on þysse eorðan syndon' stresses the physical nature, the solidity of the buildings, but, on a second reading or hearing, these lines yield up an implicit contrast with the Heavenly City, the 'sigefolca gesetu' of the final lines, which is not of this earth and cannot be seen.[26]

The immovable walls of the fort are set in opposition to the wind, the most insubstantial of things, 'on lyfte swiftust' (swiftest in the air). This superlative quality of the wind introduces a series of gnomes also linked by superlatives, but first comes a surprising reference to Christ: 'Þunar biÞ þrāgum hlūdast. Þrymmas syndan Crīstes myccle' (4: Thunder is at times loudest. Christ's powers are great). The connection between the two thoughts would seem to be a contrast: Thunder may be very loud, but Christ's powers are greater still (although the second sentence lacks a comparative). Conceivably the gnomes conceal a reference to Þórr (OE: Þunor), the thunder-god, so that the comparison would parallel that between Woden and the 'Alwalda' in *Exeter Maxims* 132. The pagan god, despite his noise, is powerless in comparison with Christ. In Norse conversion narratives, Christ is most often pitted against Þórr (Þunor).[27]

The series of superlatives which follows passes through the seasons of the year from winter to autumn;[28] then continues with some of the perennial preoccupations of gnomic verse: truth, wealth, and wisdom. A striking line, which at first sight seems to epitomize the casual nature of the links between one gnome and the next in Old English wisdom verse, follows:[29] 'Wea biÞ wundrum clibbor. Wolcnu scrīÞaÞ' (13: Misery is wondrously clinging. Clouds glide on). The tenacity of misery is finely imagined, balanced by the sense of a measured perspective on grief in the second half of the line: the thought recalls the refrain of *Deor*: 'Þæs oferēode; þisses swā mæg' (that passed by; so may this). Next comes a small cluster of gnomes capturing the ideal nobleman, then the poet embarks on a long, intricately constructed series of observations.

The theme is that of 'things in their places':

> Hafuc sceal on glōfe
> wilde gewunian. Wulf sceal on bearowe
> earm ānhaga. Eofor sceal on holte,
> tōÞmægenes trum. Til sceal on ēÞle
> dōmes wyrcean. DaroÞ sceal on handa,
> gār golde fāh. Gim sceal on hringe
> standan stēap ond gēap.
>
> (17b–23a)

A hawk must[30] on a glove — wild creature — remain. A wolf must be in a grove, the wretched lone creature. A boar must be in a wood, strong in the power of his tusks. A good man must in his homeland perform famous deeds. A javelin must be in the hand, the spear adorned with gold. A gem must stand tall and proud on a ring.

The syntax is cleverly constructed: the broader semantic range of OE 'on', in comparison with that of the modern preposition, permits both physical objects and abstract qualities to be located 'on' something or somewhere. Thus the verse is more densely patterned than a modern English version could be.[31] The idea that each object in Creation, natural (wolf, boar), human (good man), man-made (javelin, jewel) has its own appointed place, combined with the interlocking half-lines produces a satisfying sense of fitness and order; evidence of God's providential care for his Creation.[32] The strong patterning of the verse (X sceal on Y, Adjectival Phrase / Verb+Object) imitates the pattern which the poet perceives in the world around him.

The central series of gnomes is mainly concerned with the physical location of objects, but the occasional abstract or moral quality obtrudes. Thus the good man must do deeds of glory; a warrior must be loyal and wise:

> Trēow sceal on eorle,
> wīsdōm on were. Wudu sceal on foldan
> blǣdum blōwan.
>
> (32ᵇ–34ᵃ)

A warrior must have loyalty, a man wisdom. A wood must, on the earth, blossom with flowers.

As in the *Exeter Maxims*, where puns[33] occasionally provide the connection between one thought and the next, the transition here is probably[34] through an intermediate, unexpressed term: *treow* (loyalty) / **treo* (tree) / *wudu* (wood). More typically, the transitions are provided by the grammar alone; no system of contrasts or similarities can account satisfactorily for the series God; door; shield; bird.[35]

At 41ᵇ the series is arrested by a sequence of 'things which go about secretly'; the final observation about showers in 41ᵇ may be a cue for the 'þystrum wederum' of 42ᵇ:

> Þēof sceal gangan þystrum wederum. Þyrs sceal on fenne gewunian,
> āna innan lande. Ides sceal dyrne cræfte
> fǣmne hire frēond gesēcean, gif hēo nelle on folce geþēon
> þæt hī man bēagum gebicge.
>
> (42–6ᵃ)

A thief must go about in gloomy weather. A monster must live in the fen, alone within the land. A lady must, with secret craft, a woman seek out her lover, if she does not wish it to come about among the people that she is obtained with rings.

The gloomy weather provides good cover for the thief's illicit activities, just as Grendel the *þyrs* stalks 'under mist hleoþum' (under mist-banks) and 'under wolcnum' (under clouds) to Heorot (*Beowulf* 710b, 714a). Metaphorically the weather suggests the dark state of the man's soul and that of the monster, isolated from human society; he must dwell alone as an outcast, as the thief may find he must do when his crimes are uncovered. The woman's behaviour is less easy to account for; one persuasive explanation is that her lover is not sanctioned by society and cannot therefore contract with her as his wife in the normal way 'bēagum gebicge' — compare *Exeter Maxims* 81–2b, where the king obtains his queen with 'būnum ond bēagum' (with goblets and arm-rings).[36]

The description of the sea which follows may have been suggested by the implication that the woman, as in *Hávamál* 90, is headstrong and uncontrollable: as in *Exeter Maxims* 51a ff., a strong passionate nature evokes surging waters. From the sea, the poet's eye moves to the land and its beasts, thence to the skies and the stars. This sweep through the cosmos establishes a series of elemental oppositions,[37] shading into descriptions of human conflicts, first on a large scale between two armies: 'fyrd sceal wið fyrde', then on a smaller scale in individual hostilities. Strife concerns the wise man: 'ā sceal snotor hycgean | ymb þysse worulde gewinn', perhaps, as in the *Exeter Maxims* 18a–21, he can settle the feud peacefully, unlike the criminal of 56b who resolves quarrels with unlawful violence and is hanged. The death of the 'wearh' gives rise to speculation about the fate of his soul after death; the fates of all spirits are unknown.

The poem ends with a recognition of the limitations of human knowledge: 'Is sēo forðsceaft dīgol and dyrne' (62b–63: Future fate is dark and secret). In these final lines, the poet speaks of the heavenly Ruler, and the places where the elect live, the invisible city. Thus the *Cotton Maxims* move from considering the earthly king and those human cities, visible even from afar, which he must rule, to the heavenly 'rīce' (kingdom), maintained by the

'Meotud' (Ruler). Things of this earth, the *Cotton Maxims* suggest, can be observed and encapsulated in gnomic form, but those things pertaining to the other world are 'dīgol and dyrne'. No observer or wise man can tell us for certain what conditions beyond death are like.

Most distinctive in the *Cotton Maxims* is the marvellously vivid realisation of animals, humans and landscape, illustrative of the typical, coupled with the joyful recognition of the fundamental unity which underlies the variety of Creation. These natural gnomes are the counterpart of the human gnomes of the *Exeter Maxims*, which depict people engaged in all types of activity, but to characterize the *Exeter Maxims* as 'human' and the *Cotton Maxims* as 'natural' is to oversimplify. The *Exeter Maxims* are aware of man's existence in nature, as the similes drawn from the natural world make clear, just as the *Cotton Maxims* are aware of man as a natural phenomenon: the thief and the *þyrs* roam in the same murky hinterland.

4.3 THE *RUNE POEM*

Organization is imposed externally upon the contents of the *Rune Poem*[38] by the *fuþorc*-structure. Arranged in the order of the initial rune-letter, each stanza is discrete, expanding the name of the letter by description. Thus the problems of unity encountered in other Old English wisdom poems arise to a lesser extent.

Each letter is described in a stanza, generally six half-lines long, but sometimes as short as four (*Nyd*), or as long as eight half-lines (*Eolh*).[39] The stanzas are thus somewhat longer than the equivalents in the Old Icelandic and Old Norwegian *Rune Poems*;[40] the Icelandic stanza contains three half-lines, a Latin gloss, and an alliterating name for a king, while the Norwegian poem is in rhyming couplets. Longer than is optimum for the purely mnemonic poem, the Old English stanzas are expanded for didactic and lyrical purposes.

The rune-names, and thus the subjects treated in the *Rune Poem* are traditionally determined, and can be analysed into natural phenomena: animals, plants, weather; cultural items: property, the bow, the *peorð*;[41] and abstract qualities: generosity, happiness, need. Unlike the studiously unchristian Icelandic version, the *Rune Poem* frequently refers to God. Surprisingly, he is absent

from the verses concerned with abstract qualities where some moral teaching might be expected; the poem's emphasis is rather upon God the Creator,[42] who sends daylight to men, and who permits the coming of spring (74–5; 32–4):
   Other Christian references are more sombre: reminding the audience of the fact of death. In the stanza for *feoh*, the poet warns that money should be given away freely if one is to face the Lord after death: 'gif hē wile for drihtne dōmes hlēotan'. The stanza for *man* is similarly pessimistic, conscious that earthly happiness lasts but for a short time. In this it contrasts markedly with the celebratory Icelandic equivalent:

> Maðr er manns gaman   Man is the delight of man[43]
> ok moldar auki   and increase of the earth
> ok skipa skreytir   and adorner of ships.
> (*Icelandic Rune Poem* 14)

> 'Man' byþ on myrgþe   his māgan lēof;
> sceal þēah ānra gehwylc   ōðrum swīcan,
> for ðām Dryhten wyle   dōme sīne
> þæt earme flæsc   eorþan betæcan.
> (*Old English Rune Poem* 59–62)

A man is in mirth, dear to his kinsman; each of them must desert the other, for the Lord desires, by his judgement, that the wretched flesh should seek the earth.

The tone and sentiments of this verse are echoed by the long final stanza of the poem (93b–94):[44] *ear* (the grave). The tone is elegiac:

> 'Ear' byþ egle   eorla gehwylcun,
> ðonn fæstlice   flæsc onginneþ
> hrāw cōlian,   hrūsan cēosan
> blāc tō gebeddan;   blēda gedrēosaþ,
> wynna gewītaþ,   wēra geswīcaþ.

The grave is terrifying to every man, when the body, the corpse inexorably begins to grow cold, the pale one to choose the earth as a bed companion; prosperity comes to an end, joys depart, pledges are broken.

'Gebeddan' (bed-companion) is the clue that locates the context in which death is viewed; the corpse's committal to earth is, as J. R. Hall points out,[45] a negation of that most joyful of human rituals, marriage. Instead of pledging faith, feasting and taking a wife to bed, the bridal night of the corpse is spent with the cold earth. All promises 'till death us do part' now expire.

The verses concerned with other abstract qualities are not specifically Christian in tone; they take a consistently materialistic view of wealth and happiness, differing markedly from the warning against hoarding in the *feoh* stanza. The one exception is *gyfu* (generosity), a quality especially praiseworthy since it constitutes the entire substance, 'ar and ætwist' of those who have nothing else; an assimilation of the Germanic custom of gift-giving to the Christian notion of alms-giving. *Wenne*[46] (happiness) is experienced by the man who is lacking in woe, sorrow, and pain, and who enjoys other tangible benefits: 'and him sylfa hæfþ I blæd and blysse and ēac byrga geniht' (23b–24: and who himself has prosperity and joy, and also the sufficiency of cities).[47]

Nyd is a paradoxical quality: while the state of being in need is a heavy weight on one's chest 'nearu on breostan', it also has a positive aspect if heeded in time to take precautionary measures. Need can thus be a blessing: 'to helpe and to hæle'.

Other stanzas are lyrical rather than didactic: 'gēr' cited above, or the unexpected beauty which the poet sees in ice:

> 'Īs' byþ oferceald,   ungemetum slidor,
> glisnaþ glæshluttur,   gimmum gelīcust,
> flōr forste geworuht,   fæger ansȳne.
>
> (29–31)

'Ice' is extremely cold and immeasurably slippery, it glistens clear as glass, most like jewels, a floor made by the frost, beautiful to see.

The poet invites us to marvel at the extraordinary coldness and slipperiness of this marvellous substance, in a stanza radiant with light, both from the ice itself, and from the paradigms of brilliance, glass, and jewels, with which it is compared. The solidity of ice, described in the *Icelandic Rune Poem* as 'unnar þak' (roof of waves), is suggested by the image of the frost-wrought floor. Hail too is a phenomenon that evokes superlatives, the whitest of grains,[48] descending in solid form, hurled about by the wind, then melting into water.

Some stanzas are puzzling: words such as *peorð* have become obscure through the course of time, while the verses about Tir,

Ing,[49] and Ōs probably conceal references to heathen gods. Comparison with the Icelandic version of the *Rune Poem* confirms the guess that Tir, though reduced to a constellation in the Old English, was originally the Germanic god, while Ōs (Latin 'mouth') is the reflex of Áss in the Icelandic poem:[50]

> 'Ōs' byþ ordfruma   ælcre spræce,
> wīsdōmes wraþu   and witena frōfur,
> and eorla gehwām   ēadnys and tōhiht.
> (10–12)

'Ōs' is the origin of every speech, a support of wisdom and comfort of wise men, and to every warrior a blessedness and hope.

That the verse should ascribe wisdom and eloquence 'ordfruma ælcre spræce' to Ōs makes probable an identification of *Os* with Óðinn, since, as we have seen, these qualities are associated in Old Norse primarily with Óðinn.

Other stanzas imitate the riddle techniques of the Exeter Book:

> 'Āc' byþ on eorþan   elda bearnum
> flæsces fōdor,   fēreþ gelōme
> ofer ganotes bæþ;   gārsecg fandaþ
> hwæþer āc hæbbe   æþele trēowe.
> (77–80)

An oak is fodder of the flesh on the ground for children of men, it travels frequently over the gannet's bath; the ocean tests whether the oak keeps faith nobly.[51]

How is an oak food for the children of men? How can it travel across the sea? Two possible uses of the oak: provider of acorns as mast for pigs to eat, and wood for a ship, are sketched obliquely, just as *Riddle* 30a in the Exeter Book depicts a tree as natural object, Cross, ship, log, and bowl.[52] Similarly, *ior* (eel? newt?)[53] is described in paradoxical, near-riddling terms: it is a river-fish which takes its food on land, yet it has a pleasant home in the water.

Further stanzas are made vivid by their evocations of social activity. Sometimes the poet views the activities of his fellow men with a slightly ironic eye:

> 'Rād' byþ on recyde   rinca gehwylcum

sēfte, and swīþhwæt   ðām ðe sitteþ on ufan
mēare mægenheardum   ofer mīlpaþas.

(13–15)

Riding is easy for every warrior in hall, and rather strenuous for him who sits on top of a powerful horse over miles of road.

The transition between inside and outside the hall is swiftly accomplished within 14ᵃ. The contrasting adjectives are joined by 'and', rather than contrasted by 'ac', as if the warrior, sitting comfortably on the bench in hall, were suddenly transported to a saddle. Horses of the sea can be equally troublesome, as the stanza for 'lagu' warns, imaginatively extending the traditional formula of ship as 'sea-horse' to depict the steering mechanism as a bridle (63–6):

'Lagu' byþ lēodum   langsum geþūht
gif hī sculun nēþun   on naca tealtum,
and hī sǣȳþa   swȳþe brēgaþ,
and se brimhengest   brīdles ne gȳmeð.

'Ocean' seems to men to extend a long way, if they have to risk themselves in an unstable boat, and the waves terrify them very much, and the sea-stallion pays no heed to the bridle.

The simple syntax 'gif' . . . 'and' . . . 'and' emphasizes the gradual worsening of the sailors' plight: the boat is untrustworthy, the waves frightening, and the tiller defective. In the last line we expect some resolution akin to that in the 'sigel' stanza, where the 'brim-hengest' (sea-stallion), steering by the sun, finally brings the seamen to land, but no such comfort is at hand, the sailors have been abandoned to their fate.

One of the most vividly realized stanzas in the poem describes *eh* — the horse, which provides a vignette as striking as those of the *Exeter Maxims*, of horse and rider in harmony together; contrasting with the ambivalent view of riding taken in the 'rād' stanza. Other verses complete the ideal picture of warriors in fellowship together: the torch burns brightly to illuminate their merriment (16–18), the *peorð* (dice-box?) provides mirth in the beer-hall. The *eþel* (homeland) is a place of 'blæd' (prosperity) while the *yr* (bow) is an essential part of the warrior's equipment.

Counterbalancing the picture of comradeliness and security[54] are such stanzas as *lagu*, and those which evoke discomfort: falling among thorns (*þorn*) or seizing hold of the sharp *eolhx*-reed. Such physical dangers are mild in comparison with the loss of every pleasure when the body comes to its final resting place.

The *Rune Poem* is akin to the *Cotton Maxims* in its delight in the variety of natural objects: the wild ox, with his tremendous horns, a 'felafrēcne dēor' (a very brave beast); the magnificent poplar tree (*beorc*). Sixteen out of the twenty-nine verses are concerned with nature, while many of the others depict an ideally ordered society, with horses, good weapons, and enjoyment of company in hall. There is surprisingly little Christian or didactic material in the poem: two evocations of God the Creator are balanced by references to God as judge, while only a few verses are exhortatory. The poet's enthusiasm for comfort, material happiness, and prosperity is tempered by a reflection that not everyone can partake in these joys: 'wræcna gehwam' (each wretched person), must depend on the generosity of others.

Halsall suggests that the poet of the *Rune Poem*:

> recognised in the futhorc an opportunity to compose a poem about the temporal world in which he lived and its relation to the eternal world in which he hoped and believed . . . the poet was prepared to take up the challenge of forging all this mass of inherited rune lore into a Christian unity.[55]

The 'Christian unity' of the poem is, however, a product of the Christian tone of the first and last verses: few other stanzas are, or easily could be, assimilated to points of Christian doctrine or morality. Yet notwithstanding, the *Rune Poem* is finally moral in outlook: the allusions to transience, the disappearance of earthly goods, and the final horror of the grave, function as reminders that the remarkable variety of the world we see does not endure.

4.4 *FORTUNES OF MEN*

The *Fortunes of Men* begins with the birth of a child:

> Ful oft þæt gegongeð,   mid godes meahtum,
> þætte wer ond wīf   in woruld cennað
> bearn mid gebyrdum   ond mid blēom gyrwað,

tennaþ ond tǣtaþ,   oþþæt sēo tīd cymeð,
gegǣð gēarrimum,   þæt þa geongan leomu,
līffǣstan leoþu,   geloden weorþað.
Fērgað swa ond feþad   fæder ond mōdor,
giefað ond gierwað.   God āna wāt
hwæt him weaxendum   winter bringað.

(1–9)

Very often it happens, through the powers of God, that a man and a woman bring into the world a child through birth and adorn it with a complexion,[56] nurture and coax it,[57] until that time comes, the years pass, that the young limbs, the members entrusted with life, become mature. In this way, the father and mother thus carry and feed (it), give (it) gifts and clothe (it). God alone knows what the winters will bring to it as it grows up.

Born by God's grace, the child at first is simply the object of the parents' attentions. Caring for a child is time-consuming work; a series of paired alliterating verbs: 'tennaþ ond tǣtaþ'; 'fērgaþ . . . ond fēþaþ'; 'giefað ond gierwað' stress the labour involved in raising a child to healthy maturity. The man and woman now become 'fæder ond mōdor': their identity is in their relation to the new life for which they are responsible. Once grown, 'weaxendum', the child's fate is in the hands of God; the parents can protect it no more.

The child is likened to a branch of the tree which is the family, through the words 'leomu' and 'leoþu' (tree) limbs, branches. (We may compare the *Exeter Maxims* passage discussed at length in chapter 5 for a similar identification between child and tree.) Although 'tree' as a baseword is rare in Old English, in contrast to Old Norse, kennings,[58] none the less the elliptical nature of the juxtaposition of human and tree in *Fortunes of Men* and *Exeter Maxims* suggests that the identification would have been well known, if not conventional, for their audiences.

The simple fact of birth provides a logical starting-point for observations about the possibilities inherent in human existence: the fate which each child meets. The first half of the poem catalogues unpleasant deaths: the first of these is that of a man eaten by a wolf. The mother mourns her son's death: 'hinsīþ þonne | mōdor bimurneð,' looking back to the description of childhood, when the mother stood between the child and death.

Other deaths follow; some have barely a half-line of description, while others are described at greater length. Of these, the lines which have attracted most critical attention[59] are those concerned with the man who falls from the tree:

> Sum sceal on holte   of hēan bēame
> fiþerlēas feallen;   bið on flihte seþēah,
> lāceð on lyfte,   oþþæt lengre ne bið
> westem wudubēames.   Þonne hē on wyrtrūman
> sīgeð sworcenferð   sāwle birēafod,
> fealleþ on foldan;   feorð biþ on sīþe.
>
> (21–6)

One is doomed to fall, featherless, from a high tree in the wood; nevertheless he flies, he sports in the air, until he is no longer a fruit of the tree. Then, his spirit darkening, he crashes to the tree-roots, falls to the ground, deprived of life, his soul journeys away.

For a moment, the falling man poised as if in flight, the poet plays with the riddle-like enigma, 'he flies, but he has no wings'. At first the fall is graceful; like the bird of *Cotton Maxims* 38[b]–39[a], he sports in the air, 'lāceð on lyfte'. Then, less gracefully, the man is visualized as the fruit of the tree, naturally falling to the ground when ripe. Suddenly, almost callously, the poet lets the man crash to the ground. The comparisons with the featherless bird and the fruit have distracted us from the horror of the fall, until, with a crash, we are brought back to reality: the man is dead.

In contrast to this almost playful description, the fate of the hanged man in 33–42 is horribly exact: no distracting imagery mitigates the gruesomeness here. Despite the poet's observation that the corpse is 'fēlelēas' (without feeling) the suggestion that it might beat off the attacking raven with its hands, if it were able to, endows the man on the gallows with a consciousness of the indignities and suffering he must undergo as his eyes are pecked out. The earlier verb 'rīdan' (to ride) 33[60] suggests movement as the body sways; a grisly realism, down to the details of the corpse rotting, and the miasma 'wælmiste' which surrounds it, renders the passage far more explicit than the parallel description in *Beowulf*.[61]

Other deaths follow, until, at the centre of the poem, the turning-point comes, an 'edwenden' (reversal) in the sense of *Beowulf*

280, where Beowulf tells the Coastguard that he can bring a reversal in the Danish fortunes. 'Edwenden' in one's fortune can only come about through God's help, just as God is respons-ible for the miracle of conception. The parallel is made explicit through the repetition of 'mid Godes meahtum' 1ᵇ:

> Sum sceal on geoguþe   mid godes meahtum
> his earfoðsīþ   ealne forspildan,
> ond on yldo eft   ēadig wēorþan,
> wunian wyndagum   ond wēlan þicgan,
> māþmas ond meoduful   mǣgburge on,
> þǣs þe ǣnig fira mǣge   forð gehealdan.
>
> (58–63)

One, in his youth, must, through the powers of God, do away with his troubles, and in old age afterwards become blessed, live through joyful days, and receive riches, treasures and the mead-cup in the dwelling of his family, as far as any man may continue in this.

'Sum' has, until now, introduced each man doomed to die, but now it signals a man whose life, through God's help, is changed. Despite hardship, possibly exile, in youth, he survives to enjoy his old age, surrounded by family, with prosperity and status. The ideal fate: a long, happy life, is thus sketched at the outset of the second half. Now the poet is faced with a difficulty: while death comes in a myriad forms, happiness, as the *Rune Poem* tells us, is simply the absence of such threat, together with the enjoyment of wealth and home. Happiness is single, monolithic: the poem could effectively end here. However, in order to balance the catalogue of evil fates in the first half of the poem, the poet lists, some briefly, some at greater length, the different skills and attributes which the Lord instils in people. Many of these are paralleled in the Old Norse *íþróttir*, the essential accomplishments which a young nobleman must have.[62]

Two extended portraits of men with particular expertise, the hawker and the harper (80–4), balance the two horrifying deaths of the first half of the poem. The vigour of 'snellice' (boldly) and 'hleapeð' (leaps) evokes the energy with which the harpist sets to his task, while the reference to his seat, at his lord's feet, shows his secure and rightful place in the court milieu; he is not displaced and grieving like Deor in the poem of that name. There is a similar appreciation of an activity skilfully performed in *Beowulf* 864–71, which describes the warriors racing their horses back from the mere as the *scop* recites Beowulf's deeds. As in the *Exeter Maxims*, such sketches provide an assurance that society is functioning properly, that humanity is performing the tasks allotted to it, in accordance with God's will.

Fortunes of Men is close to the *Exeter Maxims* in its concern with depicting a whole spectrum of human activities. However, while the poet of the *Exeter Maxims* is content to let the range of his observations speak for him, to show how society is ordered, the poet of *Fortunes of Men* uses the fates and accomplishments in the poem to demonstrate explicitly how human lives are determined by God: 'For þon him nū ealles þonc æghwa secge, | þæs þe hē fore his miltsum monnum scrifeð' (97–8: Now let everyone thank him for this reason, for that which he has, in his mercy, decreed for men).

4.5 PRECEPTS

Precepts has a more elaborate framework than any of the Old English wisdom poems we have considered so far. The poem consists of ten pieces of advice given by a father to his son; a father who is evidently a wise man:

> Ðus frōd fæder   frēobearn lǣrde,
> mōdsnottor [mon],   māga cystum eald, [*mon* not in MS]
> wordum wīsfæstum,   þæt hē wel þunge
>
> (1–3)

Thus the wise father, a man with an intelligent mind, old in virtues, taught his noble son with wise words, so that he would prosper well.

The father's characterization resembles that of Hroðgar in *Beowulf*;[63] the age and wisdom of both men is stressed. The father is described as 'frōd', 'þoncsnottor' (wise) 'sē gomola' and 'eald' (the old man, old) while Hroðgar, in the immediate context of the homily (1700–84), is characterized as 'wīsa', 'sē snottra' (wise, the wise man), 'gamela Scylding' (the old Scylding), and 'wintrum frōd' (advanced in years).[64]

The father speaks on ten numbered occasions 'ōþre sīþe' (the second time), 'Ðriddan sȳþe' (the third time), etc.; on each occasion he may utter more than one maxim. Often the maxims grouped together are thematically related, but in the first and last utterances, a number of disparate observations are strung rather loosely together.

Precepts is generally predictable in content; its themes are obedience, loyalty to friends, avoiding sin, caution in speech, and moderation in behaviour. Yet it is the Old English wisdom poem most directly comparable to *Hávamál*'s Gnomic Poem and *Loddfáfnismál* in particular, for it is the only poem to tell its audience how it should live. The maxims of *Precepts*, like those of the *Loddfáfnismál*, are in the imperative mood, but the tone is neither peremptory nor hectoring. The commands are softened by the kindly intentions of the father, who speaks with 'mildum wordum' (with gentle words), 'þurh bliþne geþoht' (with cheerful thought). His affection for his son, the 'mōdlēofne māgan' (kinsman dear to his heart) is deep, and he is anxious about the young man's future, for he speaks on the final occasion 'torn-sorgna ful' (filled with sorrow and care.)

The first utterance urges the young man to choose the right and shun the wrong, coupled with an adjuration to love his parents and honour his elders. The elders are visualized as the youth's superiors and teachers:

> Wes þū þīnum yldrum   ārfæst symle,
> fægerwyrde,   ond þē in ferðe lǣt
> þīne lāreowas   lēofe in mōde,
> þa þec geornast   to gōde trymmen.
>
> (11–14)

Be always respectful to your elders, fairly-spoken, and let your teachers be dear to you in your heart, who most eagerly desire to encourage you to good.

We may compare this with *Hávamál* 134: 'at hárum þul | hlæðu aldregi' (never laugh at a grey-haired sage), where the undesirable course of behaviour — scoffing at the old — is clearly realized for us. Both poems share the topos of the wisdom of the aged; but in *Hávamál*, the wisdom of the old is arcane, magical lore, rather than advice, for the old man in the kitchen among the cheese-skins is a type of Óðinn hanging on the tree.[65]

In the second utterance, the father adjures the son to avoid sin: what sin is will be defined more closely in the fifth speech. The third and fourth occasions explore the idea of friendship: like *Hávamál* 120, *Precepts* 24ᵇ–26 urge that a good man, capable of giving good advice, should be chosen as a companion:

> ac þū ānne genim
> tō gesprēcan symle   spella ond lāra
> rǣdhycgende,   sȳ ymb rīce swa hit mǣge.
>
> (24ᵇ–26)

But choose to speak with someone who always is mindful of examples and teaching, whether he be powerful or not.[66]

Gaining good instruction, one of *Precepts'* principal themes, is the main reason to choose a friend; *Hávamál* 123 urges, on the contrary, that a friend should be sought out so that he will enhance one's status in the eyes of others. Both texts are equally vehement about the importance of loyalty to the friend once chosen: compare *Precepts* 29–31 and *Hávamál* 121. While *Precepts* is convinced of the absolute value of loyalty in friendship, *Hávamál* emphasizes the pain of loneliness after the friendship is broken off: 'sorg etr hjarta' (sorrow eats the heart).

The fifth utterance defines more closely the types of sin which a young man might fall into:

> Druncen beorg þē   ond dollic word,
> man on mōde   ond in mūþe lyge,
> yrre ond ǣfeste,   ond idese lūfan.
>
> (34–6)

Shield yourself from drunkenness and foolish words, wickedness of heart and lies in the mouth, anger and envy and the love of women.[67]

In *Hávamál*, the dangers of unwary speech and over-indulgence in drink, together with the perils of falling in love, are discoursed upon at some length. The worst result of such behaviour in the world of *Hávamál* is social ridicule, becoming an 'augabragð', and losing one's standing in society; for, as we have seen, the concept of sin is absent from *Hávamál*. In *Precepts*, however, the sanction against the man who commits such sins is clearly spelt out, as is the reward for piety; the figure of God as Judge is present behind each of the father's maxims: 'Hē þē mid wīte gielde | swylce þām oþrum mid ēadwēlan' (19ᵇ–20: He (God) will repay you with punishment, as he will (repay) the others with bliss).

On the sixth occasion, the father admonishes the son in the virtue of judiciousness: the task of deciding 'hwæt sȳ gōd oþþe yfel' (what may be good or evil) is devolved from the divine Judge on to the human. The ability to make right judgements is valued in *Beowulf* also: we may compare the Coastguard's statement in 287[b]–289:

> Æghwæþres sceal
> scearp scyldwiga   gescād witan,
> word ond worca,   sē þe wēl þenceð

A sharp shield-warrior of upright mind must know how to distinguish both words and deeds.[68]

Judiciousness is related to sharpness of mind in both poems: 'scearpe mōde' (*Precepts* 46[b]). Having determined the better course, this should be chosen over the sinful one, urges the father: 'ond þē ā þæt sēlle gecēos'. Hrōðgar admonishes Beowulf in similar terms, but here the alternatives are more closely defined than the universal opposition between good and evil which *Precepts* offers: Beowulf's choice is between the 'better cause' and the avariciousness of the man who forgets his duty as king and becomes prey to complacency (*Beowulf* 1724[b]–1755).

Next a distinction is drawn between the wise man and the fool, *Hávamál*'s favourite opposition. The wise man cannot enjoy himself, for he is never free from an awareness of the uncertainty of the future, but the fool's pleasure is unalloyed. The poet modifies this last sentiment: even a fool will be anxious if he knows he has an enemy. The gnome's basic proposition shares the theme of *Hávamál* 54–6, but the disconcerting conclusion which the *Hávamál*-poet draws is that it is therefore best only to be middling wise, 'meðalsnotr'. Typically, the *Hávamál*-poet transforms a traditional commonplace into an ironic challenge to the value of wisdom itself.

'Learn what you are taught' is the theme of the next utterance, while in the ninth, the father turns aside from instruction to moralize about nations who have turned away from God. As God's judgment falls heavily upon the sinful individual, so it will upon the sinful people: 'Monig sceal ongieldan | sawelsusles' (71[b]–72[a]: Many will have to pay for that with torment of the soul).

Precepts ends with the tenth utterance, glancing briefly at some of the themes from earlier in the poem: guarding against anger and sin; moderation in speech, being neither slanderous nor flattering.[69] The final adjuration, as so frequently in wisdom poetry,[70] is to remember what has been taught: 'Swā þū, mīn bearn, gemyne I frōde fæder lāre' (So, remember, my child, the teaching of your wise father).

The advice of the father shows a strong resemblance in theme to certain of the brief maxims (*monosticha*) which preface the *Disticha Catonis*. The first speech advises the son to honour his father and mother, while the second and third *monosticha* advise similarly: 'Parentes ama. I Cognatos cole' (Love your parents. Respect your kindred).

In his fifth speech, cited above, the father warns against various foolish and sinful things while the *monosticha* also warn against strange women, drunkenness, lying, and anger:

Vino tempera.	Be moderate in wine.
Meretricem fuge.	Shun a whore.
Iracundiam rege.	Control your anger.
Nihil mentire.	Do not lie.

These are the most striking correspondences between the *Disticha* and *Precepts*,[71] but they do not prove that *Precepts* has necessarily taken the *Disticha* as a model. The ten pieces of advice suggest that the poem is partly based on the Decalogue, and thus the adjuration in the first of the father's speeches to honour one's father and mother is most likely to gloss the Fifth Commandment. Likewise the admonition to avoid various occasions for sin in the father's fifth speech refers to spiritual dangers very commonly found in gnomic poetry. Since the *Disticha* were known early in England, the possibility that the author of *Precepts* may have been familiar with them cannot be ruled out, but they cannot be identified as a model for *Precepts* with any degree of certainty.

The poet of *Precepts* identifies himself with the father, just as we, the audience, are to assume the role of the son. The monologue addressed to a fictive listener is an attractive device for the presentation of wisdom material, since it enables the poet to instruct his audience indirectly and tactfully. The learning process takes place at one remove, and so the audience can assimilate the instruction without feeling that they are being criticized or lectured. Similarly, Hesiod ostensibly directs his advice in *Works and Days* to his reprobate brother Perses, while Virgil claims that the *Georgics* are intended expressly for the 'ignoros agrestis' (uninstructed farmer), and thus only indirectly for Octavian and Maecenas, the patrons of the work.

Although, like the gnomic sections of *Hávamál*, *Precepts* offers a variety of wisdom for social contexts, the wisdom of *Precepts* seems leaden and pedestrian in comparison with the light touch and colloquial voice of the Old Norse poem. Where *Hávamál* invokes the censure and mockery of one's peers as an incentive to behave wisely, the ultimate arbiter in *Precepts* is a stern God the Judge, who will weigh all actions and find them wanting. Spiritual perfection is the aim of *Precepts*, where *Hávamál* contents itself with the more easily achieved: living sensibly with the approval (lof) of others. For the modern reader, the main interest of *Precepts* may lie in the comparison with Hroðgar's 'sermon' in *Beowulf*. Hroðgar's warnings are apt and well chosen, concentrating on the specific spiritual danger, pride, which is most likely to threaten the young hero. Nothing is otiose or irrelevant, as the respectful silence with which Beowulf receives this additional gift of counsel makes plain. Shorn of the dramatic context which shapes and focuses the *Beowulf* passage, *Precepts* imparts wisdom for every day, for the ordinary youth rather than the epic hero.

4.6 *SOLOMON AND SATURN II*

The dialogue form is not used in *Hávamal* but it is found in other Eddic wisdom poems, for example *Vafþruðnismál* and *Fáfnismál*. In Old English, the dialogue is represented by the two *Solomon and Saturn*[72] poems. The aim of *Solomon and Saturn I* is to show the efficacy of the Pater Noster as a powerful charm against all kinds of evil. The poet personifies the letters of the prayer, and elaborates at extraordinary length the battles which they undertake against the spiritual enemy. The prose dialogue which separates *Solomon and Saturn I* and *Solomon and Saturn II* in MS Corpus Christi College Cambridge 422 also deals with the subject of the Pater Noster, but the second poem does not mention the prayer, and its interests range much more widely, through references to obscure Oriental legends, and gnomic observations, to exploration of the significance of Doomsday and Fate.

The wisdom dialogue is well-attested in Old Norse, where it generally takes the form of a contest in which the challenger wagers his life.[73] In the first dialogue, Saturn offers to give Solomon thirty pounds of gold and his twelve sons, if Solomon can succeed in convincing him of the truth of Christianity. In the second dialogue, no stakes are explicitly set, but in the lines normally understood as the conclusion,[74] the poet declares victory for Solomon (175–8). Although Saturn has lost the contest, he has gained in knowledge, and he seems, for the first time, to find hope of salvation. His defeat, paradoxically, is occasion for joy. The purpose of *Solomon and Saturn II* is the dramatization of the confrontation between pagan and Christian.

Solomon and Saturn are distinctively characterized: Saturn is a military leader of some renown, a 'bald breosttoga' (bold war-leader). Though of mature years and much-travelled, he is eager to learn, genuinely puzzled by the aspects of existence about which he questions Solomon. He is also persistent; when he fails to gain a satisfactory answer he will return to the matter later, rephrasing the question. Saturn represents the type of the 'wise pagan'; less learned than Hroðgar in *Beowulf*, who has arrived at a monotheistical belief and a quasi-Christian understanding of good and evil, Saturn nevertheless belongs to the same tradition.[75]

Solomon is quietly superior in his wisdom, yet magnanimous. Although his answers sometimes appear evasive or unsatisfactory, these evasions are part of the poet's plan, enabling him to develop his themes at more leisure. Saturn must be allowed to put a number of questions to Solomon if the subject under discussion is to be explored thoroughly.

The contest begins with the exchange of arcane knowledge of Oriental myths: the 'Vasa Mortis' and the still inexplicable 'weallende wulf' (raging wolf). These motifs belong to Jewish legend and Rabbinical tradition;[76] their function here is both to emphasize the exotic background of the speakers and to enhance their authority and breadth of knowledge, just as the list of spells which Óðinn knows, but will not impart, in the *Ljóðatal* completes our image of the god of wisdom as possessor of every type of knowledge. Since it is the restricted access to such knowledge which gives the wisdom its value, we may well doubt whether the poem's audience had any better idea of the 'Vasa Mortis' than we do; the obscurity is probably intentional. From such matters, the speakers move to a discussion of philosophical problems: why the evil seem to prosper, the nature of Fate, and the origin of Evil.

The poem has many gaps, but the general movement from facts and riddles to philosophical considerations can still be discerned. The central issue, with which Saturn shows an anguished preoccupation, is the eternal problem of understanding earthly suffering, a question which he approaches from a number of angles. The thrust of his questioning illustrates the struggle between opposing forces on earth; these inevitably end with the victory, albeit temporary, of the negative force. J. A. Dane sums up the structure of the poem thus:

> Saturn's emphasis is on dichotomy, struggle and the physical manifestation of conflict in the world; Solomon's replies either refer struggle to an extra-physical level, or assert a third term that offers a higher synthesis to Saturn's dichotomous imagery.[77]

While this may be true of the later section of the poem, ll. 355 onwards, it does not apply to the lines with which we are dealing here. Solomon tends simply to assert the superiority of the stronger force, confirming the dichotomy perceived by Saturn.

Saturn begins with an obvious example from the cycle of the seasons, the winter snowfall which withers the plants and starves the animals:

> Ac forhwon fealleð se snāw,   foldan behȳdeð,
> bewrīhð wyrta cīð,   wæstmas getīgeð,
> geðȳð hīe and geðrēatað,   ðæt hīe ðrāge bēoð
> cealde geclungne?
>
> (293–96ᵃ)

But why does snow fall, hide the ground, cover the shoots of plants, bind growing things, crush and restrain them, so that for a time they are shrunken with cold?

The answer is lost in one of the lacunae, but, shortly after the poem resumes, Saturn returns once more to the question of physical suffering; this time asking why sunshine is unequally distributed: 'Ac forhwon ne mōt sēo sunne sīde gesceafte | scīre geondscīnan? (331–332ᵇ: But why cannot the sun shine brightly everywhere throughout broad creation?). Solomon recognizes the real import of the question, replying with his own formulation of the problem of inequality:

> Ac forhwām nǣron eorð(we)lan   ealle gedǣled
> lēodum gelīce?   Sum tō lȳt hafað,
> gōdes grǣdig.   Hine god seteð
> ðurh geearnunga   ēadgum tō rǣste
>
> (335–8)

But why were not the riches of the earth all shared out alike among people? One man has too little, so greedy is he for good. God will seat him for his merits at rest among the blessed.

Solomon's answer plays with the paradox of two types of contrasting greed: the yearning after worldly goods, and an intense spiritual desire for Good. Such inequalities in earthly fortune will be levelled out in the next world, when the poor will have their reward. A few lines later, he returns to the physical opposition contained in Saturn's original question: fire and frost, sun and snow cannot be together; the stronger must always give way to the weaker. The assertion is an appeal to the observed facts of nature, to common-sense.

Saturn presses on, reformulating his question on the human, rather than the natural plane: why do two twins, born on the same day suffer different fates? Solomon's answer[78] recalls the opening of *The Fortunes of Men*; a mother can only protect her child from Fate for a short time, then wildness, a murderous spirit, exile, and early death may well be his lot. The only explanation that Solomon offers for this is a blank fatalism: 'ac sceall on gebyrd faran | ān æfter ānum: ðæt is eald gesceaft' (376[b]–377: but one thing must follow another in order: that is the way of Creation of old).

The generalization is unsatisfactory to Saturn, who demands to know why the young man of the previous example cannot improve his lot by attaching himself to a benevolent lord in his youth, a reflection of Old English social practices. The answer is that a fortunate man may choose a good lord: 'mildne hlāford | ānne æðeling' (a gracious lord, a prince), but the luckless may not. The implication that the 'mildne hlāford' is to be identified with Christ is not developed further, the hint is left in the minds of the audience and Saturn himself.

Finally, Saturn expressly puts to Solomon the one question towards which all others have been leading. The question is preceded by a lengthy preamble, which depicts wise men, the counsellors of the Philistines and Saturn himself, disputing over the matter, opening books and exchanging views on a single problem. Solomon breaks in to guess what the question will be, and his skill in divining what it is Saturn wishes to know further enhances his authority. The delayed revelation of the question, and the eagerness with which the matter has been discussed, signal the importance of the question which follows:

> hwæðer wære twēgra   būtan twēon strengra,
> wyrd ðe warnung,   ðonne hīe winnað oft
> mid hira ðrēanīedlan   hwæðerne āðrēoteð ær
> (418–20)

which of the two might, without doubt, be stronger, fate or foresight, when they often struggle together with their compelling force, which would weary first.

'Warnung' is found only here in this sense of 'foreknowledge, prescience', according to Bosworth-Toller; in all other instances, 'warnung' means 'warning', 'admonition'. Menner denies that 'wyrd ðe warnung' has any connection with Boethius or Augustine;[79] anxious to identify some 'native Germanic' elements in the poem, he seizes upon the phrase as an expression of a strictly Germanic destiny and foresight. Saturn's pre-occupation with *wyrd* is, Menner thinks, to be regarded as evidence of 'the deep-rooted Germanic belief in the power of destiny', although he concedes that the poet probably had no clear idea of the meaning of *wyrd* in the pagan system of belief.

But the very terms in which Saturn formulates his question: 'wyrd' (fate, future events),[80] and 'warnung' (foresight, fore-knowledge), betray his awareness of the existence of the philosophical problem of the interaction of providence and foreknowledge, as outlined by Boethius in *De consolatione philosophiae* V. III.[81] Put briefly, the fictive Boethius wants to know whether God's foreknowledge (*warnung*) causes the future (*wyrd*) to happen, or whether He has foreknowledge of what is to come, simply because it *is* to come. Which is cause and which effect: 'hwæðer wære . . . strengra', and how can either position be reconciled with the notion of free will? The complexity of the problem which prompts Saturn's question cannot be reduced to a simple belief that 'Wyrd biŏ ful ārǣd' (Fate is inexorably fixed),[82] which is how Solomon's answer attempts to paraphrase it. Saturn has an inkling of the problem to which the Boethian theory of God's Providence is the answer.

Solomon nods to the Germanic belief that Fate is inexorable, asserting that *wyrd* is hard to change, 'Wyrd biŏ wended hearde' in 427, but the sage continues by pointing out the implications of the Boethian position for the individual: the wise man who understands the relationship of Fate and Providence will be able to mitigate the effects of Fate through his friends' help:

> and hwæŏre him mæg wīssefa   wyrda gehwylce
> gemetigian,[83]   gif hē biŏ mōdes glēaw,
> and tō his frēondum wile   fultum sēcan,
> ŏēhhwæŏre godcundes   gǣstes brūcan
>
> (430–3)

and yet the man wise in soul may deliberate upon everything which happens, if he is prudent in heart, and may wish to seek help from his friends, even though he may partake of the divine spirit.

The wise man who considers carefully will see that all that happens to him, even ill fortune, is to be regarded as an opportunity to increase his wisdom. As Lady Philosophy explains to the fictive Boethius, everything that happens, 'wyrda gehwylce' is an ultimate good:

> And therefore, she (Philosophy) said, 'a wise man ought not to take it ill, every time he is brought into conflict with fortune, just as would not be fitting for a brave man to be vexed every time the sound of war crashed out. Since for each of these the difficulty is itself the occasion, for the latter of increasing his glory, for the former of further fashioning his wisdom. And this is indeed why virtue is so called, because relying on its own powers it is not overcome by adversity. (IV. VII, (p. 379)).

Even though he understands the nature of divine Providence, 'godcundes gǣstes'[84] the wise man may, in practical terms, look to his worldly friends for assistance when adverse fortune comes.

Saturn seems to be satisfied by this response, for he next enquires into the origin of *Wyrd,* now to be understood specifically as 'evil fortune'.[85] Solomon completes the equation 'Fate'='evil fate'='evil' and narrates the story of the Fall of Lucifer. This story accounts for the two types of spirit, the guardian angel and the opposing demon, who follow a man through life, seeking to influence him for good or evil. The manuscript ends shortly after this passage; the conclusion normally supplied for the poem is a fragment from earlier in the manuscript.

Gnomic Elements

In the course of Saturn's quest for the solution to the 'Boethian' problem, few strictly gnomic observations are made. Solomon moralizes, apparently prompted by the 'weallande wulf' (raging wolf):

> Dol bið sē ðe gǣð   on dēop wæter,
> sē ðe sund nafað   nē gesegled scip,
> nē fugles flyht,   nē hē mid fōtum ne mæg
> grund gerǣcan.
>
> (216–19ᵃ)

Foolish is he who goes on deep water, who does not have the skill of swimming, nor a ship with sails, nor the flight of a bird, who cannot reach the bottom with his feet.

The gnome follows a familiar Old English pattern, paralleled in the *Exeter Maxims* and in the conclusions to *The Wanderer* and *The Seafarer,* but the simple maxim is expanded to cover all expediencies, even, apparently, the most unlikely — an ability to fly — by which the foolish man might save himself.

Later Saturn appears to echo the *Cotton Maxims:*[86] 'Nieht bið wedera ðīestrost, nēd bið wyrda heardost, | sorg bið swārost byrðen, slǣp bið dēaðe gelīcost' (303–4: Night is the darkest of weathers, need the hardest of conditions,[87] sorrow the heaviest burden, sleep is most like death). This series of superlatives is immediately preceded by a missing leaf, so the context is obscured; Solomon adds a comment to the effect that leaves are green only for a short time, then they fall and rot.[88] Just so do the sinful, hoarders of treasure, fall to the ground and perish. The superlatives, like the sequence 'forst sceal frēosan . . .' (frost must freeze . . .) in the *Exeter Maxims,* are incontrovertible truths; by their self-evident nature they validate the less easily accepted wisdom which the poem presents elsewhere.

Other questions are couched in riddle terms:

> Ac hwæt is ðæt wundor   ðē geond ðās worold færeð,
> styrnenga gæð,   staðolas bēateð . . .
>   him tō mōse sceall
> gegangan gēara gehwelce grundbūendra,
> lyft flēogendra,   laguswemmendra,
> ðria ðrēotēno   ðūsendgerimes.
>
>   (273–4; 279ᵇ-282)

But what is that wondrous thing which travels through this world, it goes exorably, it beats upon the foundations . . . every single year there must go as food for it three times thirteen thousand of land-dwellers, fliers in the air and sea-swimmers.

The solution to the riddle is Old Age, who finally brings all creatures to their knees.[89] The exactness of the figures, three times thirteen thousand, recalls the curious precision of the facts in the *Prose Dialogues* of *Solomon and Saturn*.[90]

In *Solomon and Saturn II* the poet seems to have intended to dramatize a confrontation between a Christian and a virtuous pagan. The poet's knowledge of paganism was no doubt drawn from the secular literature that he knew, poems such as *Beowulf*, and might be represented as a heroic belief in the power of *Wyrd*,[91] a fate which was inexorable, but whose operations could be modified or arrested by courage, and its concomitant, fame: 'Wyrd oft nereð | unfǣgne eorl, þonne his ellen dēah!' (*Beowulf* 572ᵇ-73: Fate often saves the undoomed warrior, when his courage is sufficient!).

Like Boethius, Saturn is concerned with fundamental questions: the inequalities of Fortune and the power of fate. There is one major difference from Boethius, however. Boethius draws a distinction between the good man and the wicked, asking why the good man should suffer adversity, while the wicked prosper. However, since he is a pagan, Saturn does not think in terms of the good man and the wicked man; the notion of Good and Evil as moral absolutes is absent from Saturn's thinking, as it is absent from *Hávamál*. The opposition of 'gōde oððe yfle' (good or evil) (355) is reserved for the fortune which overtakes the twins, not for the characterization of the twins themselves, a strictly pragmatic understanding of the terms.

Saturn's formulation of the central problem, placing in opposition 'wyrd' and 'warnung', is surely Boethian; the *De consolatione* may have been a direct model for the poem, with Saturn representing the fictive Boethius and Solomon taking the role of Philosophy; such a model might also have suggested the dialogue structure. More probably, the poet of *Solomon and Saturn II* knew *De consolatione philosophiae*, as would many of his educated contemporaries, and assumed that his audience would recognize his use of Boethian ideas[92] placed in the mouth of a virtuous pagan.

Menner suggests that the Germanic wisdom and riddle contest may have influenced *Solomon and Saturn II*,[93] noting the occurrence of some stylistic formulas found in the *Riddles* and in the questions of *Vafþrúðnismál, Alvíssmál,* and *Heiðreks saga.*[94] However, it seems most probable that the poet would have made use of traditional formulas available to him in Old English for the asking of riddling questions: there is no necessity to assume a direct link with a common Germanic ancestor. Wisdom contests are also known from outside the Germanic area: the legendary contest between Hesiod and Homer attests to a Greek tradition, while in Ireland we find the tenth-century *Colloquy of the Two Sages.* The actual dialogue form of the poems is to be related to Latin models rather than the Germanic wisdom contest. Ultimately descended from Plato's dialogues (which were of course unknown to the Anglo-Saxons), the dialogue was adopted by the early Christian writers as a vehicle of theological debate, of which Boethius' *De consolatione philosophiae* is only one among many.

The Old English poets amalgamate Germanic tradition, biblical forms, and classical devices in the presentation of wisdom in verse. The topos of the sage from whom wisdom is received may be Germanic, reinforced by the Solomonic tradition of the Bible, while the dialogue, possibly influenced by a native wisdom-contest tradition,[95] is founded on the classical dialogue as debate form, inherited from Latin. The Old English poets have taken whatever seemed useful to them from the traditions with which they were familiar and created a number of frameworks around which they could structure the various types of wisdom material which they wished to present.

Notes

1. e.g. the references to Wōden, Þunor, and Ōs in *Exeter Maxims, Cotton Maxims,* and *Rune Poem.*

2. e.g. Williams, *GP*, 89, 93, 107, and 112–13.

3. Text cited from *ASPR* iii: *The Exeter Book* ed. G. P. Krapp and E. V. K. Dobbie (London and New York, 1936).

4. R. McGregor Dawson, 'The Structure of the Old English Gnomic Poems', *JEGP* 61 (1962), 14–22; N. F. Barley, 'Structure in the Cotton Gnomes', *NM* 78 (1977), 244–9.

5. Dawson, 'Structure', 22, and see also Hansen, *SC*, 160.

6. The contention that 'progression by opposites . . . is the organizing principle behind lengthier (sc. than *Beowulf*'s gnomic passages) gnomic poems such as *Maxims I* and *II*', as asserted by C. Karkov and R. Farrell, 'The Gnomic Passages of *Beowulf*', *NM* 91 (1990), 303, ignores the frequency with which juxtaposition of like things is the nexus between one gnomic unit and the next.

7. Barley, 'Structure', 245.

8. Hansen, *SC*, 157–62.

9. See below, ch. 5 for the nexus between Creation and nature-wisdom.

10. Hansen, *SC*, 158–9.

11. 'Onge' is a *hapax legomenon*. B-T (Supplement) relates it to 'ange, ænge' (anxiously, painfully).

12. In a recent note, F. M. Biggs and S. McEntire argue that the blindness is to be construed as spiritual rather than physical. However, the context of illness, 'Lēf mon lǣces behofað', (the sick man needs a doctor) would seem to suggest that the blindness is real. 'Spiritual Blindness in the Old English *Maxims I* part 1', *NQ* 35 (1988), 11.

13. See B-T, s.v. 'gifre'.

14. Such sharp breaks are paralleled in *Háv.* however; between 14 and 15; 57 and 58; 79, 80, and 81.

15. For more detailed analysis of OE Nature gnomes, see below, ch. 5.

16. J. Mann, 'Proverbial Wisdom in the *Ysengrimus*', *NLH* 16 (1984), 93.

17. 'Dēop dǣda wǣg': Krapp and Dobbie translate as 'The deep way of the dead'. Shippey, *PW*, follows C. Brown, '"Poculum Mortis" in Old English', *Speculum*, 15 (1940), 389–99, in taking 'wǣg' as 'cup', thus 'deep is the cup of death'; 'wǣg' would mean 'wave', parallel with 'sund'. I prefer Krapp and Dobbie's interpretation; the sea is traversed by the dead in a funeral ship?

18. 'Holen' (holly) forms the wood for the funeral pyre, as Krapp and Dobbie suggest, although Malone's suggestion that 'holen' should be taken as 'chief', paralleled by *The Wanderer* 31 'lēofra geholena', is also attractive ('Notes on Gnomic Poem B of the Exeter Book', *MÆ* 12 (1943), 65–7).

19. Although 'ōs' in *The Rune Poem* probably conceals a reference to Woden.

20. Cf. *Buf.* 175 ff. where the poet castigates the Danes for turning to the worship of idols 'wīgweorþunga' after Grendel has manifested himself.

21. P. Lendinara, '*Maxims I* 146–51: A Hint of Funeral Lamentation', *NM* 74 (1973), 214–16, suggests that the insincerity of the wolf's mourning is a parody of the false grief of the hired mourner.

22. Hansen, *SC*, 176.

23. *Menologium* and the *Cotton Maxims* are both to be found in manuscript in Cotton Tiberius B. 1 and are edited in *ASPR* vi, *The Anglo-Saxon Minor Poems*, ed. E. V. K. Dobbie (London and New York, 1942). For a closer examination of the *Menologium*, see below, ch. 5.

24. See J. K. Bollard, 'The *Cotton Maxims*', *Neophilologus*, 57 (1973), 179–87.

25. It is conceivable that the author had the Augustinian opposition in mind.

26. The movement from 'visibilia' to 'invisibilia' is noted by S. B. Greenfield and R. Evert, '*Maxims II*: Gnome and Poem', in L. E. Nicholson and D. W. Frese ed. *Anglo-Saxon Poetry: Essays in Appreciation. For John McGalliard* (Notre Dame, Ind., 1975), 340. We might also compare *Buf.* 50b–52.

27. *Njáls saga* 102, where the poet Steinunn challenges the missionary Þangbrandr, for

example.

28. In 'Oaks, Ships, Riddles, and the Old English *Rune Poem*', *ASE* 19 (1990), 103–16, P. Sorrell remarks on the interaction of this kind of gnome and the riddle, the gnome furnishing the answer to the question 'what is most . . . ?' There is a similar series in *Solomon and Saturn II* 303–4, discussed below, ch. 4. 6.

29. Krapp and Dobbie emend 'wea' to 'weax', transforming a fine line to a banality. See F. C. Robinson, 'Understanding an Old English Wisdom Verse: *Maxims II* Lines 10 ff.', in L. D. Benson and S. Wenzel ed. *The Wisdom of Poetry: Studies in Early English in Honor of Morton W. Bloomfield* (Kalamazoo, Mich., 1982), 1–11.

30. I translate 'sceal' as 'must'; the sense is close to 'is by nature'. Greenfield and Evert translate this passage, inelegantly, if accurately, 'is typically'. For discussion of the semantic range of 'sceal' and 'biþ' in OE gnomic poetry, see M. Nelson, '"Is" and "Ought" in the Exeter Book *Maxims*', *Southern Folklore Quarterly*, 45 (1984 for 1981), 109–21, and see introduction.

31. The gnomes in the series can take one of two forms: either (i) (Noun) sceal on (Place), (Adjectival Phrase), or (ii) (Noun) sceal on (Place), (Verb + Complement). The variants are not allocated according to the topic of the gnome, although there is a tendency for human subjects (the good man, the king) to take model (ii) performing some characteristic action.

32. T. D. Hill, 'Notes on the Old English *Maxims I* and *II*', *NQ* NS 17 (1970), 447.

33. See R. Frank, 'Some Uses of Paranomasia in Old English Scriptural Verse', *Speculum*, 47 (1972), 207–26.

34. Dawson, 'Structure', 21

35. Shippey, *PW*,14

36. A. L. Meaney, 'The "ides" of the Cotton *Gnomic Poem*', *MÆ* 48 (1979), 23–39; J. A. Dane, '"on folce geþeon"', *NM* 85 (1984), 61–4.

37. Hill identifies Eccles. 23: 15 as the source of this section.

38. Text cited from M. Halsall ed., *The Old English Rune Poem: A Critical Edition* (Toronto,1981).

39. Halsall suggests that the variations in stanza length are connected with the ancient tripartite division of the runes into 'ættir', groups of eight named for the rune with which they begin. *The Old English Rune Poem*, 51–2.

40. The Icelandic and Norwegian *Rune Poems*, although shorter than the Old English poem, have similar names for most of their runes, differing in *ur, þorn* (*þurs*), and *cen* (*kaun*). The poems are dated by B. Dickins ed., *Runic and Heroic Poems* (Cambridge, 1915), 6–7, thus: the Old English poem, 11th c.; the *Norwegian Rune Poem*, late 13th c.; the *Icelandic Rune Poem*, 15th c. See M. Clunies Ross, ' The Anglo-Saxon and Norse "Rune Poems" A Comparative Study', *ASE* 19 (1990), 23–40 for a persuasive reading of the Norse poems, locating them in the gnomic and wisdom traditions.

41. The meaning of *peorð* is still obscure. Clearly it is a good; accordingly, most scholars have adopted Schneider's suggestion 'dice-box'. K. Schneider, *Die Germanischen Runennamen: Versuch einer Gesamtdarstellung* (Meisenheim am Glan, 1956).

42. See below, ch. 5 for examination of the importance of God the Creator in other OE wisdom poems.

43. Cf. *Háv.* 47[6], see above, ch. 1.3.

44. Although in the traditional English *fuþorc* order, *ear* preceded *iar* (Halsall, *The Old English Rune Poem*, 59), the poet reverses the runes here in order to end the poem with the finality of Death.

45. J. R. Hall, 'Perspective and Word-Play in the Old English *Rune Poem*', *Neophilologus*, 61 (1977), 458, notes the metaphor of sexual union.

46. On the name 'wen' rather than 'wyn', see E. G. Stanley, 'Notes on the Text of *Christ and Satan*, and on the *Riming Poem* and the *Rune Poem*, chiefly on *wynn, wen* and *wenne*', *NQ* 31 NS (1984), 443–53.

47. This material definition of happiness is reiterated, but ultimately rejected, by the narrator in *The Seafarer*, who contrasts the pleasant existence of the town-dweller with his own privations (ll. 27–30).

48. Cf. both the Norwegian and Icelandic *Rune Poems*: 'hagall er kaldastr korna', 'hagall er kaldakorn' (hail is the coldest of grains, hail is a cold grain).

49. M. Osborn, 'Old English "Ing" and his Wain', *NM* 81 (1980), 388–9 suggests that the rune can actually be drawn through the constellation of Boötes, which follows the Plough 'wæn' across the sky.

50. S. B. Greenfield, *A Critical History of Old English Literature* (New York, 1965), 193 suggests that the *double entente* is intentional.

51. J. R. Hall, 'Perspective', 456 sees a pun on 'trēow' (faith) and 'trēow' (tree / wood), so that the line can be read 'whether the oak keeps faith nobly' or 'whether the oak-ship has good timber'.

52. See P. Sorrell, 'Oaks, Ships, Riddles'.

53. M. Osborn and S. Longland, 'A Celtic Intruder in the Old English *Rune Poem*', *NM* 81 (1980), 385–7 suggest that *iar* may be a beaver; Sorrell, 'Oaks, Ships, Riddles', 111 suggests a 'hippopotamus'.

54. Cf. Shippey, *PW*, 20.

55. Halsall, The Old English Rune Poem, 56.

56. Shippey, *PW*, 59, 129 translates 'mid blēom gyrwað' as 'clothes them in fleshly form', but C. J. E. Ball and A. Cameron, in 'Some Specimen Entries for the Dictionary of Old English', in *A Plan for the Dictionary of Old English* ed. R. Frank and A. Cameron (Toronto and Buffalo, 1973), 329–47, show that 'bleoh' has the meaning 'shape' only in connection with supernatural entities. Where it is used in a human context, it means 'complexion', 'colouring', or 'appearance'. Here there seems to be an echo of anarchaic conception of creation as endowing a new being with 'bleoh': cf. *Vǫluspá* 18 and further E. C. Polomé, 'Some Comments on *Vǫluspá*: 17–18.' in *Old Norse Literature and Mythology: A Symposium* ed. E. C. Polomé. (Austin, Tex., 1969), 264–90.

57. Both these verbs are *hapax legomena*: 'tennan' is glossed by Grein, *Sprachschatz*, as 'locken?' (to attract) encouraging the child to walk, while B-T suggests 'kindle' in a figurative sense. 'Tǣtan' in Grein is given as 'liebkosen' (to caress), while B-T offers 'to gladden, make cheerful'.

58. See H. Marquardt, *Die altenglischen Kenningar* (Halle, 1938), 233 and 244.

59. N. D. Isaacs, 'Up a Tree: To See The Fates of Men', in L. E. Nicholson and D. W. Frese edd., *Anglo-Saxon Poetry: Essays in Appreciation for John C. McGalliard* (Notre Dame, Ind.,1975), 363–75 interprets the tree-climbing as a shamanistic ritual.

60. The identification of the gallows with a horse is evidenced in Oddr Snorrason's *Oláfs saga Tryggvasonar* ch. 21.

61. *Bwf.* 2444–59.

62. See A. Crozier, 'Old West Norse *íþrótt* and Old English *indryhtu*', *Studia Neophilologica*, 58 (1986), 3–10, and above, ch. 2.1.

63. See E. T. Hansen, 'Hroðgar's "Sermon" in *Beowulf* as Parental Wisdom', *ASE* 10 (1982), 53–67; id. '*Precepts*, an Old English Instruction', *Speculum*, 56 (1981), 1–16, and *SC*, ch. 2.

64. See Hansen, *SC*, 61 and B. S. Cox, *Cruces of Beowulf* (The Hague, 1971), 143.

65. See above, ch. 1.5.

66. Cf. *DC* IV[15]

67. See above, ch. 1.5 for parallel with *Háv.* 79.

68. See below, ch. 7; also R. E. Kaske, 'The Coastwarden's Maxim in *Beowulf*: A Clarification', *NQ* NS 31 (1984), 16–18.

69. A theme frequent in the *DC*; cf. also *Háv.* 45, 92 and above, ch. 1.5 for a different view of flattery. *Háv.* agrees that slander is harmful, however: cf. *Háv.* 118, above, ch. 1.6.

70. Cf. the closing adjuration of *Hugsvinnsmál*, and the refrain of the *Loddfáfnismál.*

71. Other correspondences include: monosticha 27: 'Quae legeris memento (remember what you read), cf. *Precepts* 61. *DC* 1[9]: on admonishing one's friend if he commits wrong, cf. ibid. 17–18. *DC* III[1]: on the value of learning, cf. utterance 8.

72. Text from *The Poetical Dialogues of Solomon and Saturn*, ed. R. J. Menner (New York, 1941).

73. As Óðinn does in *Vafþrúðnismál* 19; compare also *Grímnismál* and the riddle contest of *Hervarar saga*.

74. See K. Sisam's review of Menner's edition in *MÆ* 13 (1944), 33.

75. The topos of the wise pagan has been studied extensively in ON: e.g. L. Lönnroth, 'The Noble Heathen: A Theme in the Sagas', *SS* 41 (1969), 1–29. In OE there is less evidence of the topos. See, however, *The Earliest Life of Gregory the Great*, by an anonymous monk of Whitby, ed. B. Colgrave (Lawrence, Kans., 1968), and G. Paris, *La Légende de Trajan*, Bibl. de l'école des hautes études, 35 (Paris, 1878) who cites material from Paulus Diaconus and John Diaconus.

76. See Menner, *Poetical Dialogues*, Introduction, 22–3 and 59–62.

77. J. A. Dane, 'The Structure of the Old English *Solomon and Saturn II*', *Neophilologus*, 64 (1980), 600.

78. Shippey, *PW*, 22 notes the parallel.

79. Menner, *Poetical Dialogues*, 138.

80. B. J. Timmer, '*Wyrd* in Anglo-Saxon Prose and Poetry', *Neophilologus*, 26 (1941), 220, n. 1 argues from the later occurrence of 'wyrd sēo swīðe', l. 434, that 'wyrd' is used in *Solomon and Saturn II* in an anachronistic sense, recreating the pagan understanding of *Wyrd* as virtually a personified goddess of Fate. I contend that the poet understood *Wyrd* in a Boethian sense, 'fata', events that happen in the sublunary sphere under the direction of Providence.

81. Boethius, *Theological Tractates and the Consolation of Philosophy*, ed. and tr. H. F. Stewart, E. K. Rand and S. J. Tester, Loeb Classical Library (London and Cambridge, Mass., 1923; repr. 1973).

82. *The Wanderer* 5b .

83. 'Gemetigian' is derived from 'metan' (to measure); it can mean 'to moderate, regulate, mitigate', or, according to B-T, a second meaning, 'deliberate on, meditate upon', 'measure in the mind' is also available. In context, it seems more probable that Solomon intends to suggest that a man can come to understand the workings of Fate, if he has the advantage of Christian knowledge, rather than that he can alter his destiny.

84. Shippey, *PW*, 99 translates 'godcundes gǣstes' as 'Holy Spirit', but the 'divine spirit' is surely Providence here, rather than an anachronistic notion of the Holy Spirit.

85. I disagree with R. Woolf, 'The Devil in Old English Poetry', *RES* NS 4 (1955), 1–12, who claims that the identification of *wyrd* with the devil at this point is incontrovertible' (p. 10).

86. See n. 26 above.

87. I interpret the plural of *wyrd* in Timmer's sense ('*Wyrd* in Anglo-Saxon Prose and Poetry', 216) as 'events' rather than 'fates'.

88. Hill, 'The Falling Leaf and Buried Treasure: Two Notes on the Imagery of *Solomon and Saturn*', *NM* 71 (1970), 571–6 identifies the image as patristic.

89. Cf. the story of Þórr wrestling with Elli (Old Age) in *Gylfaginning* ch. 46–7.

90. J. E. Cross and T. D. Hill ed., *The Prose Solomon and Saturn and Adrian and Ritheus* (Toronto, 1982).

91. Used here in the sense in which Alfred understood it: Timmer, '*Wyrd* in Anglo-Saxon Prose and Poetry', 24–33.

92. A. D. Horgan, '*The Wanderer*: A Boethian Poem?' *RES* 38 (1987), 40–46 demonstrates the presence of Boethian ideas in *The Wanderer*.

93. Menner, *Poetical Dialogues*, 58.

94. See above, ch. 2, n. 27.

95. The only evidence of a native wisdom-contest tradition in OE apart from this poem is the aborted framework of the *Ex. Max.* See above, ch. 4. 1.

5 GNOMIC POETRY AND THE NATURAL WORLD: NATURE AS AN AESTHETIC

The purpose of wisdom and its literature is to suggest a scheme
of life in the broadest sense of the word, to ensure its continuance, to predict its variations and to associate humanity with
the fundamental rhythms of nature. It is an attempt to control
life by some kind of order, to reduce the area of the unexpected
and the sudden.

Morton Bloomfield
'Understanding Old English Poetry', *AnM* 9 (1968), 17

Gnomic poetry frequently concerns itself with the natural world
and man's relation to it, as distinct from those precepts which
provide a guide to man's conduct as a social being. In such
contexts as Hesiod's *Works and Days* and Virgil's *Georgics*, the
recording of observations about natural phenomena serves a
clearly educational and informative purpose, but in Old English
poetry the purpose of such observations as we find in the *Cotton
Maxims*, for example, is less immediately clear. What might the
origin of such poetry be, and how might it have been regarded by
the peoples who preserved it?

Anthropological investigation into gnomic verse suggests that
the origin of wisdom poetry — and in particular wisdom verse
dealing with natural phenomena — lies in the magico-religious.[1]
After natural elements have been named, they are classified:
taxonomies constructed, relating, by contrast or comparison, one
object to another. The natural object may then become a focus
for further mental activity, legends may be woven or rituals
developed about it. Here origins may be invented for the object;
for knowledge of the origin of the thing, or of its characteristics,
gives power not only over the object itself, but also creates an
immanent power within the knower himself, which he may deploy
in other ways. In the *Kalevala*, the divine beings Väinämöinen and
Joukahainen take part in a contest in which Väinämöinen
demonstrates the superiority of his knowledge and his magical
powers. Joukahainen assumes that his extensive knowledge of
origins will be enough to overcome Väinämöinen:

> I know the origin of the tom-tit, I know the tom-tit is a bird,
> the hissing adder a snake, the roach a fish of the water,
> I know iron is brittle, black soil sour,
> boiling water painful, being burned by fire bad.
> Water is the oldest of ointments, foam of a rapids oldest of magic
> nostrums,
> the Creator himself the oldest of magicians, God the oldest of
> healers.[2]

Though Joukahainen boasts that he knows of the Creator, and then claims to have been present when the earth was being created, Väinämöinen, who is older by far, knows that he was not. With Joukahainen's claim to knowledge thus proven suspect, Väinämöinen's store of powerful spells[3] impels Joukahainen into a bog from which he is only released when he promises to marry his sister to the old man.

In the Indian *Laws of Manu*,[4] the divine Manu is approached by sages who ask him to reveal the sacred laws. Manu begins with an account of the Creation of the universe by Brahma, then details the origins of living creatures:

> Cattle, deer, carnivorous beasts with two rows of teeth, *Rakshâsas*, *Pisâkas*,[5] and men are born from the womb.
>
> From eggs are born birds, snakes, crocodiles, fishes, tortoises, as well as similar terrestrial and aquatic animals.
>
> From hot moisture spring stinging and biting insects, lice, flies, bugs, and all other (creatures) of that kind which are produced by heat.[6]

In order to validate the laws which he is about to lay down for human conduct, Manu must show how all the universe, from the highest of the worlds to the smallest plant or creeping creature has been created in an ordered hierarchy by Brahma. Thus if Man is to escape from the cycle of existences and become one with Brahma, he must conform to that order as it is laid down in the Laws regulating human existence.

In Old Norse, the composers of wisdom poetry are obsessed with facts about phenomena: winter, summer, day, night; their names and their ancestry, where they come from and where they are to be found. Over and over again, the variants of the primeval act of Creation, the ordering of the universe by gods, or the dismemberment of the cosmic giant Ymir, are rehearsed: *Vǫluspá* 4–6, *Vafþrúðnismál* 20–35, *Grímnismál* 40–1. The ancestry of the Norns is a matter of urgent importance to the hero Sigurðr. Knowing such facts is a pre-requisite of kingship; discovering the truth of them is the task of the god of wisdom himself.[7]

Little consciousness of any such origin for nature gnomes, if they were once magical or pagan-religious in significance, remains in the Old English *Exeter* and *Cotton Maxims*. However, it has been suggested that the use of *sceal* as a gnomic auxiliary in the nature gnome may be religious in function.[8] *Sceal* is employed in human gnomes[9] to recommend a course of action for humans in their social environment, often with a strong implication of obligation: 'Cyning sceal mid cēape   cwēne gebicgan, | būnum ond bēagum' (*Exeter Maxims* 81–2a: A king must obtain a queen with a bride-price, with cups and rings).

A choice is implied: the king may choose to kidnap or carry off his queen, rather than obtain her legally and peacefully. *Sceal* with the meaning 'is obliged to, ought to' makes good sense in the human gnome, where an alternative and undesirable course of action can be posited. But how are we to read *sceal* in the nature gnomes? 'Forst sceal frēosan, fyr wudu meltan, | eorþe grōwan' (*Exeter Maxims* 71–2b: Frost must freeze, fire burn up wood, the earth bear growth). An alternative is also implied, that frost may choose not to freeze, or fire to burn. Thus *sceal* has a prescriptive value; it reiterates that natural objects are under a divinely imposed obligation to continue performing their natural functions: to say that a thing *sceal* be so is to cause it to continue to be so.[10] By incorporating statements of the natural properties of things into poetry, perhaps, as Bloomfield suggests, the poet is ensuring the continuance of life according to the observed patterns, keeping at bay the forces of dissolution, and implying that nature is, at least in part, within his control.

In Old English any such pre-Christian religious intention in nature gnomes has been overlaid by an aesthetic of the natural. The phenomena in the *Cotton Maxims* catalogue are observed in their proper habitats, performing their appointed functions. Yet the list is not a dry catalogue of types of plant and creature: the poet takes delight in the variety and abundance of nature, in the contrasts and patterns which it affords and in his insight into the life of other creatures:

> Hafuc sceal on glōfe,
> wilde gewunian.   Wulf sceal on bearowe,
> earm ānhaga.   Eofor sceal on holte,
> tōþmægenes trum.
>
> (*Cotton Maxims* 17ᵇ–20ᵃ)

A hawk shall — on a glove, wild creature — dwell.[11] A wolf shall be in the forest, a miserable, solitary creature. A boar shall be in the wood, strong in tooth-power.

The hawk is poised on the glove, a miraculous thing, for the wild creature does not normally dwell with men. The three half-lines are a concentrated characterization, telling us all we need to know of the civilized, courtly pursuit, suggested by the glove, and the tension between wildness and taming. A contrasting hawk is that in *Battle of Maldon* 7–8: 'hē lēt him þā of handon   lēofne flēogan | hafoc wið þæs holtes,   and tō þǣre hilde stōp' (Then he let the dear hawk fly from his hand to the wood, and advanced to the battle).

 This hawk is returned to its natural wild state; precious it may be to its owner, but now the time for such noble amusements is past: Offa's kinsman must advance to the fight. The hawk of *Battle of Maldon* exists to point both the aristocratic nature and the resolution of its owner; the *Cotton Maxims* hawk exists for itself. The wolf (18ᵇ–19ᵃ) unusually, is seen sympathetically as a miserable, lonely outcast — an 'ānhaga', like the protagonist of *The Wanderer*, the boar is bold because he knows that he can trust in his tusks.

 In 26ᵇ–27ᵃ the dragon is regarded with admiration: 'Draca sceal on hlǣwe, | frōd, frætwum wlanc' (A dragon shall be in a barrow, wise and old, exulting in his treasures). Old and wise, and pleased with his amassed treasure, the dragon is like any human warrior. Similarly, the dragon in *Beowulf* is a magnificent creature, neither loathsome nor terrible, until its function as treasure-guardian is trespassed upon by a human, and it has to leave its natural place, where it broods quietly over its hoard. Death is the result, but, even after the monster's death, the poet evokes for a moment the dragon in its splendour:

> Nalles æfter lyfte   lācende hwearf
> middelnihtum,   māðmǣhta wlonc,
> ansȳn ȳwde.
>
> (*Beowulf* 2832–4ᵃ)

Not at all would he go playing in the air in the middle of the night,
exulting in treasure, show his appearance.

If the nature gnomes originated in a magical or religious context,
it is unlikely that they would have been preserved in the Christian
period unless they served another use.[12] It may be that the poet of
the *Cotton Maxims* wrote down these verses 'simply because he
liked them for themselves' as Shippey suggests,[13] but I think it
more probable that Old English poets used them as an aesthetic
tool, for particular literary purposes.

B. C. Williams's suggestion that the *Cotton Maxims* are preserved
as a kind of metrical exercise[14] is generally discounted by scholars.
The formulas of the Cotton nature gnomes would not be
particularly useful to a poet seeking ready-made building blocks
for his poems, since the half-lines which describe any one natural
phenomenon do not alliterate with each other. Yet the creatures
and the scenery observed in the *Cotton Maxims* reappear in other
Old English poems, often described with similar images and
vocabulary as in the gnomic poems.

I have compared above the poet's admiration for the dragon
sporting in the night-skies in *Beowulf* with that of the poet of the
Cotton Maxims; an admiration of the beast for what it is, as distinct
from what it does. The splendour of the dragon sporting in the
night-sky remains with the audience longer than the carrion
tipped ignominiously over the sea-cliff. Earlier, the *Beowulf*-poet
makes a gnomic observation about the nature of dragons, using
the traditional lore about dragons encapsulated in the *Cotton
Maxims*:

>   Hē gesēcean sceall
> (ho)r(d on) hrūsan,   þǣr he hǣðen gold
> wara ð wintrum frōd,   ne byð him wihte þȳ sēl.
>   (*Beowulf* 2275[b]–2278)

He must seek out a hoard in the earth, where he guards heathen gold,
wise in winters,[15] nor is he one whit the better for that.

Similarly, the *Beowulf*-poet twice employs the image of ice as a
restraining bond, locking up nature, first in 1131–4, and then to
describe the melting of the sword found in the den of Grendel's
mother:

> Þæt wæs wundra sum,
> þæt hit eall gemealt,   īse gelīcost,
> ðonne forste bend   Fæder onlǣteð,
> onwindeð wǣlrāpas,   sē geweald hafað
> sǣla ond mǣla.

(*Beowulf* 1607–11)

That was a miracle, that it all melted, most like ice, when the Father re-
leases the frost's bond, looses the fetters of the deep, He who has power
over times and seasons.

We may compare the image of ice locking up the elements in
frost-bonds which only the Creator can undo in *Exeter Maxims*
71–5. The portrayal of nature, and of human society, which the
Exeter and *Cotton Maxims* give is an 'absolute irreducible reality',[16]
a static tapestry of the world as it has been, is, and shall be, as a
background to narrative action in Old English poetry, upon
which the dynamic of narrative is superimposed.

Thus far we have considered descriptions of typical natural
phenomena in Old English gnomic verse. I now wish to examine
man's relationship with, and place in, the natural world, the
unchanging background to his activities. Bloomfield predicates a
third function of wisdom poetry, as the association of 'humanity
with the fundamental rhythms of nature'. Man apprehends these
'fundamental rhythms' necessarily through his own time-bound
consciousness, imposing a human calendar on the natural cycle of
the seasons. This impulse to relate human time to nature is found
across many wisdom literatures, and takes various literary forms:
the instructional agricultural poem, the calendar poem, or the
more philosophical meditations on the eternal and the transient
which we find in Old English.

In the *Laws of Manu*, after the origins of the universe and all
created things have been rehearsed, Bhrigu, who has succeeded
Manu as instructor-figure, expounds the system by which time is
measured, from one 'nimesha' (a twinkling of an eye) to a 'yuga',
an entire cosmic cycle, which is but as a minute in the existence of
Brahma. Only after time has been explained can the different
duties of the castes, and the laws applicable to each, be given.
Time provides the transition between the hierarchies apparent in
the natural world and the ordering of the human world.[17]

Works and Days takes human activity, and its appropriate time (*kairos*), as its theme and organizing principle. Towards the beginning of the poem, as an explanation of why work is necessary, Hesiod expounds a myth of the progressive degeneration of the ages; these, like the four 'yugas' in the *Laws of Manu*, lead to the present Iron age (*Kali yuga*) of strife and injustice (ll. 176 ff.), in which ceaseless toil and unnaturally short lives are men's lot. Hesiod uses the calendar of the farmer's year (ll. 383–616) as a basis for the central part of the poem; when the cycle of the year is completed, Hesiod goes on to prescribe the right time for sea voyages, and marriage. In l. 767 onwards, the auspicious days for various activities are given: begetting and bearing children — advice also found in the *Laws of Manu* — the best day for broaching a cask of wine, or for shipbuilding.

Virgil's *Georgics* are related to *Works and Days*[18] in that they give agricultural instruction specific to the season of the year for each aspect of farming: tillage, the planting of trees, nurture of beasts, and bee-keeping. Virgil does not use the seasonal cycle to organize his material as systematically as Hesiod does, but rather bases his poem on the different areas of a farmer's work. Although he makes frequent reference to the time of year, no particular order is adhered to in discussing sowing, reaping, or ploughing.

In the Old English *Menologium*,[19] in the same manuscript as the *Cotton Maxims*,[20] the calendar of the Church's year virtually suppresses the seasonal cycle, beginning with the birth of Christ in December, whereas Hesiod begins at the start of the agricultural year: the time for ploughing. Although the cycle of Church feasts and saints' days gives the *Menologium* its structure, the older pagan names for the months, as they are found in Bede and the *Prose Martyrology*,[21] are also used; an older pagan time-cycle clearly underlies the Christian one.[22]

The poet of the *Menologium* moves swiftly from one church feast to another, yet he cannot resist a lyrical passage describing the arrival of summer in May:

> swylce ymb fyrst wucan,
> butan ānre niht,   þætte yldum bringð
> sigelbeorhte dagas   sumor tō tūne,
> wearma gewyderu. Ðænne wangas hraðe
> blōstmum blōwað,   swylce blis astīhð
> geond middangeard   manigra hāda

> cwicera cynna,   cyninga lof secgað
> mænifealdlice,   mærne bremað
> ælmihtigne.
>
> (*Menologium* 87–95a)

Thus after the space of a week, except for one night, summer brings for men sun-bright days to the dwellings, warm weather. Then meadows quickly bloom with flowers, then this joy arises throughout the earth, of the many orders of living creatures, they praise the king in manifold ways, celebrate the glorious Almighty.

Traditional descriptive formulas such as we find in *Beowulf*, *The Seafarer*, and the *Exeter* and *Cotton Maxims* poems[23] are brought together to give a vivid picture of all Creation praising its Creator, rejoicing in the warmth of summer. Although people and animals are seen here as equally joyful, the poem lays particular emphasis elsewhere on the coming of a new season as it affects human settlements, using repeatedly such phrases as 'ūs tō tūne' (to the dwellings for us), 'sigeð tō tūne' (comes to the settlement), 'to folce' (to the people), 'niða bearnum' (for the sons of men) to mark out the perception of time passing as especially human.[24]

The description of May above is paralleled by the departure of the sun in November:

> Siððan wintres dæg   wīde gangeð,
> on syx nihtum,   sigelbeorhtne genimð
> hærfest mid herige   hrīmes 7 snāwes
> forste gefeterad   bē frēan hǣse,
> ðæt ūs wunian ne mōton   wangas grēne,
> foldan frætuwe.
>
> (*Menologium* 202–7a)

After winter's day has passed, after six nights, the autumn captures the sun-bright one with an army of frost and snow, fettered with frost by the Lord's command, so that no green fields can remain to us, adornments of the earth.

'Sigelbeorhtne' echoes 'sigelbeorhte' in the earlier passage, while the fruitful, burgeoning fields of May are contrasted with the November meadows, bereft of any colour. In a striking metaphor, the poet imagines the meadows invaded by an army of frost and snow, and the sun taken prisoner. The effect of autumn on men is emphasized by the metaphor of captivity which links brilliantly with the image — as we have seen, a traditional one — of frost as an oppressive fetter upon the earth and waters. Possibly the image has suggested the unusual metaphor of the frost and snow as an army to the poet.[25]

While a relatively late poem in the view of the *ASPR* editors, the *Menologium* again shows how the traditional images stored in nature gnomes, can be incorporated into different sub-species of the genre of wisdom poem, here in a lyrical visualization of spring and autumn.

Thus humanity associates itself with nature, by recognizing and adapting to the 'fundamental rhythms' of the seasonal cycle, as in Hesiod, or by imposing its own time-scheme on them, as in the *Menologium*. The *Exeter* and *Cotton Maxims* take a less formally structured approach to the association of human and natural, an aesthetic and philosophical approach which integrates man, nature and the perceived universe into a single comprehensible system.

The human and the natural are placed side by side for comparison, the effect being to emphasize the essential wholeness and unity of the world. Humans and trees are juxtaposed:

> Tū bēoð gemæccan.
> Sceal wīf ond wer in woruld cennan
> bearn mid gebyrdum. Bēam sceal on eorðan
> lēafum līþan leomu gnornian.
>
> (*Exeter Maxims* 23ᵇ–26)

Two people are mates. A woman and a man must bring into the world a child through birth. A tree must lose its leaves on earth, the limbs mourn.

At first, the leap from human to tree seems arbitrary, but in nature ('in woruld', 'on eorðan'), people and trees both participate in the same cycle of birth and decay. The child will die, perhaps prematurely (l. 31), but, like the leaves of the tree, new children will replace those lost. Significantly, the emotion which the parents 'wīf ond wer' must feel at losing their child is transferred to the tree, 'leomu gnornian'.[26] This transference diminishes the grief at the death of a child which might otherwise overwhelm the restrained and objective tone of the poem. A tree cannot, after all, mourn greatly, and it is assured of new growth next year. The identification of tree and human is confirmed by the poet's use of the word 'magutimbor' (timber of kin) in stanza 33.

In *Exeter Maxims* 51–6, the tumultuous spirit of man is compared with a storm at sea:

> Stȳran sceal man strongum mōde.[27]   Storm oft holm gebringeþ,
> geofen in grimmum sǣlum.   Onginnað grome fundian
> fealwe on feorran tō londe,   hwæþer hē fæste stonde.
> Weallas him wiþre healdað,   him bið wind gemǣne.
> > Swa biþ sǣ smilte
> > þonne hȳ wind ne weceð,
> swā bēoð þeode geþwǣre   þonne hȳ geþingad habbað.

A strong mind is to be restrained. Often a storm brings the sea, the ocean into furious states. The angry dark (waves) begin to rush from afar to land, yet he[28] may stand firm. The cliffs withstand them, they both feel the wind in common. As the sea is calm, when the wind does not stir it up, so are nations peaceable when they have become reconciled.

Although the passage begins with the temperament of the individual, focusing on an unchecked propensity to violence, the comparison with the storm permits a transition to the tempestuous spirit of nations. The turbulent spirit must be held back, just as the cliffs resist the violence of the waves; the natural inclinaions of the powerful temperament are equated with waves, while self-control is symbolized by the buttress-like cliffs. The poet returns to the human, but on a different scale, to nations rather than individuals. The comparison is now made explicit through 'swā . . . swā' (as . . . as), whereas in l. 51 the mere juxtaposition of the strong spirit and the forces of the storm was enough to establish the relation between them.[29]

These two examples show how, on a symbolic level, the natural and human are subject to the same forces and participate in the same cycles. Yet the *Exeter* and *Cotton Maxims* do not explore the themes of transience and mutability as do *The Wanderer* and *The Seafarer*. There is no real sense of loss in the world of the *Exeter* and *Cotton Maxims*. Even the mourning tree knows it will put forth leaves again; children will be replaced. Time does not pass; man and nature are displayed in a timeless universe, where everything is frozen at its most typical and in its proper place: salmon swimming in the river, the Frisian sailor's wife waiting for her husband. The gnomic auxiliaries *bið* and *sceal* mark this static moment as apart from the ordinary tense-system with its opposition of then and now. The *Maxims* use the equivalent of the cinema freeze-frame technique: arresting change so that relationships, structures, hierarchies, and order may be examined, 'the area of the unexpected and sudden' thus reduced.[30]

The figure of the Creator stands outside frozen time. The poet of *Exeter Maxims* is aware that time can be arrested only in poetry, and that outside it, the facts of human mortality and Divine immortality are inescapable:

> Meotud sceal in wuldre. Mon sceal on eorþan
> geong ealdian. God ūs ēce biþ.
> Ne wendeð hine wyrda, ne hine wiht dreceþ
> ādl ne yldo ælmihtigne.
>
> (*Exeter Maxims* 7–10)

The Creator shall be in glory. Man on earth must, young, grow old. God is eternal for us. Events do not change him, nor do sickness nor old age oppress him at all, the Almighty.

'God ūs ēce biþ' (God is eternal in his relation to us), he is what we are not. Man perceives in God the unobtainable Eternal, in nature an immortality through the recurrence of the typical. He himself is a creature who partakes in both.

If we accept that the origin of the nature gnome lies in observation and classification of natural phenomena and cycles, it seems probable that the nature gnomes of the *Maxims*, particularly the *Cotton Maxims* series 17b–50, belong to the oldest tradition of gnomic verse, albeit probably not in their tightly structured manuscript form. The Old English poet who put them together with verse praising God's creativity in bringing into existence the 'feorhcynna fela' (many forms of life) (*Exeter Maxims* 14a), which the nature gnomes depict, may have seen them, as Hill suggests,[31] as reflecting 'God's providential order'. Thus the poet was able to incorporate them into an inner structure within the traditional colloquy form of the wisdom poem, an inner structure which follows Cædmon's hymn of praise as model:

> God sceal mon ǣrest hergan,
> fǣgre, fæder ūserne,   forþon þe hē ūs æt frymþe getēode
> līf ond lǣnne willan.

(*Exeter Maxims* 4^b–6^a)

First God should be praised, fittingly, our Father, for he established for us at the beginning life and transient joy.

By associating the nature and human gnomes of *Exeter Maxims* with a hymn of praise, the poet is, consciously or unconsciously, once again emphasizing the importance of origins. Control over nature comes from knowing how natural objects originated, in the divine creative impulse. As in the *Laws of Manu*, before something new is undertaken, and new rules for existence promulgated, the original creative act must be rehearsed.[32] The Old English poet here manifests an archaic tendency.

The poets of the *Maxims* may well have regarded his gnomes as displaying the variety of created life within a divinely imposed ordering, but there is no reason to assume on that account that the gnomes must necessarily be of Christian origin. The impulse to record and observe, and thus to acquire the ability to control the mysterious and unpredictable in nature, is both universal and older than Christianity. To read *Exeter* and *Cotton Maxims* exclusively in Christian terms is to view too narrowly the cultural background which has produced them, and to ignore the ancient and universal tradition which lies behind them.

Notes

1. For anthropological approaches to the Anglo-Saxon wisdom poems: N. F. Barley, 'Structure in the *Cotton Gnomes*', *NM* 78 (1977), 244–9; id. 'A Structural Approach to the Proverb and Maxim, with Special Reference to the Anglo-Saxon Corpus', *Proverbium*, 20 (1972), 737–50; and id. 'Anthropological Aspects of Anglo-Saxon Symbolism', D.Phil. thesis (Oxford, 1974). See also L. L. Remly, 'The Anglo-Saxon Gnomes as Sacred Poetry', *Folklore*, 82 (1971), 147–58.
2. *The Kalevala* tr. F. P. Magoun, Jr. (Cambridge, Mass., 1963), Poem 3.
3. Väinämöinen's spells, like those of the *Ljóðatal*, remain unarticulated; although we see their effects, we do not hear them sung.
4. *The Laws of Manu* ed. G. Bühler, Sacred Books of the East, 25 (Oxford, 1886).
5. *Rakshāsas* and *Pisākas* are different types of demon.
6. *The Laws of Manu*, I^43–5.
7. As in *Grímnismál* and *Vafþrúðnismál.*
8. L. C. Gruber, 'The Agnostic Anglo-Saxon Gnomes: *Maxims I* and *II, Germania* and .the Boundaries of Northern Wisdom', *Poetica*, 6 (1976), 23–45.
9. For a definition of human gnomes, see Introduction.
10. Hansen, *SC*, 164–5: 'if the ideal or hortatory sense of the gnomic verb [*sceal*] is

understood here, then these normally inanimate forces are recategorized and imbued with choice, a human characteristic.'

11. See above ch. 4, nn. 30 and 31 for discussion of the two syntactic patterns in this series of gnomes.

12. See W. J. Ong, *Orality and Literacy* (London, 1982), 46: 'oral societies live very much in a present which keeps itself in equilibrium or homeostasis by sloughing off memories which no longer have present relevance'.

13. Shippey, *PW,* 22

14. Williams, *GP,* 109

15. For dragons as preternaturally wise creatures, see discussion of Fáfnir, above, ch. 2.5.

16. Remly, 'The Anglo-Saxon Gnomes', 153

17. *The Laws of Manu:* I^{64}.

18. G. Kromer, 'The Didactic Tradition in Virgil's *Georgics*', *Ramus,* 8 (1979), 7–21. Also D. Wender, 'From Hesiod to Homer by Way of Rome', ibid. 59–64.

19. *The Menologium, ASPR* vi: *The Minor Anglo-Saxon Poems,* ed. E. V. K. Dobbie (London and New York, 1942).

20. MS Cotton Tiberius B.i.

21. *The Old English Prose Martyrology* ed. G. Herzfeld, EETS OS 116 (London, 1900).

22. I differ from N. Howe, 'The Old English Catalogue Poems', *Anglistica,* 23; Copenhagen, 1985), 74: 'The *Menologium* poet refrained from fusing his religious material with any native poetic convention, and thus did not radically alter the accepted framework of the religious calendar.'

23. Cf. *Ex. Max.* 111–12 for warm summer weather; *The Seafarer* 48; *Bwf.* 97–8.

24. Hansen, *SC,* 120 notes the prevalence of these deictics.

25. Though we may compare the virtuoso — and quite gratuitous — description of winter in *Andreas:* the 'hāre hildestāpan' (grey-haired warrior). ll. 1255–62.

26. The parallel with *The Fortunes of Men* is noted above, ch. 4.4. See also below, ch. 6.1 for a parallel in *Sonatorrek.*

27. Cf. *The Seafarer* 109ª and *Háv.* 18$^{4-5}$.

28. 'He': the referent is not clear, for 'lond' is neuter. The *ASPR* editors suggest the emendation of Holthausen, 'hit', as a way out of the difficulty.

29. J. W. Earl, '*Maxims I,* Part I', *Neophilologus,* 67 (1983), 279 finds a good parallel in the *Pastoral Care,* and links both with the imagery of *The Seafarer.*

30. Remly, 'The Anglo-Saxon Gnomes', 151.

31. T. D. Hill, 'Notes on the Old English *Maxims I* and *II*', *NQ* NS 17 (1970), 447.

32. M. Eliade, *Myth of the Eternal Return,* tr. W. Trask (Paris, 1949), 76.

6 GNOMES IN ELEGY

Although its origin is often hidden and mysterious, once gained, social wisdom interpenetrates every part of human existence, from advice on the buying of dogs to the revelation of what will survive of us after death. Just so, gnomes form part of the stylistic repertoire of other genres, sounding a 'gnomic key' which relates the narrative or elegiac to a universal dimension, approving, confirming, contradicting, or warning. This chapter considers the gnomic voice in Old Norse and Old English elegy.

6.1 OLD NORSE ELEGY

There is a rich variety of elegiac verse in Old Norse — memorial lays for kings and earls, elegy for dead friends or relatives, and elegiac monologues attributed to characters from heroic legend, reflecting the tragic nature of their story. In some of these poems, a gnomic element plays a significant part, for elegy, with its double task of lament and praise for the dead, will almost always contain elements of both tradition and spontaneity: the recognition that bereavement is universal combined with the shock of the loss of the individual. The complexity of elegy in Old Norse is illuminated by M. Alexiou's study of ritual lament in Greek tradition; it takes account of living practice, as well as ancient sources.[1]

Alexiou makes a distinction between lament and praise-poem, which approximates to Mustanoja's earlier analysis of the mourning songs in *Beowulf*:[2] the song of the twelve warriors circling *Beowulf*'s pyre, and the lament of the old woman.[3] In Greek these are termed *thrênos* and *góos*; *thrênos* was a set dirge, composed and performed by professional mourners, while the *góos* was the spontaneous weeping of kinswomen. The *threnoi* are characterized by:

> calm restraint, gnomic and consolatory in tone, rather than passionate and ecstatic. The *góos*, on the other hand, while less restrained, was from Homer onwards more highly individualised,

and since it was spoken, rather than sung, it tended to develop a narrative, rather than a musical form.[4]

The lament can be seen primarily as expressing a physical need for the articulation of grief: in the *góos* a spontaneous, individual articulation, in the *thrênos* a ritualized expression of a communal or social sense of loss. Yet in the ritual, there is a movement towards the consolatory, an attempt to impose logic or order upon the chaotic feelings of grief and loss, a necessity if communal life is to continue. In Greek tradition, as, it seems, in Germanic, the *góos*-type songs were associated with women, the *thrênos*-type rather with men,[5] but both had the function of helping the bereaved adjust once again to the world of the living.

Alexiou's analysis of types of lament in Greek helps to clarify the range of elegy which we find in Germanic literature, and helps to identify the function of the gnomic elements: they work to distance and to generalize, and so impose a degree of control over the incomprehensible fact of death and loss. While this is the main function of wisdom material in Old English elegy,[6] in Old Norse the mourner is seldom consoled for his or her loss, nor does the wisdom serve to give a perspective to grief. In certain cases, on the contrary, the gnomes intensify the sense of loss.

Women's Laments

The closest parallels to the *góos*-type lament in Old Norse are the monologues associated with Oddrún, Guðrún, and Sigrún in the *Poetic Edda*.[7] The laments of Guðrún and Sigrún are carefully shaped and stylised poetic representations of an immediate expression of grief, the spontaneity of which is a dramatic artifice. There is no attempt to distance grief in these laments through consoling gnomic reflection such as we find in the refrain of *Deor*: 'þæs oferēode, þisses swā mæg' (that passed, so may this.)[8] Rather the laments give release to the pain by recalling the dead in glowing, idealized terms: a sublimation of emotion in the ideal which seems to be an alternative to gnomic generalizations. Order and rationalization are produced by the imagery, and the use of parallel syntactic constructions.

In *Oddrúnargrátr*, like *Guðrúnarhvǫt*, the heroine laments events in the past, the elegiac circumstances giving rise to a narrative recital, a 'tregrǫf' (chain of woes), *Guðrúnarhvǫt* 22⁵. That the tragedies of Oddrún's life are in the past lends a perspective which generates a gnomic observation in the last stanza: 'maðr hverr lífir I at munom sínom' (*Oddrúnargrátr* 34⁵⁻⁶: every man lives to suit his own desires).

Oddrún's final remark seems to take responsibility for her own fate, a generalization which would scarcely be comforting. Nor indeed is it true that Oddrún has caused her own tragedy, or instigated events in the drama of the Gjukungar, as Guðrún and Brynhildr have: on the contrary, Oddrún represents herself as a passive victim of fate. Rather the gnome pronounces on the fates of the other figures in the story; its function is a dramatic one: to sum up all the happenings rehearsed in the poem with a satisfyingly conclusive generalization.

Egill's Sonatorrek

The women's 'elegies' are poetic representations of utterances which a heroic character is imagined to have made. In the poetry of Egill Skalla-Grímsson, we find a quasi-historical representation of elegy: the *Sonatorrek*, a poem articulating a deeply felt personal grief at the death of the poet's two sons.

The emotions which flare up in the *Sonatorrek* are almost uncontrollable sorrow and rage, separated by reflective passages such as stanzas 11–12 where Egill considers the potential in his son, or the difficult stanza 15 in which he apparently pours scorn on those who accept financial compensation in lieu of revenge. The poem begins as an effort to control these emotions, a control achieved finally through Egill's self-conscious awareness of the value of his own poetic activity in making a memorial for his dead. At first, Egill finds, in his impotent melancholy, that the very act of making the poem is laborious, even hopeless:

Mjök erum tregt	Greatly is it grievous for me
tungu að hræra	to move the tongue
eða loftvætt	or the weight of air
ljóðpundara;	of the song-measurer;
esa nu vænligt	there is not now probability
of Viðurs þýfi	of Viðurr's stolen prize
né hógdrægt	nor is it easily drawn
ór hugarfylgsni.	from the mind's refuge.

(*Sonatorrek* 1)

Egill blames Óðinn who has given him the gift of poetry for
breaking faith with him, 'of sleit við mik', and permitting his sons
to be taken; yet by the end of the poem, he accepts that this very
gift is Óðinn's recompense to him for his loss:

þó hefr Míms vinr	though Mím's friend (Óðinn)
mér of fengnar	has provided me
bǫlva bœtr	with compensations for griefs
ef ek betra telk.	if I reckon up the better aspect.
	(23⁴⁻⁸)

The imagery permits further externalization, a therapeutic
distancing of his loss; from the wonderfully realized visualization
of Egill's family as trees,[9] to the conceit of the fifth stanza, the
metaphor is used to integrate and unify the poem's chief
concerns: family and language:

Þvít ætt mín	for my clan
á enda stendr	stands at its close
hræbarnir	beaten into corpses
sem hlynir marka:	like the maples of the forest:
	(4¹⁻⁴)

. . . þat berk út	. . . that I bring out
ór orðhofi	of the sanctuary of words
mærðar timbr	timber of praise
máli laufgat.	leafy with speech.
	(5⁴⁻⁸)

The tree imagery in these verses (picked up again in 21, 'ættar
ask' (ash of the clan), 'kynvið' (kin-wood)), contrasts the dead
wood of Egill's clan — 'hræbarnir' — with the living, verdant
branches of poetry, and binds together both his loss (the 'bǫlva'
of 23) and his recompense, 'bœtr'. The balance of loss and gain
thus created begins to provide a consolation for the old man, so
that in the final lines of the poem he is able to wait stoically and
even cheerfully for death.

Catharsis also comes about through the reasoned thoughts
which are often gnomic in substance, if not always in form.
Clearly, Egill was familiar with gnomic themes: the value of
brothers (13),[10] the good son, and the mercenariness of kinsmen
run through the poem. Generalized, gnome-like statements
spring from his own understanding of his situation:

esa karskr maðr	he is not a cheerful man who
sás köggla berr	has to carry the little bones
frænda hrørs	of the corpse of kinsmen
af fletjum niðr.	down from the hall-floor.

(4)

Just so, in *Hávamál*, Óðinn's experiences, of drunkenness and of women, give rise to gnomes. As a figure with pronounced Odinic traits, it is particularly appropriate that Egill should follow the example of his patron.

Sonatorrek is not an unreasoning wail of despair, as it has sometimes been characterized. M. C. van den Toorn[11] has pointed out the frequent hypotactical constructions in the poem's syntax: the use of 'þótt' (though), 'ef' (if), and 'þvít' (since) as evidence of 'kausal-logisch' (causal-logical) reasoning in Egill's argument with himself: that he should find the courage to die in time, to wait for Hel on the headland, rather than rush headlong towards her by starving himself to death.[12] Such hypotaxis is highly typical of *Hávamál*'s Gnomic Poem also: the argument of the *ljóðaháttr* strophe often pivots around 'þvíat' in l.4, providing support for a proposition put in the first half-verse.[13]

K. von See has suggested[14] that *Hávamál* was known to Egill, and cites several parallels:

(i)   *Sonatorrek* 22²⁻⁴ with *Hávamál* 89⁷⁻⁹: 'tryggr at trúa honum';
(ii) *Sonatorrek* 20⁶⁻⁸ with *Hávamál* 22: 'vamma varr';
(iii) *Sonatorrek* 25 with *Hávamál* 15: 'glaðr . . . bíðr bana';
(iv) *Sonatorrek* 17 with *Hávamál* 72. 'ali . . . nið . . . iðgjǫld'.

The first of these expressions, 'tryggr at trúa honum' (trusting (enough) to trust him) is more closely paralleled, as von See acknowledges, by *Hávamál* 110, for both *Sonatorrek* and *Hávamál* 110 query the wisdom of trusting Óðinn; *Hávamál* 89 is merely the climax of the list of untrustworthy things and lacks any especial Odinic resonance. The possible parallel in item (ii) is simply the collocation 'vamma varr' (wary of blemish), found in *Hugs-vinnsmál* 21, but not in the *Hávamál* verse, where the phrase is 'hann era vamma vanr' (he is not lacking in blemishes).[15] Item (iii) offers a better parallel, for the theme is similar in both poems: the cultivation of cheerfulness until death comes. In reworking a similar maxim to that of *Hávamál* to express his own hard-won resolution to continue living, Egill shows the presence of gnomic ideas and phrasing influence even the most personal of poetry.

While Egill may well have known *Hávamál* or similar gnomic poems, the difference in sentiment between *Sonatorrek* 17 and *Hávamál* 72 makes it impossible to assert that he is alluding directly to *Hávamál*. *Hávamál* 72 points out that only relatives erect memorial stones, even if only a posthumously born son. Certainly both verses share some vocabulary — 'niðr' (kinsman), 'alinn' (raised), but the thought is not really similar: *Hávamál* expresses no grief, for no son is lost. Rather the verse is a sardonic concession that sons may have some use after all, despite their general unreliability (*Hávamál* 88¹⁻³).

The hypothetical father in *Hávamál* is already dead, and can get no other benefit from his son. Von See adduces as further evidence of indebtedness the fact that 'iðgjǫld' (recompense) is found in verse only here, and in *Hávamál* 105; however, the word is attested in prose several times. That *Sonatorrek* and *Hávamál* should share vocabulary does not prove that Egill is citing from the poem; it suggests that the discussion of psychological and spiritual attributes in both poems calls forth the type of specialized abstract vocabulary discussed above in chapter 3.1.

In stanza 17, Egill engages with proverbial wisdom more directly, with the traditional generalizations which others might accept as consolation. Since 16 is defective, we cannot be certain whether the 'auk' (also) of 17¹ does not refer back to another folk-saying in the previous verse, now lost:

Þat's auk mælt	It is also said
at engi geti	that no man can get
sonar iðgjǫld	recompense for a son
nema sjálfr ali	unless he himself beget
enn þann nið	offspring again
es öðrum sé	who for the other may be
borinn maðr	a man born
í bróður stað.	in the place of a brother.

Egill's situation has two striking parallels: Óðinn's loss of Baldr, and the Old Man in *Beowulf* whose son has been hanged, all sharing the theme: replacement of a dead son. In the *Vǫluspá* account, this is easily accomplished.¹⁶ Váli is born able to fight when one night old: vengeance for Baldr is swift. *Beowulf* shares the 'vengeance' motif with *Vǫluspá*: the Old Man is inconsolable, for the death of his son is a judicial punishment: no vengeance could be taken even if he had another son to perform it. Miserably he wanders through the empty rooms of his dwelling where all feasts and entertainments have ceased: 'Gesyð sorhcearig   on his suna būre | wīnsele wēstne . . .' (*Beowulf* 2455–6ᵃ: He gazes sorrowfully at his son's quarters, the deserted wine-hall . . .). 'Nis þǣr hearpan swēg, | gomen in geardum, swylce ðǣr īu wǣron' (*Beowulf* 2458ᵇ–2459: Nor is there the sound of the harp, entertainment in the dwellings, as there was once).

Similarly in *Sonatorrek* 18 all human companionship is distasteful to Egill. Always misanthropic, Egill has lost those few people: parents, sons, brother, whom he loved. His son has departed to seek his other kin, gathered in Valhǫll:[17] 'burr's Bileygs í bœ' (my son is in the Weak-sighted One's castle). The social focus of Egill's life, where his kinsmen are to be found feasting round the board, is no longer on earth, but in Óðinn's hall. Nor does the Old Man in *Beowulf* wish to have more children (2451ᵇ–2453ᵃ) Egill too refuses to consider begetting sons as a replacement — the traditional advice to those whose child dies — no recompense, 'iðgjǫld', will be accepted for the lost sons. Far from finding comfort in the common, proverbial folk-knowledge 'volksläufige Spruchswissen', as von See suggests,[18] Egill turns away from proverbial wisdom and seeks consolation instead in his poetic art.

With its jerky sequence of thought, *Sonatorrek* conveys a spontaneous and deeply emotional outpouring of grief. Yet poetic control is maintained, by the exigencies of the form and the use of consciously integrated imagery, moral argument, and reminiscence in an intellectual attempt to impose order on the chaos of feelings. One form of consolation is considered: proverbial wisdom, rooted in experience, but it is rejected for a resentful acknowledgement that Óðinn gives as well as takes. No easy escape into clichéd gnomic consolation is permitted to Egill: the conclusion that bereavement is inevitable and must be borne is uncongenial to the ferocious old warrior. The gnomic undercurrent to the poem sketches an ideal of how life should be: Egill should be enjoying an honoured old age, surrounded by his kin. Instead the gnomic themes intensify Egill's apprehension of loss:

no longer has he a faithful brother, promising sons, nor can new ones be got.

Memorial Eulogy: Eyvindr's Hákonarmál

Beside the elegiac monologues of the Edda, and the two poems of Egill, we also find praise and memorial poems for kings and jarls. *Hákonarmál*, composed for Hákon the Good by Eyvindr skáldaspillir, no doubt shortly after the death of Hákon in battle against the Eiríkssons in 960, provides the most important example in Old Norse of the use of gnomic material in elegy. Eyvindr does not lament the loss of the individual alone; there is also a political dimension to be explored: the achievements of the ruler during his reign and expectations for the future.[19]

Hákonarmál and *Hávamál* are clearly related: not for nothing was Eyvindr known as 'skáldaspillir', plunderer of poets, yet he puts his borrowings to fresh and exciting use. The peculiar atmosphere of foreboding which hangs over Hákon's entry into Valhǫll is quite unlike that of *Eiríksmál*, usually posited as *Hákonarmál*'s model,[20] where Óðinn bustles about, eagerly anticipating his guest, and Eiríkr enters confidently, sure of his welcome. Hákon, by contrast, seems unwilling to enter at all (15):

Ræsir þat mælti	Then spoke the king
— vas frá rómu kominn,	— he was come from battle,
stóð allr í dreyra drifinn	he stood all drenched in gore
'Illúðigr mjök	'Very hostile
þykkir oss Óðinn vesa:	Óðinn seems to us:
séumk vér hans of hugi.'	we fear his displeasure.'

Hákon's reluctant approach recalls the tension with which another hall is regarded in *Hávamál* 1, in which hostility may also be waiting. In *Hákonarmál*, as in *Hávamál*, the initial doubts about the welcome are soon dispelled; in both poems hospitality is offered, and the visitor — still wary —makes himself at home. *Hávamál* counsels the visitor to a strange hall never to let his caution lapse for a moment:

Enn vari gestr, . . .	The cautious guest …
þunno hlióði þegir,	is silent with finely-tuned hearing,
eyrom hlyðir,	he listens with his ears
en augom skoðar	and looks about with his eyes
	(*Hávamál* 7[1,3–5])

Nor is Hákon yet completely trusting:

'Gerðar órar',	'Our armour',
kvað enn góði konungr	said the good king,
'viljum vér sjálfir hafa.	'we will keep ourselves.
Hjálm ok brynju	Helmet and corslet
skal hirða vel.	shall be kept well.
Gott es til görs at taka.'	It is good to grasp what's ready.'
	(17)

This recalls *Hávamál* 38, perhaps with a verbal echo in 'görs' and 'geirs':

Vápnom sinom	From his weapons ought
skala maðr velli á	a man on the open plain not
feti ganga framarr;	to move a foot-length away;
þvíat óvist er at vita,	there's no knowing for certain,
nær verðr á vegom úti,	when he's out on the road,
geirs um þorf guma.	when a man will need his spear.

Although the setting is different — the protagonist of *Hávamál* out in the country, Hákon in Valholl — the thought is the same. *Hákonarmál* 19 echoes *Hávamál* again:

Góðu dœgri	On a good day
verðr sá gramr of borinn	is that prince born who can
es sér getr slíkan sefa.	get himself such a spirit.
Hans aldar	His life
mun æ vesa	will ever be
at góðu getit.	given good report.

This sentiment, and particularly the phrase 'es/er sér (um) getr', recalls the emphasis in *Hávamál* on gaining reputation by one's own independent efforts, notably in *Hávamál* 8, 9, and, most importantly, since *Hákonarmál* 21 shows that Eyvindr knew this verse, in *Hávamál* 76. After 'Deyr fé', etc. come the lines:

en orztírr	but glory
deyr aldregi	never dies
hveim er sér góðan getr	for him who gets himself good (fame).

Eyvindr is not, however, talking of reputation, 'lof', or 'dómr' here, but of 'sefi' (spirit, soul, mind). The *Hávamál* collocation of 'er sér góðan getr' with 'lof'/'orztírr' is deliberately varied in order to emphasize the aspect of Hákon's character which seemed most important to Eyvindr: the quality of Hákon's inner nature, rather than his external fame, touched upon in the following verse. The word 'sefi' belongs to the pre-Christian psychological vocabulary frequently instanced in *Hávamál*;[21] it is not easy to gauge its precise connotations from the pre-Christian contexts in which it occurs, nor is it clear how Eyvindr means us to understand this phrase. He may be referring to some kind of spiritual development in Hákon, in learning the value of compromise in the matter of Christianizing Norway.[22] This interpretation is borne out by the use of 'slíkan', referring back to the preceding verse, hence a spirit which was wise enough to preserve the pagan sanctuaries. Eyvindr must have been making a particular point here, since he has made a deliberate change from his source, from 'orztírr' to 'sefa'.

In 21, Eyvindr reshapes lines from *Hávamál*. K. von See[23] has suggested that the *Hávamál* verses are dependent on the *Hákonarmál*, which in turn cites *The Wanderer* ll. 108 ff. He argues that *Hákonarmál* is closer to *The Wanderer* than *Hávamál* is to *The Wanderer*, from the similarity of 'eyðisk land ok láð' (land and people are laid waste) to l. 110 of *The Wanderer*, 'eal þis eorðan gestæl īdel weorþeð' (all the foundations of this world become empty). As regards the *Hávamál* stanzas 76 and 77[1-3], von See maintains that l. 3 has 'ohnehin mit dem altenglischen Text nur entfernte Ähnlichkeit' (only a distant similarity to the Old English text).

But, in my view, 'deyr sjálfr it sama' (the very self must die) is similar to 'hēr bið mon læne' (here man is transient) in *The Wanderer* 109, as it stands in context, at least as similar as *The Wanderer* 110 is to 'eyðisk land ok láð'. If the poet of *Hávamál* has taken the 'Deyr fé' lines from *Hákonarmál*, as von See suggests, lines in turn derived from *The Wanderer*, then it would be an extraordinary coincidence that the *Hávamál* poet's own expansion of the lines, using a sentiment not found in *Hákonarmál*, 'deyr sjálfr it sama' should be so similar to the thought 'hēr bið mon læne' which follows the comparable lines in *The Wanderer*. Thus the *Hávamál*-poet has 'accidentally' hit upon the 'original' continuation! The explanation would seem to be, as Heusler suggests in 'Sprichwörter in den eddischen Sittenge-dichten', that both *Hávamál* and *The Wanderer* are citing a common Germanic source here.[24]

The verse may be translated thus:

Deyr fé,	Cattle are dying,
deyja frændr,	kinsmen are dying,
eyðisk land ok láð;	land and realm laid waste;
síz Hákon fór	since Hákon went
með heiðin goð	with the heathen gods[25]
mǫrg es þjóðum þjeuð.	greatly has the nation been enslaved.

The deaths of the cattle and the kinsmen are made directly contingent on the passing away of Hákon. It is not only the loss of Hákon which Eyvindr laments here, but also the passing of the old gods; Hákon takes them to death with him. The Eiríkssons were Christians, and set about destroying the sanctuaries which Hákon, as Eyvindr pointedly remarks, had taken pains to preserve.

Eyvindr's use of gnomic material in *Hákonarmál* is twofold: in 17 he demonstrates Hákon's common-sense, using *Hávamál*-type maxims to endorse the king's decision, an illustration of the royal *sapientia* celebrated in 19. In 21, he uses a quotation from *Hávamál* about worldly transience to epitomize the current political situation. We all know, he seems to suggest, that all things are mortal, but now our king is gone, we see the terrible evidence of this familiar truth in our land. While the *Hávamál* continuation of these lines, stressing the glory of the departed warrior, plays a counterpoint in the audience's ears,[26] Eyvindr contrasts an inglorious present of slavery and destruction. There is no consolation to be found here; rather Eyvindr makes a subtly subversive attack on the new masters of Norway, the sons of Eiríkr. Dramatic use is made of the maxims and situations which Eyvindr found in *Hávamál*, not primarily to impose a rationalizing order on a personal grief, but to compose a deeply felt political poem.

6.2 OLD ENGLISH ELEGY

Elegy in Old English ranges from personal lament to philosophical consideration of worldly transience. At one extreme, *Wulf and Eadwacer* and *The Wife's Lament* correspond most nearly to the Greek *góos*; like *Guðrúnarkviða I* and *Oddrúnargrátr*, these poems are spoken by women.[27] Just as *Oddrúnargrátr* ends with a gnomic observation summing up what Oddrún has learned from the unfolding of the tragedy of the Gjúkungar, so the speaker of *Wulf and Eadwacer* concludes with a gnome illuminating the relationship with her husband as she now understands it, after her exploration of her feelings towards both Wulf and Eadwacer in the course of the poem. The other extreme: the meditative lament, is represented by *The Wanderer* and *The Seafarer* (see below).

Praise-poems are to be found in Old English also; for example, the brief memorial verses of the *Anglo-Saxon Chronicle*. But while these usually constitute a — not entirely uncritical — record of the achievements of the king,[28] they are not normally substantial nor poetically ambitious enough to permit the heightening of the figure of the individual king through gnomic generalizations, as in *Hákonarmál*.

Personal Laments

Wulf and Eadwacer

Wulf and Eadwacer is a brief, highly allusive lament, spoken by a woman who is separated from her lover, Wulf, and afraid for his safety; in the last lines of the poem, she taunts her husband, Eadwacer, with the failure of their marriage, exultantly declaring its end with the dispatch of their child.[29]

Wulf and Eadwacer has a deceptive simplicity. All the background and the details of the story have been cut away, leaving the emotions of the speaker in sharp relief, longing for her lover while fiercely defying her husband. There is an unusual and imaginative use of language; the poet exploits the ambiguities inherent in the vocabulary to emphasize the tensions in the woman's attitude both to Wulf and to her husband. So in the first line, Wulf is described as 'lāc' for the woman's people, a gift, but also an offering or sacrifice: 'Lēodum is mīnum swylce him mon lāc gife; | willað hȳ hine āþecgan, gif hē on þrēat cymeð' (*Wulf and Eadwacer* 1–2: It is as if my people are being given an offering; they will receive him if he comes among an armed troop).

The people are willing to 'āþecgan' (receive/devour)[30] this gift, but, ironically, with a hostile reception in which the 'gift' will become a sacrifice — he will be attacked and killed. The ambiguity of meaning in the first lines is resolved in 7, by the repetition of the woman's prophecy, after the 'wælhrēow' (cruel in slaughter) nature of the tribe is made clear.

The refrain 'ungelīc is ūs' (we are separated/our fates are different) punctuates the poem like a wail of despair. It establishes the themes of separation and togetherness, physical union and emotional alienation which climax at the end of the poem in the gnomic observation: 'Þæt mon ēaðe tōslīteð þætte nēfre gesomnad wæs, ǀ uncer giedd geador.' (*Wulf and Eadwacer* 18–19: That may easily be put asunder, that which was never joined, our song together).

The gnome plays with the marital injunction of the Bible, Matthew 19: 6: 'What therefore God has joined together, let no man put asunder',[31] riposting to the Biblical admonition with a logical corollary: our union can easily be destroyed for it was no union. The gnome puns on 'gesomnad', from 'gesomnian' (to unite, join in a relationship) and 'gesomnad', from 'somnian' (to compose a song or poem). Thus 'giedd' is used both with its literal meaning, 'song, poem',[32] continuing the sense of 'somnian', and as a metaphor for the marriage, referring back to the primary meaning of 'gesomnian' (united in wedlock).

The woman is telling Eadwacer, whom she now addresses directly, 'Gehȳrest þū Ēadwacer?' (Do you hear, Eadwacer?) that theirs has never been a true marriage, they have never been in harmony with one another, as the different elements of a 'giedd' should be, and that in the eyes of God, they have not been 'gesomnad': in their case the marriage bond may be sundered without breaking God's law. The only result of their union, the 'hwelp' (pup), wolf-eaten/Wulf-abducted, is also destroyed: 'Uncerne earmne hwelp [MS earne] ǀ bireð wulf tō wuda.' (*Wulf and Eadwacer* 16b–17: Our wretched pup the wolf/Wulf is carrying to the wood), or perhaps torn asunder, 'tōslīteð', for wolves[33] are notorious for tearing at their prey. With the loss of the child, the marriage is at an end: nothing now remains to hold them together.

The gnomic conclusion of *Wulf and Eadwacer* transforms the Biblical ideal of marriage into a comment on an individual marriage — a comment the more telling since the language used echoes the phrasing of the Gospel verse.[34] The lines do not directly contradict the Bible, but point out that not all marriages are unions truly made by God. There is no consolation to be gained for either Eadwacer or the woman from these lines: punning in wry bitterness, they represent a terrifyingly courageous evaluation of the death of a marriage.

The Wife's Lament

The Wife's Lament is a 'giedd'; a lament like that of *The Seafarer*, which is deeply rooted in the speaker's own tribulations. Thus there is little that is gnomic in the main part of the poem (23–4): 'eft is þæt onhworfen, is nū   swā hit nō wǣre' (that has all disappeared as if it never were) briefly provides a reflective gloss on the woman's experiences. Then suddenly, in 42–50ᵃ, comes an unexpected gnomic passage:

> Ā scyle geong mon   wesan gēomormod,
> heard heortan geþōht,   swylce habban sceal
> blīþe gebǣro,   ēac þon breostceare,
> sinsorgna gedreag,   sȳ æt him sylfum gelong
> eal his worulde wyn,   sȳ ful wīde fāh
> feorres folclondes,   þæt mīn frēond siteð
> under stānhliþe   storme behrīmed,
> wine wērigmōd,   wætre beflōwen
> on drēorsele.

Always ought a young man to be serious of mood, the thought of his heart resolute, likewise he must have a cheerful manner, also anxiety at heart, a multitude of sorrows, whether he is solely dependent on himself for all his joy in the world, or whether he is outcast, in a far-off nation, where[35] my friend sits under a rocky cliff, frozen by the storm, my friend weary-hearted, surrounded by water in a desolate hall.

What is the purpose of this apparently arbitrary comment? The movement of thought seems to be as follows: the speaker considers the qualities desirable in a young man under all circumstances, and then, in the syntactically parallel pair of clauses introduced by 'sy' . . . 'sy', contrasts the 'geong mon' who is able to find happiness in the world through his own efforts, with the lot of the man, exiled and unhappy, like the speaker's 'freond', a transition from gnomic generalization back to the individual only made with difficulty. Conceivably the tradition of gnomic reflection in lament had become so conventional that it was felt a moral had to be tacked on somewhere, contextual incongruity notwithstanding.

The poem concludes with another gnome: 'Wā bið þām þe sceal | of langoþe   lēofes ābīdan.' (52b–53: Woe is it for that person who must experience longing for a loved one.).

Deor

Deor is a short lament spoken by a man, the complaint of a minstrel who has lost the favour of his lord. The poem has a reflective refrain: 'þæs oferēode, þisses swā mæg' (that passed, this may also),[36] which unifies the disparate allusions of the stanzas, pulling the focus of *Deor* away from the famous individuals of history and legend, back to the narrator's own plight, and synthesizing the two into a perception of the passing of sorrow with time.

Elegiac Meditations

The Wanderer

The Wanderer describes the reconciliation of grief and life through the acquisition of a stoical wisdom: the exchange of disillusion with the transient hopes of the world for confidence in the immutable comfort of God, the only gold-friend, 'goldwine' who will not die. The poem opens with a celebrated gnome:

> Oft him ānhaga   āre gebīdeð,
> Metudes miltse,   þēah þe hē mōdcearig
> geond lagulade   longe sceolde
> hrēran mid hondum   hrīmcealde sǣ,
> wadan wræclāstas: wyrd bið ful ārǣd.
>
> (*The Wanderer* 1–5)

Often the solitary man waits for/experiences grace, the mercy of the Creator, though with heart full of care, for a long time, he must travel the seaways, move with his hands the rime-cold sea, journey on paths of exile: Fate is completely determined!

The central theme, the meditations of the 'ānhaga', opens with an exploration of the tension between speech and silence. As in *Hávamál*, speech is viewed ambivalently, but while in the Norse poem, the pressure to speak and thus reveal one's character comes from one's peers gathered in the hall, who want to 'freista' (try the quality of) (2[6]) the newcomer, in *The Wanderer* the urge to speak is internal and must be suppressed by the self. Both poems are conscious of the nobility of silence: 'Þagalt ok hugalt | skyli þjóðans barn . . . vera' (silent and thoughtful a prince's child should be) says *Havamál* 15¹⁻³; in *The Wanderer* silence is the hallmark of the noble: 'indryhten þēaw'. Thus the narrator must struggle to reconcile his need to speak out, to make a 'sōðgiedd' (true song) about himself, with his apprehension that such behaviour is inappropriate. Images of locking up and concealment are employed, a theme continued in 20ᵇ 'feterum sǣlan' (secure with fetters) and 'gebindað' (bind) 40ᵇ.

Now the narrator lists his sorrows: these are less his present discomforts, unlike the tangible winter cold and dangerous seas which the Seafarer must face, but rather his longing for benefits once enjoyed, but now denied. Good advice, 'lēofes lārcwidum' is one of these; the counsel of a friendly lord, 'winedrihten'. Such wisdom, tested and passed on by an older generation, is no longer available to him; now a man must become wise through experience. While in *Hávamál*, it is association with others, knowledge of different types of man which confers wisdom:

Sá einn veit —	That man alone knows —
er víða ratar	who roams widely
ok hefir fjǫlð um farit,	and has travelled a good deal,
hverio geði	what sort of mind
stýrir gumna hverr —	each man has —
sá er vitandi er vits.	he who is master of his wits.

(*Hávamál* 18)

in *The Wanderer* wisdom is learned in solitude: 'Swā cwæð snottor on mōde, gesæt him sundor æt rūne.' (*The Wanderer* 111: So said the wise in heart, he sat apart in secret meditation.)

The acquisition of wisdom is seen as an almost passive process, accruing to the man who has had 'wintra dæl in woruldrice' (his share of winters in the world). The experienced wise man is defined in the catalogue³⁷ of qualities which follows. Moderation is the key:

Wita sceal geþyldig:
ne sceal nō tō hātheort,   ne tō hrædwyrde,
ne tō wāc wiga,   ne tō wanhȳdig,
ne tō forht, ne tō fægen,   ne tō feohgifre,
ne nǣfre gielpes tō georn   ǣr hē geare cunne:
beorn sceal gebīdan,   þonne hē bēot spriceð,

> oþþæt, collenfcrð, cunne gearwe
> hwider hreðra gehygd hweorfan wille.
>
> (*The Wanderer* 65^b-72)

A wise man must be patient: nor too passionate nor too swift to speak, nor too unreliable a warrior, nor too despairing, nor too fearful, nor too servile, nor too avid for money, nor too eager to boast before he knows for certain: a man must wait, when he makes a vow, until, bold-hearted, he knows well in which direction the thoughts of the spirit will turn.[38]

Patience stands out as an essentially Christian virtue from a list summarizing a secular wisdom, valid for the man who still serves and fights with the *comitatus*, with its ritual vows and boasts. These qualities are those to which a worldly man can aspire: social values, like those of the Gnomic Poem, in which parallels to most of these sentiments can be found.[39] The definition of the wise man as one who does not speak out too quickly looks forward to the poem's conclusion in 112 ff.

The ultimate end of this knowledge, the section concludes starkly, is nothing but a fuller understanding of the terrible desolation of worldly existence, a sense of devastation in which *Hákonarmál* shares:[40] 'Ongietan sceal glēaw hæle hū gæstlic bið | þonne eal þisse worulde wela wēste stondeð.' (*The Wanderer* 73–4: The wise man must perceive how terrible it will be when all the riches of this world stand waste.)

A second figure, little differentiated from the first speaker, 'sē þonne þisne wealsteal wīse geþōhte' (he who wisely considered the foundations of the world), is introduced at 88, a man 'frōd in ferðe' (wise in spirit). Generalizing from the first speaker's personal experience of severance from his own lord and meadhall, through lament for a horse, warrior, lord: all that is lost, he concludes that 'hēr' (here) all things are transient (108–10). 'Hēr' implies an elsewhere, a place with which the empty 'īdel' world may be contrasted. This contrast forms the basis for the poem's conclusion.

The final lines of *The Wanderer* offer two possibilities: that of the man who is virtuous, 'til', and of the man for whom it is 'wel':[41]

> Til bið se þe his trēowe gehealdeð, ne sceal næfre his
>   torn tō rycene
>   beorn of his brēostum ācȳþan, nemþe hē ǣr þā bōte cunne,

eorl mid elne gefremman. Wel bið þām þe him āre sēceð,
frōfre tō Fæder on heofonum, þær ūs eal sēo fæstnung stondeð.

(The Wanderer 112–15)

Virtuous is he who keeps his faith,[42] nor should he ever make known his resentment[43] too quickly from his heart, unless he, the warrior, previously know the remedy, how to carry it out with zeal. Well is it for him who seeks mercy, comfort from the Father in heaven, where for us all security lies.

The 'til' man knows the benefit of keeping the promises he has made to others, and of keeping his resentments to himself until he has decided how they may be remedied, virtues not necessarily Christian, for the man who is still concerned with life in the world. The man for whom it is 'wel' has passed beyond such earthly considerations, placing all his trust in the Father in heaven, a resolution anticipated in the opening lines of the poem: the lonely man who waits for grace will receive it.

The Wanderer, more so than *The Seafarer*, is consistently gnomic in tone, for it is a meditation on experience and the wisdom which arises from it; each new thought builds gradually, if sometimes fitfully, towards the homiletic conclusion. The gnomic mood is created through two principal techniques: the first of which is the use of maxims as markers of the conclusion of a particular train of thought, signalling a transition to a new area of concern. Thus the opening verse paragraph, delineating the plight of the solitary man, arrives at the conclusion 'wyrd bið ful āræd' (fate is inexorably fixed). So it must seem to the man who has not yet experienced grace. Line 36b: 'Wyn eall gedrēas' (joy has all perished) draws together the lost joys of life in hall and the companionship which the narrator can no longer enjoy. Lines 62b–65a mark a movement from the consideration of lost joys and the vision of absent companions to the definition of wisdom in 65bff. with:

Swā þes middangeard,
ealra dōgra gehwām drēoseð and fealleð.
Forþon ne mæg weorþan wīs wer, ær hē āge
wintra dæl in woruldrīce.

Thus this earth, every single day, falls and declines. Therefore a man can never become wise, before he has had his share of winters in this world.

106–7 epitomize the wise man's apprehension of human existence: 'Eall is earfoðlic   eorþan rīce, I onwendeð wyrda gesceaft weoruld under heofunum.' (All is full of hardship in the kingdom of earth, the decree of fate alters the world under heaven.) These platitudes provide a memorable summary of the observations which have preceded them; in this they resemble the proverb-type final *Vollzeile* of some of the *Hávamál* stanzas: 'half er ǫld hvar' (men are half and half (wise and foolish) everywhere), or 'glík skolo gjǫld gjǫfum' (gifts should be repaid with like ones): but these, unlike the predictable Old English maxims, have a sharp, witty point.

A second characteristic which helps to create the gnomic tone of *The Wanderer* is the rapid alternations between first and third person. We have seen in *Hávamál* how the narrator 'ek' (I) 'becomes' Óðinn at will, confirming the identification by using the third person. In the Old English poem, a generalized third person is introduced to act as a foil to the first-person speaker: 'wāt se þe cunnað' (he knows who has tried it) (29b). This figure can vouch for the truth of the first person's observation that sorrow is a cruel companion; 'se þe sceal his winedryhtnes I lēofes lārcwidum longe forþolian' (he who must forgo for a long time the counsels of his dear, friendly lord) of 37–8 likewise confirms the Wanderer's despair at the loss of his lord. The attitudes of the third persons are all consistent with those expressed by the 'ic' persona, and thus the effect of these interchanges is to blur the distinctions between the third-person characters and the narrator, so that they all become facets of a single consciousness, viewed with varying degrees of detachment.[44] This blurring underlines the poem's conclusion that worldly experience will lead all men — if they live long enough to grow wise — to the same realization, for they will all experience loss and destruction. The only solution is to be found in heaven: 'þǣr ūs eal sēo fæstnung stondeð' (where for us all security is to be found).

The Seafarer

Wisdom does not lie at the heart of *The Seafarer* as it does in *The Wanderer*. The development of thought in the poem is from a concrete portrayal of the hardships experienced in sea-voyaging, contrasted with the comfort of life on land, to an apprehension of the emptiness of existence and a resolution to set out on another voyage: a pilgrimage.[45] Yet, despite the vivid physicality which distinguishes *The Seafarer*, the poem shares some of the pre-occupations of *The Wanderer*, particularly in the closing lines.

The Seafarer does not employ the brief, pithy maxims of *The Wanderer* to conclude a movement in the poem's thought; instead the conjunctive phrase 'forþon' (so, therefore) is used to effect transitions,[46] but however it is interpreted, 'forþon' does not provide a closely argued, logical sequence of thought. The gnomes are concentrated in the conclusion and in the lengthy examination of 'lof' (reputation) in 72 ff; but a gnomic tone is established, as in *The Wanderer*, by alternations between third persons. Where in *Hávamál* we would expect a fully formed gnome of the type: 'hinn er sæll er . . .' (That man is happy who . . .) (8), in *The Seafarer*, the third person is evoked in order to make a specific contrast (12b-15):

> þæt se mon ne wāt
> þe him on foldan   fægrost limpeð,
> hū ic earmcearig   īscealdne sæ
> winter wunade . . .

The man whose lot is cast most happily on land does not know how I, wretched and miserable, passed the winter on the ice-cold sea . . .

Although the observation sounds as if it will become a gnome, the universalising element is absent.

There is not quite the same blurring between the first person and third person characters as in *The Wanderer*, 'se þe āh līfes wyn' (he who possesses the joy of life) in 27 is explicitly contrasted with the 'ic' of the poem's opening. In 39–41, we assume that the 'mōdwlonc man' (proud man) who enjoys various advantages in life is to be identified with 'se þe āh līfes wyn' from 27 above, and thus to be contrasted with the first person narrator. Yet in 42, we find that this man too experiences anxiety about his seafaring:

> for þon nis þæs mōdwlonc   mon ofer eorþan . . .
> þæt he ā his sæfōre   sorge næbbe,
> tō hwon hine Dryhten   gedōn wille.
>
> (*The Seafarer* 39, 42–3).

for this reason there is not a man so proud on the earth . . . that he does not always have anxiety about his seafaring, as to what the Lord will bring him to.

No man is so content with his lot that there is not some lurking anxiety which gnaws at him. This pessimistic view of earthly contentment prepares for the final resolution of the poem, in which the Seafarer decides to set out anew, on a journey both literal and allegorical, to seek 'elþēodigra eard' (a land of foreigners). There is a contrast with the positive use to which the pattern: 'No man is so ... that ...' is put in *Hávamál* 71, where we are told that even the deaf man can fight, and the man with no hands can be a herdsman. The 'mōdwlonc mon' occupies a medial position between 'se þe āh līfes wyn' — the 'sēftēadig secg' (man happy in comfort)[47] of 56a, incapable of imagining, let alone experiencing, the vicissitudes of seafaring, and the third person who is well aware of the physical and spiritual implications of voyaging. The alternations between grammatical persons in *The Seafarer* are more clearly definable, and less subtly used than in *The Wanderer*.

The catalogue structure, as we have seen characteristic of the wisdom poem, occurs only in 40–5 to list the 'līfes wyn' which will be as nothing to the man who intends to put to sea, 'se þe on lagu fundað'. The formula 'ādl oþþe yldo oþþe ecghete' (sickness or old age or violence) in 70 is a shorthand description of the different kinds of death enumerated in *The Wanderer*, and in fuller detail in *The Fortunes of Men*, typical of homiletic writing.[48]

The consideration of the Christian significance of 'lof' (praise) in 72 ff. is unique to *The Seafarer* among Old English wisdom poems. The impeccably heroic sentiment of *Hávamál* 76 and 77:

en orztírr	but glory
deyr aldregi	never dies
hveim er sér góðan getr.	for him who can get himself a
	good (reputation).
	(*Hávamál* 76[4–6])

ek veit einn	I know one thing
at aldri deyr,	which never dies,
dómr um dauðan hvern.	fame for every dead man.
	(*Hávamál* 77[4–6])

is reworked in *The Seafarer* 72–80b:

For þon þæt (bið) eorla gehwām æftercweþendra
lof lifgendra lāstworda betst,

þæt hē gewyrce, ǣr hē on weg scyle,
fremum on foldan wið fēonda nīð,
dēorum dǣdum dēofle tōgēanes,
þæt hine ælda bearn æfter hergen,
and his lof siþþan lifge mid englum
āwa tō ealdre, ēcan līfes blǣd,
drēam mid dugeþum.

Therefore for every warrior, the best reputation after death is the praise of the living, those who speak afterwards, that, before he passed away he should perform great and daring deeds on earth, against the malice of fiends/enemies, and against the devil, so that the children of men praise him afterwards, and his praise later live with the angels, for ever and ever, the glory of eternal life, joy among the host.

Hávamál's thought is general in application: good reputation (dómr) and glory (orztírr)[49] are undying; they defeat death. *The Seafarer* uses a broadly similar generalization about the heroic life for a specifically Christian purpose — 'lof' defeats, not only physical death, as do the pagan 'dómr' and 'orztírr', so that generations to come praise the memory of the departed man, 'ælda bearn æfter hergan', but Christian 'lof' also persists in the eternal Life, 'his lof siþþan lifge mid englum'. While the *Hávamál* verse does not specify an enemy who must be striven against, *The Seafarer* plays with the ambiguity of 'fēond' — human enemy or hellish fiend — making concrete the spiritual foe, 'dēofol' against whom the battle must be waged.

The greatest concentration of gnomic material is to be found in the closing lines of the poem, unfortunately corrupt in the manuscript and difficult to interpret. Lines 103–8 are comparable in structure to the final lines of *The Wanderer*, using the 'X biþ þām þe . . .' (X is he who . . .) construction so characteristic of Old English wisdom poetry. The lines contrast the foolish 'dol' whose reward is death, and the blessed 'ēadig' who has lived humbly, and whose reward is heavenly grace, 'sēo ār of heofonum'.[50]

These lines (103–8) would form a satisfying conclusion to the poem, but in fact the poem continues for another fifteen or so lines, the first seven of which contain three gnomic statements:

Stīeran mon [MS mod] sceal strongum mōde and þæt on
staþelum healdan,

and gewis wērum wīsum clǣne.
Scyle monna gehwylc mid gemet healdan
wiþ lēofne and wiþ lāþne . . . bealo.
þēah þe hē hine wille fȳres . . . fulne
oþþe on bǣle forbærnedene
his geworhtne wine. Wyrd biþ swīþre [MS swire]
Meotud meahtigra, þonne ǣnges monnes gehygd.

                                        (*The Seafarer* 109–11)

A man must control a strong temperament and keep it firm-rooted, be true to men, pure in habit. Every man should act fittingly toward the dear one, and with malice toward the hated one, though he will (see?) the friend he has made burned on the pyre, or in the foulness of the fire. Fate is stronger, the Creator mightier, than any man's thought.)

The first of these gnomes — 109ᵃ — is usually emended as above, to a form virtually identical with *Exeter Maxims* 51ᵃ: 'stȳran sceal mon strongum mōde'.⁵¹ Lines 110–15ᵃ are extremely difficult to interpret. Lines 110–12 seem to imply that good should call forth good, and hatred malice — an unchristian moral reminiscent of 'glík skolo gjǫld gjǫfum' (a gift shall be repaid with a like one) in *Hávamál* 46. Lines 113–15ᵃ suggest a death after death, consignment to the flames of hell, paralleling the physical burial described in 97–102, which is also introduced with a concessive clause. 'Wyrd biþ swīþre [MS swire], Meotud meahtigra, | þonne ǣnges monnes gehygd' suggests *Cotton Maxims* 4ᵇ–5ᵃ: 'Þrymmas syndan Crīstes myccle. | Wyrd byð swīðost, . . .' (Christ's powers are great. Fate is very strong . . .). The gnome provides a smooth transition to the homiletic closing lines of the poem, which exhort the reader to consider how he may reach the eternal bliss awaiting him in heaven.

The Wanderer considers the traditional wisdom which comes to the man who has experienced much, but finally advocates faith in God: eternal security and divine grace are preferable in the face of the inescapable mortality which is the poem's lesson. *The Seafarer*'s progression is less straightforward. While *The Seafarer* is undeniably Christian in sentiment, the inclusion of unchristian values (in 111–12 above) indicates that 'neutral' traditional wisdom and Christian faith can co-exist in this poem, as in the Old English wisdom poems, without strain. While 104–12 offer practical advice for life, 115–16 emphasize that larger powers than those of mankind are at work in human existence, and thus the divine, as well as the earthly, must be taken into account. The narrator of *The Seafarer* does not achieve the detachment of the *Wanderer*-persona (l. 111): 'Swā cwǣð snottor on mōde ǀ gesǣt him sundor æt rūne.' (So spoke the wise in heart, and sat apart in meditation.) The ordinary wisdom of this earth is still of value to him.

Both *The Wanderer* and *The Seafarer* concern themselves, to a greater or lesser extent, with the wisdom to be gained from human experience — a preoccupation of *Hávamál* also. Obvious homiletic features: the formulaic 'ādl and yldo' (sickness and age), the reworking of the heroic theme of reputation (lof) in *The Seafarer* 73–6, the final gnome 'Wel bið þām þe . . .' (Well is it for him who . . .) of *The Wanderer*, and the closing sentiments of *The Seafarer* demonstrate that Christian conventions could easily be assimilated to the features already present in the native tradition. Thus the capacity for gnomic modes of thought inherent in the elegiac genre may have attracted both foreign, Christian, and homiletic elements and native wisdom conventions, expanding and altering the genre to make possible the poetry of ideas which *The Wanderer* and *The Seafarer* represent.

Notes

1. M. Alexiou, *Ritual Lament in Greek Tradition* (London, 1974).
2. T. F. Mustanoja, 'The Unnamed Woman's Song of Mourning over Beowulf and the Tradition of Ritual Lament', *NM* 68 (1967), 1–13. See also R. Frank, 'Old Norse Memorial Eulogies and the Ending of *Beowulf*', in *The Early Middle Ages, Acta*, 6 (1979), 1–19.
3. See C. J. Clover, 'Hildigunnr's Lament' in J. Lindow, L. Lönnroth, and G. W. Weber ed., *Structure and Meaning in Old Norse Literature*, (Odense, 1986), 141–83.
4. Alexiou, *Ritual Lament*, 103
5. See J. R. J. North, 'The Pagan Inheritance of Egill's *Sonatorrek*', *Poetry in the Scandinavian Middle Ages*, 7th International Saga Conference (Spoleto, 1988), 289–300 and Pagan Words and Christian Meanings, Costerus New Series, 81, (Amsterdam and Athens, Ca., 1991), 46–62 .
6. See below, ch. 6.2.
7. *Oddrúnargrátr, Guðrúnarkviða I*, and *Helgakviða Hundingsbana II*. For comparisons with OE 'Frauenlieder', see J. Harris, 'Elegy in Old English and Old Norse: A Problem in Literary History', in *The Vikings*, ed. R. T. Farrell (London, 1982), 157–64, and K. Malone, 'Two English *Frauenlieder*', *CL* 14 (1962), 106–17. In 'Women's Songs, Women's Language: *Wulf and Eadwacer* and *The Wife's Lament*', in H. Damico and A. Hennessey Olsen ed., *New Readings on Women in Old English Literature* (Bloomington, Ind., 1990), 193–203, P. Belanoff suggests that the language of these two poems, in partiuclar its polysemy, indicates a 'differentness' of genre.
8. 'Þæs' and 'þisses' should be taken as genitives of point of time from which, 'It passed over from that; it can from this.' B. Mitchell, *Old English Syntax* (Oxford, 1985) i. §§ 1404–5.

9.   Cf. *The Fortunes of Men* above, ch. 4.4 and *Ex. Max.*, above, ch. 4.1.

10.   There are a number of proverbs about the advantage of having a brother in Germanic tradition: *Ex. Max.* 174–6; *Njáls saga* ch. 152; *Grettis saga* 82, Saxo, i. bk. v., 128.

11.   M. C. van den Toorn, '*Egils saga* als dichterische Leistung', *ZfdPh* 77 (1958), 46–59.

12.   *Egils saga*, ch. 78.

13.   *Hávamál* 1^5, 56^7, 9^4, 12^4, 38^4, etc.

14.   K. von See, '*Sonatorrek* und *Hávamál*', *ZDA* 99 (1970), 25–33.

15.   Von See, ibid. 32, thinks that 'vanr' and 'varr' had become virtually interchangeable in this collocation.

16.   *Vǫluspá* 32–33.

17.   Following Nordal's emended text, *ÍF*, iii. 253.

18.   Von See, '*Sonatorrek* und *Hávamál*', 32 suggests that the wisdom and outlook of *Hávamál* confirm 'bestätigt', Egill's own state of mind.

19.   Cf. the memorial poem for Eadgar in the *Anglo-Saxon Chronicle*, i. ed. B. Thorpe (London, 1861), 217–19.

20.   *Eiríksmál* is generally assumed to have preceded *Hákonarmál*, except by von See. See A. Wolf, 'Zitat und Polemik in den *Hákonarmál* Eyvinds', in *Germanistische Studien*, ed. J. Erben and E. Thurnher, Innsbrucker Beiträge zur Kulturwissenschaft, 15 (Innsbruck, 1969), 9–32; ibid. 9 for a summary of previous critics who give *Eiríksmál* the priority. Von See's opposing view is put in 'Zwei eddische Preislieder: *Eiríksmál* und *Hákonarmál*' in *Festgabe für U. Pretzel* (Berlin, 1963), 107–17, in which he discounts *Fagrskinna*'s account of the genesis of *Hákonarmál*. *Hákonarmál* is cited from *Heimskringla*; *Eiríksmál* cited from *Anglo-Saxon and Norse Poems*, ed. N. Kershaw (Cambridge, 1922).

21.   See above, chs. 3.1 and 3.2.

22.   *Hákonarmál* 18 and *Heimskringla, Hakonar saga góða*, chs. 13–18. For evidence of the Eiríkssons' attitude towards the old religion, see *Heimskringla, Haralds saga gráfeldar*, ch. 2.

23.   Von See, *Die Gestalt*, 48–50.

24.   *KS*, 109. See, however, von See's latest word on the subject in CS, 137–8, where he reiterates his argument, and Evans's response, MCS, 134–5.

25.   The phrase 'fara með' + acc. means 'to go with, accompanied by', with an idea of continuing movement — e.g.: Kormákr 1, 7 (*Sigurðardrápa*): 'Hroptr fór með Gungni' (Hroptr (Óðinn) journeyed with Gungnir (his spear)). The phrase 'fara með' + dat. is found in Sigvatr 11, 17, where it means 'live together with': 'Fórk með feðrum þeira . . . beggja' (I was with both their fathers). In the other instances, the accusative object is something taken with the subject on a journey: hence Hákon takes the old gods with him on his journey into the unknown.

26.   Von See, 'Zwei eddische Preislieder', 112.

27.   See K. Malone, 'Two English *Frauenlieder*', *CL* 14 (1962), 106–17.

28.   See the memorial poem for Eadgar in the *Anglo-Saxon Chronicle*.

29.   What happens to the child is debatable. Possibly the woman exposes it, and a wolf carries it off. The alternative explanation is that Wulf has taken the child — to kill it, or to raise it in outlawry.

30.   For the possible meanings of 'áþecgan' and 'þecgan', (receive, take), see Grein, *Ordbog*.

31.   The biblical context is that of the Pharisees asking Jesus for his opinion of divorce.

32.   For 'giedd' and its relationship to Old Norse 'geð', see J. R. J. North, 'Words and Contexts: An Investigation into the Meanings of Early English Words by Comparison of Vocabulary and Narrative Themes in Old English and Old Norse Poetry', Ph.D. thesis (Cambridge, 1987), 30–7 and *Pagan Words and Christian Meanings*, 39–51

33.   Cf. *Exeter Maxims* 146–51.

34.   Both 'gesomnad' and 'tosliteþ' are used in the surviving OE versions of Matthew 19: 6: Quod ergo Deus coniunxit, homo non separet. 'Ne getwæme nan mon ða þe God gesomnade', *The West Saxon Gospels: A Study of the Gospel of St. Matthew. with the Texts of the Four Gospels*, ed. M. Grünberg (Amsterdam, 1967); 'ðæt God gegeadrade monn ne

toslite', *Lindisfarne Gospel* in *Die Vier Evangelien in altnorthumbrischer Sprache*, ed. K. W. Bouterwek (Gütersloh, 1857).

35. MS 'þæt'; Imelmann's emendation, as noted by the *ASPR* editors, seems preferable.
36. For the literal translation see above, n. 8.
37. See N. Howe, *The Old English Catalogue Poems*, Anglistica, 23 (Copenhagen, 1985).
38. A. D. Horgan, '*The Wanderer*: A Boethian Poem?', *RES* 38 (1987), 40–6 plausibly identifies this passage as based on *De consolatione philosophiae*, IV. VI.
39. The warrior who is 'ne tō wāc' may be compared with the 'vígdjarft' (bold in war) prince's son of *Háv.* 15^3; the man who is 'ne tō wanhydig' with the man who is 'glaðr ok reifr' (cheerful and merry), *Háv.* 15^{4-6}. The man who is not 'feohgifre' is the subject of *Háv.* 40^{1-3} while *Háv.* 6 ff. adjure silence, the opposite of the rash words of the vow in *The Wanderer* 70.
40. Cf. *Hákonarmál* 20–1 for a corresponding sense of desolation.
41. B. Huppé, '*The Wanderer*: Theme and Structure', *JEGP* 42 (1943), 516–38 notes that the man who is 'til' is not identical to the man for whom it is 'wel', though I am reluctant to classify the first as 'heroic' and the second as Christian, as Huppé does.
42. 'Trēowe' may be 'faith' in a Christian sense, or simply mean 'promise', 'pledge'.
43. 'Torn' (resentment) may be linked back to 'se hrēo hyge' (the fierce thought) 16 as Dunning and Bliss suggest, *The Wanderer*, 107.
44. This technique may be contrasted with the vivid portraits of types in the *ExeterMaxims*, the man who does not get enough to eat in 111–14, or the blind man of 39^a–44.
45. D. Whitelock, 'The Interpretation of *The Seafarer*', in C. Fox and B. Dickins ed. *The Early Cultures of North-West Europe: H. M. Chadwick Memorial Studies* (Cambridge, 1950), 259–72. (repr. in J. B. Bessinger and S. J. Kahrl ed. *Essential Articles for the Study of Old English Poetry* (Hamden, Conn., 1968), 442–57).
46. Although Gordon claims that 'the difficulty of translating *for þon* in *The Seafarer* has been exaggerated' (*The Seafarer*, 57) looking ahead in 58^a to the correlative 'for þon' in 64^b in order to provide the sense 'therefore' . . . 'because' contributes to our sense that the progress of thought in *The Seafarer*, if not actually illogical, is at least somewhat disjointed in comparison with *The Wanderer*.
47. MS 'efteadig', but see Gordon's note, (ibid. 40) for the advantages of Grein's emendation.
48. Cf. Hroðgar's 'homily', *Beowulf* 1763–8.
49. I reject von See's claim that 'orztúrr' must be interpreted in a Christian sense, *Die Gestalt*, 47–8. That it had a pre-Christian sense is evidenced by its use in Egill's *Hofuðlausn* 6 ff.
50. For this type of construction, see above, ch. 4.1.
51. *Hav.* 18^{4-6} has a comparable idiom, 'hverju geði | stýrir gumna hverr' (what sort of spirit each man controls).

7 GNOMES IN NARRATIVE VERSE: OLD ENGLISH AND OLD NORSE

Gnomes are more frequently used in the long narrative poems in Old English than in the briefer narrative poems of the Edda. Yet comparatively few attempts have been made to analyse or classify the gnomic material found outside the recognized 'wisdom poems'. Some scholars have tended to regard such gnomes when they occur in narrative verse as ornamental devices, fulfilling no significant function, apart from providing a ready-made introduction or conclusion,[1] while others see them solely as mechanisms by which the action of the narrative may be endorsed, or related to familiar norms of behaviour: 'Third, it [the narrative voice] authenticates men's moral behaviour on a continuing basis from past to present, crystallizing its concern in maximic forms and formulas'.[2]

Close analysis of *Beowulf*, *Andreas*, and *Guðlac* A and B, the narrative poems which make most skilful use of gnomes, should throw a clearer light on the types of gnomes used, and thus illuminate the various functions which they perform in narrative verse. No other Old English narrative poems use gnomes at all extensively. *Exodus*, although the most heroic in temper of the religious poems, tends to employ biblical exempla, the stories of Abraham and Noah's flood, to relate the action of the poem to universal Christian themes. Cynewulf, perhaps surprisingly, eschews the use of gnomes for comment, or to approve and validate the actions of his characters. Perhaps since both Juliana[3] and Elene are saints, whose actions find favour with God, there is no need for the sanction of the narrator; to presume to pass judgement on the saints and Apostles might be felt impertinent.

Beowulf, *Andreas*, and the *Guðlac* poems represent variations of the heroic in Old English. *Beowulf* is a primary text of heroism in secular life, while *Andreas*, closely modelled on *Beowulf*,[4] demonstrates heroic endurance in a Christian calling. In *Guðlac*, the saint is a warrior for God, fighting against the devils who try to drive him from his fenland retreat; passive suffering is equated with heroic action, while success is to be attributed to faith in God, not personal merit. Themes of courage, kingship, and loyalty, expressed in gnomic form, were equally germane to the secular and to the saintly hero. Gnomes may be spoken by characters within the poem, or, with equal frequency, the narrators, notably of *Beowulf* and *Atlakviða*, may use them to comment on the action of the plot. For analysis of gnomic comments made by the narrative voice in *Beowulf*, see below, at 7.3.

7.1 THE HEROIC: *FORTITUDO*

The Pagan Heroic

The gnomes which urge fortitude in the Norse hero may be assigned to two broad types. The first is instigatory; it urges courage, resistance to the enemy and vigour in attack, while the second, recognizing the hopelessness of the hero's situation, is often uttered before a futile attack or during the battle itself; it admits the power of fate, and recommends resignation and sustained courage in the face of overwhelming odds.

Typical of the first group of gnomes are those uttered by Brynhildr and Guðrún. Brynhildr, unrelenting in her ferocity, demands that Sigurðr should be killed. To the oaths which her husband and brother-in-law have sworn to Sigurðr: 'tóc við trygðom | tveggia bræðra'[5] (*Sigurðarkviða in skamma* 1[5-6]: He took oaths from both the brothers), she opposes a savage image of Sigurðr's young son as a wolf, who should, like Sigurðr, be killed:

scalat úlf ala	the young wolf
ungan lengi;	must not be reared for long.
hveim verðr hǫlða	to which man
hefnd léttari,	will revenge be easier,
síðan til sátta,	to settle the matter later,
at sonr lifi?	than if the son live?

(*Sigurðarkviða in skamma* 12[3-8])

By likening Sigurðr's son into a wolf, perhaps an ironic echo of Sigrdrífa's advice to Sigurðr in *Sigrdrífumál* 35, Brynhildr tries to convince Gunnarr that the entire clan must be exterminated, for, like the proverbial wolf, they represent a lurking danger.[6] After Sigurðr's death, Brynhildr laughs:

Hló þá Brynhildr . . .   Then Brynhildr laughed . . .
eino sinni   once only
af ǫllum hug.   with all her heart.

(*Brot af Sigurðarkviða* 10[1, 3–4])

Guðrún retaliates with a threat that Brynhildr's triumph will not
last for long: 'heiptgjarns hugar ǀ hefnt skal verða.' (*Brot af
Sigurðarkviða* 11[7–8]: for vindictive thoughts revenge must be
exacted).

Other gnomes of action are more nuanced: Hamðir observes
that the best way to fight is without injury to oneself: a reference
to his mother's revenge on Atli, achieved only at the cost of great
sorrow to herself:[7]

svá skyldi hverr ǫðrom   so ought every man to bring about
verja til aldrlaga,   the death of others
sverði sárbeito   with a wound-biting sword
at sér ne striddit.   so that he does not injure himself.

(*Hamðismál* 8)

Gnomes expressing fatalism are to be found in the final verses of
Hamðismál (30): 'kveld lifir maðr ekki ǀ eptir kvið norna' (no man
outlives the evening, after the Norns's decree); in *Atlamál* 46:
'skǫpom viðr manngi!' (no man can withstand fate!); and,
similarly phrased, in *Grípisspá* 53, as Sigurðr sets off to fulfil the
prophecies of Grípir. Although, contrary to his own expectations,
he returns safely and successfully from the peril, Skírnir's stoical
remarks to his horse as he departs on the dangerous mission of
wooing Gerðr for Freyr sum up the pagan spirit of resignation:

Kostr ro betri   The choices are better
heldr en at klǿkkva sé,   than that one should be snivelling,
hveim er fúss er fara;   for him who is eager to depart;
eino dǿgri   for on one day
mér var aldr um skapaðr   was my life-span shaped
ok allt líf um lagit.   and all my life laid down.

(*Skírnismál* 13)

These pagan gnomes of the heroic temperament find their reflex
in Old English also, in both secular and Christian narrative.
Heroic fatalism, courage in desperate circumstances, is easily
transformed into the resignation and endurance of the saint and

martyr, while gnomes urging courage and fortitude might be applied to any warrior.

The Warrior King

Gnomes which define and endorse a heroic course of action are most frequent in the speeches of Beowulf and Wiglaf. The precariousness and shortness of life, a preoccupation of *Hávamál*, in *Beowulf* becomes 'existential' and idealistic. Such moments of reflection obtrude at the moment of action, in the hero's thoughts or in the comments of spectators or the narrator:

> Sēlre bi∂ æghwǣm,
> þæt hē his frēond wrece,   þonne hē fela murne.
> Ūre æghwylc sceal   ende gebīdan
> worolde līfes;   wyrce sē þe mōte
> dōmes ǣr dēaþe;   þæt bi∂ drihtguman
> unlifgendum   æfter sēlest.
>
> (*Beowulf* 1384ᵇ–1389)

It is better for every man that he avenge his kinsman than that he mourn greatly. Each of us must experience the end of life in this world; let he who can achieve renown before death; that is best for every warrior when his life is gone.

Beowulf seeks to comfort Hro∂gar after the death of Æschere, offering a definition of heroic behaviour which contrasts action with inaction. His intention is to brace the old king, and indeed, at the conclusion of Beowulf's speech: 'Āhlēop ∂ā se gomela, ǀ Gode þancode' (the old man leapt up then, thanking God). Two courses of action: mourning and revenge, are postulated; Beowulf chooses the second. By implication, Hro∂gar is left with the first, since he can no longer fight. The gnome has both a contextual function: establishing an appropriate reaction to a violent attack, and a subtextual theme, one which informs the whole poem: the impotence of an old king against forces which threaten the security of his kingdom. As Hro∂gar is now, so Beowulf will become.

The theme of fortitude is interwoven with notions of reciprocal obligations and loyalty: an old king must be helped by younger warriors, whose loyalty he has encouraged in the past through his generosity; Hro∂gar says he had assisted Beowulf's father Ecgþeow when he was fleeing a feud; Beowulf repays that debt.

The key role which generosity plays in the establishment of such reciprocal obligations is introduced by the narrative voice very early in the poem, as soon as the first young prince, Scyld's son, Beowulf, appears:

> Swā sceal (geong g)uma   gōde gewyrcean
> fromum feohgiftum   on fæder (bea)rme,
> þæt hine on ylde   eft gewunigen
> wilgesīþas,   þonne wīg cume,
> lēode gelæstan;   lofdædum sceal
> in mægþa gehwære   man geþēon.

(*Beowulf* 20–5)

So must a young man bring it to pass through liberality, with splendid gifts in his father's possession, that when war may come, willing comrades may stand by him again in his old age, the people obey him; in every tribe a man ought to prosper through deeds of glory.

Hroðgar is not to be blamed for his inability to ward off the attacks of Grendel's kin; old age comes to all of us — another gnomic assertion:

> Þæt wæs ān cyning
> æghwæs orleahtre,   oþ þæt hine yldo benam
> mægenes wynnum,   sē þe oft manegum scōd.

(*Beowulf* 1885ᵇ–1887)

That was a king blameless in every way, until old age, which often has harmed many a man, took from him the joys of his strength.

Yet when Beowulf's time comes, the support which should have been forthcoming is lacking: 'Wergendra tō lȳt | þrong ymbe þēoden' (Too few warriors pressed about the prince) (2882ᵇ–2883ᵃ). Wiglaf bitterly reproaches the cowardly warriors for their failure to come to Beowulf's aid against the dragon. They have not provided the loyalty which an old king is entitled to expect from his warriors: Beowulf has wasted 'wrāþe forwurpe' (2872ᵃ) the many gifts which they have received from him. By their cowardice they have thrown away all hope of future gifts or a relationship with a lord, for everyone will taunt them with their shame; 'flēam ēowerne, | dōmlēasan dæd' (your flight, the inglorious deed) (2889ᵇ–2890ᵃ). The gnomic conclusion is finely placed as a dramatic climax: 'Dēað bið sēlla | eorlum gehwylcum þonne edwītlīf!' (*Beowulf* 2890ᵇ–2891: Death is better for every warrior than an ignoble life!). 'Dēað', following immediately on 'dōmlēasan dǣd' ironically counterpoints the maxim cited above: 'wyrce sē þe mōte | dōmes ǣr dēaþe'. Beowulf's standards are not those of his followers.

Such cowardice contravenes the codes of behaviour which the gnomes steadily asserted by the narrator and uttered by the poem's characters have explicitly stated are appropriate for a man: 'Swā sceal man dōn!' (So should a man do!) (1535b); 'swā sceal mǣg dōn' (so should a kinsman do) (2166b). From the Coastguard's maxim, 287b–289, through the gnomes cited above, to the narrator's approving comment on Wiglaf:

> Fēond gefyldan — ferh ellen wrǣc —
> ond hī hyne þā bēgen   ābroten hæfdon,
> sibæðelingas;   swylc sceolde secg wesan,
> þegn æt þearfe!

> (*Beowulf* 2706–9ª)

They felled the foe — force drove out his life —and then they both had slain him, the noble kinsmen; so should a warrior be, a thegn at need!

a web of gnomes is woven across the surface of the poem, establishing a consistent system of standards by which the actions of the characters should be judged. The poet of *Atlakviða* similarly applauds the courage of Hǫgni and Gunnarr: 'svá skal frœkn | fjándom verjaz' (so should a man defend himself against enemies) is his approving comment as Hǫgni kills seven before he is captured, and Gunnarr's refusal to disclose the secret of the treasure is praised in similar terms.[8]

The gnomic statements in *Beowulf* also delineate the different expectations of the young man and the old king: reinforcing the thematic contrasts of youth and age, and their accompanying virtues of strength and wisdom,[9] which inform the poem.

The Saint

The gnomic paradigm of heroic behaviour is reconstructed for the Christian hero. The old heroic vocabulary is reapplied in new Christian gnomes exhorting to a heroic life, as a warrior of God: 'ellen' (vigour), 'wrǣcsīð' (journey of revenge), 'sigorspēd' (victory), and 'dōm' (reputation) all form part of the vocabulary of *Andreas* gnomes, while 'oretta' (warrior) and 'compian' (to fight) are found in *Guðlac* A. These gnomes are not borrowed from the Bible, but coined by the Old English poets to encourage the loyalty of the Christian warrior, saint, or layman, to his lord.

Andreas, like *Beowulf*, is a poem of action: the saint sets off on a dangerous sea-journey to the land of the cannibalistic Mermedonians, where he suffers torture for the sake of the Lord. Andreas assures his companions that they will survive the tempest which threatens their ship, if they have 'ellen' (strength, zeal), here to be equated with Christian fortitude:

> Forþan ic ēow to sōðe   secgan wille,
> þæt næfre forlǣteð   lifgende God
> eorl on eorðan,   gif his ellen dēah.
>
> (*Andreas* 458–60)

Wherefore I wish to tell you in truth that the living God never deserts a warrior on earth if his courage is good.

This gnome seems to represent a Christianization of the heroic sentiment with which Beowulf comments on his swimming-match with Breca: 'Wyrd oft nereð unfǣgne eorl, | þonne his ellen dēah!' (*Beowulf* 572b–573: Fate often saves the undoomed warrior, when his courage is good!). While Fate may save ('nereð') the warrior who is not yet fated to die, God is always present with ('næfre forlǣteð') his servants, he will never desert them. Both gnomes are confidently uttered, but to the audience of *Andreas*, if they recalled the *Beowulf*-gnome, the difference between the uncertainty as to whether an impersonal Fate will snatch one from peril, and trust in a personal God to be always at one's side, must have been striking. There is a similarity of context too, for Andreas is encouraging his companions in the face of their perilous sea-journey, ironically unaware that Christ is aboard the vessel; both gnomes moralize from the experiences of men struggling against the might of waves.

The reward for the Christian hero is still victory, 'sigorspēd'. As Andreas realizes the identity of the pilot who has brought him safely to shore, he exclaims:

> Þǣr is help gearu,
> milts æt mǣrum,   manna gehwylcum
> sigorspēd geseald,   þām þe sēceð tō him.
>
> (*Andreas* 907–9)

There help is ready, mercy from the glorious one, victory granted for every man that seeks it of him.

In comparison with the flexibility of the gnomes in *Beowulf*, the *Andreas*-poet's usage tends to be rather mechanical. Gnomes provide a weighty-sounding conclusion to an exhortatory speech or account of heroic action; the formal qualities of a gnome lend it conviction, even if the moral drawn does not always spring immediately from the preceding lines. At the prayer of the invisible Andreas, the weapons of the Mermedonians, about to slaughter and devour a young man, all melt in their hands like wax, 'wexe gelīcost'. The poet approves the thwarting of the heathens:

> Gode ealles þanc,
> dryhtna dryhtne,   þæs hē dōm gifeð
> gumena gehwylcum,   þāra þe gēoce tō him
> sēceð mid snytrum,   þær bið symle gearu
> frēod unhwilen,   þām þe hīe finden cann.
>
> (*Andreas* 1150–4)

Thanks be wholly to God, the Lord of Lords, for he grants glory to all men who wisely seek succour from Him, there eternal peace is ever ready for him who can obtain it.

Remarkable though the miraculous melting is, it has little to do with the granting of 'dōm' (glory) or eternal peace to Andreas or the heathen.

In *Guðlac* A, the hero is a soldier who, prompted by his good angel, has given up the military life to become a hermit in the fens. The spot he chooses is an abode of demons, the pagan land-spirits[10] of the desert place. The fiends try to drive Guðlac out, but he stands his ground. The poet approves:

> Swā sceal oretta   ā in his mōde
> Gode compian   7 his gǣst beran
> oft on ondan   þām þe eahtan wile
> sāwle gehwylcre   þær hē gesǣlan mæg.
>
> (*Guðlac* A 344–7)

So must a warrior always in his heart fight for God, and bear his spirit often in wrath against him who wants to persecute every single soul, wherever he may bring that about.

The demons renew their assault, trying to ensnare the saint by treachery, just as a human foe might, a parallel assisted by the dual meaning of 'feond' (fiend/enemy):[11]

> wā bið feonda þeaw,
> þon(ne) hȳ sōðfæstra   sāwle willað
> synnum beswīcan   7 searocræftu(m).

(*Guðlac* A 565b–567)

Such is the custom of fiends when they want to ensnare a truth-fast soul with sins and cunning devices.

Guðlac B shows the warrior-saint in his final battle, against Death himself, the insuperable enemy:

> Dēað nēalǣcte,
> stōp stalgongum,   strong ond hreðe
> sōhte sāwelhus.   Cōm se seofeða dæg
> ældum ondweard,   þæs þe him in gesonc,
> hāt, heortan nēah,   hildescurum
> flacor flānþracu,   feorhhord onlēac,
> searocǣgum gesōht.

(*Guðlac* B 1139b–1145a)

Death approached, stepped forward with stealthy pace, strong and stern, sought the lodging of the soul. The seventh day came to men, when the flickering force of arrows in battle-showers pierced into him, hot, close to the heart, unlocked the life-hoard, attacked by cunning battle-keys.

Guðlac's death torment is realized in dramatic terms, with violent and complex imagery. Death advances to battle, his aim to capture the building in which the soul is contained. After seven days' struggle, the arrows which Death shoots at Guðlac become the cunningly made keys which permit the enemy to open the treasure house, and pillage the hoard (life) within.

After Guðlac's fall at the hands of this enemy, his disciple brings news of the saint's death to Guðlac's sister, then speaks a lament for him:

> Ellen biþ sēlast   þām þe oftost sceal
> drēogan dryhtenbealu,   dēope behycgan
> þroht, þēoden gedāl,   þon(ne) sēo þrag cymeð
> wefen wyrdstafum.   þæt wāt se þe sceal
> aswǣman sarigferð   wāt his sincgiefan

holdne bihveledne.   He sceal hēan þonan
gēomor hweorfan.   þām bið gomenes wāna
ðe þa earfeða   oftost drēogeð
on sārgum sefan.

(*Guðlac* B 1348–56)[12]

Courage is best for him who most often must endure the loss of a lord,
he must deeply consider oppression, deprivation of his prince, when the
time comes, woven with fate's decrees. He knows who must grieve,
sorrowful in spirit, that his loyal treasure-giver (is) buried. He must
humbly depart from thence, mourning. He who must most often endure
hardships in a sorrowful soul, lacks joy.

Gnomes impose control over the disciple's grief; they make its
articulation bearable by distancing the immediate pain. The joyful
aspect of death for a Christian, belief in departure to a heavenly
home, contained in Guðlac's final message to his sister that they
will meet again in heaven, is given almost in parentheses. It is
difficult to feel that the disciple himself is convinced that Guðlac's
death could be a matter for rejoicing:[13] 'Huru ic swiðe ne ðearf |
hinsīþ behlehhan.' (*Guðlac* B 1356b–1355a: Indeed I have no need
at all to rejoice at his journey hence).

Although the poem breaks off towards the end of the disciple's
speech, there is a clear return to sentiments of grief and loss in
the last lines. The poet of *Guðlac* B uses the gnomic convention
in elegy to depict appropriate behaviour for a mourner.
Traditional wisdom concerning the grief of those left behind is
placed beside, but not integrated with, a Christian understanding
of the meaning of death. The courage 'ellen' which must be
found is a courage of endurance, as in *Andreas* 460, rather than
the heroic courage needed by the mourner who must take
revenge.

7.2 THE HEROIC: *SAPIENTIA*

In addition to fortitude: the courage to hazard one's life in
Beowulf, the endurance of martyrdom for the saint, the hero
needs *sapientia*: 'miklis er á mann hvern vant | er manviz er'
(much is a man lacking, if he lacks common-sense), as Sǫrli points
out in *Hamðismál*.[14] In *Beowulf*, it is primarily the practical

application of wisdom, in making judgments about other people and events to come, which attracts gnomic comment.

The first character called upon to show wisdom, to exercise his individual judgement is the Coastguard:

> Æghwæþres sceal
> scearp scyldwiga   gescād witan
> worda ond worca,   sē þe wēl þenceð.
>
> (*Beowulf* 287b–289)

A bold shield-warrior of upright mind must always know the difference between words and deeds.[15]

The Geats' action in arriving without permission at the Danish harbour is capable of hostile interpretation: but their courteous speech and Beowulf's demeanour persuade the Coastguard that their initially threatening appearance may have been deceptive. The gnome acknowledges this possibility, but also functions as a warning: the visitors' further deeds had better bear out their words, for their actions will be under scrutiny. This interpretation is supported by: 'Ic þæt *gehȳre*,   þæt þis is hold weorod | frēan Scyldinga.' (*Beowulf* 290–1a: I *hear* that this is a troop loyal to the lord of the Scyldings) (my italics).

Words are easily uttered and heard; actions are unequivocal. With the gnome, the Coastguard justifies the action which he is about to take; its placing at the beginning of the Coastguard's speech marks the moment of decision, it is the pivotal point around which his attitude swings, from suspicion to trust with reservations.

Beowulf himself advocates travel as a means of self-discovery, in a more thoughtful gnome than the modern equivalent: 'travel broadens the mind'. This subtle and acute variant suggests that the man who travels benefits only as far as his innate capacity and potentialities permit:[16] 'feorcȳþðe bēoð | sēlran gesōhte   þǣm þe him selfa dēah' (*Beowulf* 1838b–1839: Distant lands are better sought by a man who has ability in himself).

If Hroðgar's son, Hreðric, were to visit the Geatish court, he would find a friendly reception. Beowulf flatters the boy: such a fine prince would do well abroad. Yet the advice carries a subtextual warning, just as Fáfnir's information about Norns and *Ragnarǫk* does: Hreðric should seek asylum with the Geats if Hroðulf usurps the throne, a hint which cannot be given more openly. The remark is designed to show Beowulf's political acumen, just as, on his return to Hygelac's court (2020–69), Beowulf predicts the outcome of Hroðgar's peacemaking attempts with Ingeld, with another gnomic remark. We know from *Widsið* l. 6 that Beowulf's forebodings about the Heathobards proved correct, and from Saxo that Hroðulf would act as Beowulf suspected.[17] Thus the apparently innocuous remark about foreign travel finds its place in the complex web of inter-dynastic rivalries which characterizes the later part of *Beowulf*.

Curiously, Hroðgar's 'homily', the climax of the theme of wisdom in *Beowulf*, actually contains no gnomes at all.[18] Although the homily's themes: the responsiblities of kingship and a warning against pride, are frequent in wisdom literature,[19] the message is vividly personal, not a sermon of generalized import. Hroðgar's speech is part of Beowulf's reward for killing Grendel's mother; a gift of the old king's wisdom[20] concerning a danger which, now more than ever, threatens Beowulf, a danger which is expressed in martial-Christian terms (1745 ff.).

Beowulf is pre-eminent, 'geboren betera' (1703a), his fame has spread across the seas and he will be a saviour to his people. The praise and prophecy modulate immediately into an account of the wickedness and royal tyranny of Heremod. Out of this flows a moralizing example of a man, blessed by God with prosperity, who sinks so far into complacency that he falls into the sin of avarice. Finally he comes to believe that nothing can harm him:

> nō hine wiht dweleð
> ādl nē yldo, nē him inwitsorh
> on sefa(n) sweorceð nē gesacu ōhwǣr
> ecghete ēoweð, ac him eal worold
> wendeð on willan;
> *Beowulf* 1735b–1739a)

nor does sickness nor old age hinder him, nor does inner sorrow darken his soul, nor does strife anywhere bring about violence, but all the world turns according to his desire.

The cowardly man in *Hávamál* 16 also thinks he can live for ever, if he avoids fighting, but:

elli gefr hánum,	Old age gives him
engi frið,	no peace,
þótt hánum geirar gefi	even if spears do.

The difference in tone between the wisdom of the Gnomic Poem and *Beowulf* is neatly illustrated here. Hroðgar is deeply serious, producing a carefully meditated reflection on worldly fortune and complacency, based partly on his own experiences, while the *Hávamál*-poet, well aware of the irony, laughs at the coward's folly. However great his strength and renown now, fate will eventually overtake Beowulf, Hroðgar warns, in a catalogue of possible deaths   (1761ᵇ–1768), paralleled in *Fortunes of Men* and *The Wanderer* 80ᵇ–84. The homily is brought to a close with reference to Hroðgar's own experience: he too thought that he was safe from danger, until the depredations of Grendel began. The three exempla Hroðgar gives, one historical, one typical, one personal, seem to invite a gnomic, moralizing conclusion: 'therefore . . .', but the homily ends in praise of God for the victory over Grendel.

7.3 THE NARRATIVE VOICE

Beowulf is characterized by an idiosyncratic narrative voice, commenting on and interpreting the action of the poems: this 'authenticating voice'[21] employs gnomes both to comment on the plot and to link it with the material contained in the poem's digressions.

As *Beowulf* is a Christian poem, the Christian preoccupation with divine control and ordering pervade the 'existential' field of heroic action: the saint's life, typified by the *Guðlac* poems, has in turn cross-fertilized the secular epic. The demonstration of God's eternal presence and concern with the world, both in the past of the poem and in the contemporary moment of the audience, is a function performed by the gnomes in the narrative voice. When God and Beowulf's 'mōd' (spirit) have put an end to Grendel, the voice observes:

> Metod eallum wēold
> gumena cynnes,   swā hē nu git dēð.
> Forþan bið andgit   æghwær sēlest,
> ferhðes foreþanc.   Fela sceal gebīdan
> lēofes ond lāþes   sē þe longe hēr
> on ðyssum windagum   worolde brūceð!
> (*Beowulf* 1057ᵇ–1062)

The Creator ruled mankind completely, as he still does now. For that reason, discernment is everywhere best, forethought of spirit. Many pleasant and hateful things must he endure, who, for a long time here, uses the world in these days of strife.

The last lines of the observation, the alternation of 'lēofes and lāþes' in this world, fit the context well: the horror of Beowulf's fight with Grendel has been succeeded by rejoicing, joy in which a sombre note will be sounded by the tale of Hildeburh's sorrow which follows, and, which in a surprising twist, is destroyed by the sudden attack of Grendel's mother. The relevance of 'andgit' and 'ferhðes foreþanc' at this point is not especially clear: these qualities have, as Burlin points out,[22] played little part in the fight against Grendel.

As Wiglaf desperately tries to keep Beowulf alive after the dragon-fight, the poet comments rightly, yet sympathetically, on the hopelessness of the endeavour; resignation should be the response: 'wolde dōm Godes   dǣdum rǣdan | gumena gehwylcum,   swa hē nū gēn dēð.' (*Beowulf* 2858–9: The judgement of God would determine the deeds of every man, as it still does now.) With the forward movement of 'swā hē nū git/gēn dēð', into the audience's own time, the poet merges the world of *Beowulf* with the 'now' of his audience. *Beowulf* may be a tale of 'in gēardagum' (in bygone days), but the effect of these gnomes is to suggest continuity: what was valid then is still relevant today.

Also characteristic of the narrative voice of *Beowulf* is a sceptical attitude towards human nature; an ironic recognition of the realities of life. As he reflects on the fate of Grendel, fleeing Beowulf's grip, to the 'dēofla gedrǣg' (abode of devils) that is his home, the narrator provides an ironic moralization upon humanity's futile efforts to escape death:

> Nō þæt ȳðe byð
> tō beflēonne   — fremme sē þe wille —
> ac gesēcan sceal   sāwlberendra
> nȳde genȳdde,   niþða bearna,
> grundbūendra   gearwe stōwe,
> þǣr his līchoma   legerbedde fæst
> swefeð æfter symle.
>
> (*Beowulf* 1002b–1008a)

Nor is that easy to flee — let him try it who will — but he must seek, (one) of the soul-bearers, constrained by necessity, of the sons of men, of the earth-dwellers, a place made ready, where his corpse, sound on its bed of death, sleeps after the feast.

The image of the weary corpse, asleep on the bed of death, is particularly apt, for it anticipates the scene in the monsters' lair where, having survived the fight with Grendel's mother, Beowulf finds Grendel's body. We see here the psychologically acute understanding of human nature which informs the whole poem, and, in the belief expressed that death is inescapable, 'fremme sē þe wille', the tone for the second half of the poem is established. It is inevitable that old age should have deprived Beowulf of his full strength, as Hroðgar had been (1858b–1887), and thus, as Hroðgar had predicted, even Beowulf finds that death is inescapable. The passage cited above, 'Nō þæt ȳðe byð' is echoed in the second movement of the poem, but where before the desperate fleeing creature was Grendel, now it is Beowulf who must give ground before the slayer:

> Ne wæs þæt ēðe sīð,
> þæt se mǣra   maga Ecgþēowes
> grundwong þone   ofgyfan wolde;
> sceolde (ofer) willan   wīc eardian
> elles hwergen,   swā sceal ǣghwylc mon
> ālǣtan lǣndagas.
>
> (*Beowulf* 2586b–2591a)

Nor was that an easy step, that the glorious kinsman of Ecgþeow should consent to yield that ground; he must against his will inhabit a dwelling elsewhere, thus must every man forsake fleeting days.

The language is similar in its emphasis on the reluctance with which living creatures give up their tenacious hold on life, to seek a dwelling elsewhere, but while the first gnome is mildly ironic, suggesting Grendel's folly in hoping he can outwit his fate, the second is informed by a gentle pity, an understanding that a great man's parting from life cannot be easy.

The homiletic elements in *Beowulf* have often been noted; the gnomes of the narrative voice share also certain constructions with religious wisdom poetry. The narrator's condemnation of the Danes' idolatry is syntactically similar to the gnomic conclusions of *The Wanderer* and *The Seafarer*.[23]

Wā biþ þæm þe sceal
þurh slīðne nīð sāwle bescūfan
in fȳres fæþm, frōfre ne wēnan,
wihte gewendan! Wēl bið þæm þe mōt
æfter dēaðdæge Drihten sēcean
ond to Fæder fæþmum freoðo wilnian!

(*Beowulf* 183ᵇ–188)

Woe is it for him who must send forth his soul in a dire, distressful way
into the embrace of the fire, who shall have no hope of solace nor of any
change! Well is it for him who, after the day of death, shall seek the Lord,
and ask for comfort in the Father's embrace.

Such gnomes are highly typical of Christian wisdom verse,
although secular gnomes with the same structure also occur.[24]
That this formulation is part of the Germanic wisdom tradition is
shown by *Muspilli* 25–7:[25]

uue demo in uinstri scal sino uirina stuen.
prinnan pehhe: daz ist rehto paluuic dink
daz der man harh ze got enti imo hilfa ni quimit.

Woe is him who must atone for his crimes in darkness, burn in hellfire,
that is a truly terrible thing when a man prays to God and help does not
come to him.

While the structure of many *Beowulf*-gnomes is traditional, their
vocabulary is often unusual. Some *hapax legomena* are to be found
in the gnomic passages: striking expressions such as 'inwitnet'
(net of malice) 2167, 'bongār' (slaughtering spear) 2031, and
'edwītlīf' (life of shame) 2891 are unparalleled elsewhere;
'freoðuwebbe' (peace-weaver) 1942 is found otherwise only in
Widsið l. 6. The unusual vocabulary tends to occur where a gnome
is used to generalize from one of the poem's many digressions,
encapsulating the digression's relevance to the main plot. This
suggests that the poet is re-fashioning the traditional gnomes in
his own words, for the moralizations are particularly well-suited to
their contexts.

Beowulf's scepticism about the peace between the Danes and
the Heaðobards, sealed by the marriage of Freawaru and Ingeld,
is summed up in 2029ᵇ–2031:

Oft seldan hwǣr
æfter lēodhryre   lȳtle hwīle
bongār būgeð   þēah sēo brȳd duge!

It is usually a rare thing when a little while after the fall of a prince the murderous spear sinks to rest, though the bride may be of worth!

'Bongār' is a particularly striking word, for it is an old spear-warrior, 'eald æscwiga' (2042ᵃ) who will incite a younger Heaðobard to begin the quarrel again. Beowulf's remarks about the likelihood of fresh strife between the Danes and the Heaðobards resonate through the rest of the poem, for his observations are equally applicable to the later history of the Swedes and the Geats.

Certain gnomes are designed to contrast characters in the digressions with those in the main plot: Þryð is to be contrasted with Hygd, and, more indirectly, with Freawaru, who is also a peaceweaver, 'freoðuwebbe':²⁶

Ne bið swylc cwēnlīc þēaw
idese tō efnanne,   þēah hīo ǣnlicu sȳ,
þætte freoðuwebbe   fēores onsǣce
æfter ligetorne   lēofne mannan.
(*Beowulf* 1940ᵇ–1943)

Nor is such a queenly virtue for a lady to perform, though she be peerless, that a peaceweaver should deprive a dear man of life after a pretended injury.

Another gnome, approving Beowulf's action in handing over his treasures from Denmark to Hygelac, apparently contrasts him with Heremod, the exemplar of the bad king in Hroðgar's sermon:²⁷

Swā sceal mǣg dōn,
nealles inwitnet   ōðrum bregdon
dyrnum cræfte,   dēað rēn(ian)
hondgesteallan.
(*Beowulf* 2166–ᵇ2169ᵃ)

So should a kinsman do, by no means weave a malicious net with secret cunning for another, prepare the death of a close companion.

The gnomes of *Beowulf* tend to follow the main plot quite closely;

they are not generally incorporated into the digressions and allusions, except where, as in the examples cited above, they explicitly contrast the behaviour of one of the protagonists of the main plot with a character in a digression: Hygd with Þryð; Beowulf with Heremod, acting as an integrating device. The Swedish war material and Hygelac's fatal adventure among the Franks are not moralized.

The account of Beowulf's swimming contest with Breca is punctuated by Beowulf's gnomic exclamation 'Wyrd oft nereð . . .' (Fate often saves . . .). Together with a reference to sunrise: 'Lēoht ēastan cōm, | beorht bēacen Godes' (Light came from the east, bright beacon of God),[28] (569b–570a) the gnome integrates the Breca tale into the main plot, by linking it with the themes of God's Creation, and ordering of the world, and of the value of courage in adversity, themes which we find expressed in gnomes elsewhere in the poem.

The poet of *Beowulf* uses gnomes to begin, conclude, and to punctuate various narrative units. The contrasting themes of youth and age, wisdom and strength are thrown into relief by gnomic observations, and these in turn serve to illuminate the ethical patterns of right and wrong. They impart an inevitability to the development of the plot, and reinforce the reality of the world of the poem for the audience of a later time. The *Beowulf* poet's use of gnomic material is both original and sophisticated; the gnomes are integrated into the thematic patterns of the poetry with the same skill that the poet displays in constructing *Beowulf*'s overall design.

Notes

1. Williams, *GP*, 33: 'They [gnomes in *Beowulf*] had become conventional stop-gaps or roundings of periods.

2. S. B. Greenfield, 'The Authenticating Voice in *Beowulf*', *ASE* 5 (1976), 60. Other examinations of the gnomes in *Beowulf* are those of K. Malone, 'Words of Wisdom in *Beowulf*', in W. D. Hand and G. O. Arlt ed., *Humaniora* (Locust Valley, NY., 1960), 180–94; R. B. Burlin, 'Gnomic Indirection in *Beowulf*', in *Anglo-Saxon Poetry: Essays in Appreciation. For John C. McGalliard*, L. E. Nicholson and D. W. Frese ed. (Notre Dame,Ind., 1975), 41–9; T. A. Shippey, 'Maxims in Old English Narrative: Literary Art or Traditional Wisdom?', in *Oral Tradition, Literary Tradition: A Symposium*, ed. H. Bekker-Nielsen *et al.* (Odense, 1977), 28–46; and C. Karkov and R. Farrell, 'The Gnomic Passages of *Beowulf*', *NM* 91 (1990), 295–310; see also M. S. Fukuchi, 'Gnomic Statements in Old English Poetry', *Neophilologus*, 59 (1975), 610–13, for a more general examination of gnomes in Old English narrative.

3. *Juliana* 224b, exceptionally, has a gnomic assertion, 'þæt is sōð cyning' (he is the true King).

4. It is now assumed that the author of *Andreas* was familiar with *Beowulf*; see (among others), K. R. Brooks's introduction to his edition of *Andreas and The Fates of the Apostles*(Oxford, 1961); A. G. Brodeur, 'A Study of Diction and Style in Three Anglo-Saxon Narrative Poems', in *Nordica et Anglica: Studies in Honor of Stefán Einarsson*, ed. A. H. Orrick (The Hague, 1968).

5. Texts of *Sigurðarkviða in skamma* and *Brot af Sigurðarkviða* from *Edda, Die Lieder des Codex Regius nebst verwandten Denkmälern*, i. *Text*, ed. G. Neckel, 5th edn. rev. H. Kuhn (Heidelberg, 1983).

6. See above, ch. 2.6 and cf. *Reginsmal* 137–8: 'er mér fangs von | at frekom úlfi' (I have expectation of difficult dealings with a hungry wolf).

7. Citation, and stanza numbering, for *Atlakviða* and *Hamðismál* from Dronke, *PE*, 86.

8. *Atlakviða* 3210–12.

9. For the importance of the opposition strength: wisdom in *Beowulf*, see R. E. Kaske, '*Sapientia et Fortitudo* as the Controlling Theme of *Beowulf*', *SP* 55 (1958), 423–56.

10. The preoccupation of the demons with their rights over the land which Guðlac has chosen for his hermitage suggests that they are akin to the 'landvættir' (land-spirits) of Old Norse; *Óláfs saga Tryggvasonar* ch. 33; *Egils saga* ch. 57 and *Landnamabók*, *ÍF* i. 313.

11. An ambiguity also exploited in *The Seafarer*, l. 75. See above, ch. 6.2.

12. Text from J. Roberts ed., *The Guðlac Poems of the Exeter Book* (Oxford, 1979); punctuation is from *ASPR* iii.

13. Cf. *The Wanderer*, where there is similar use of gnomic generalization; however, in that poem, the 'loss of a lord' topos is used for metaphorical purposes. See also F. M. Biggs, 'Unities in the Old English *Guðlac* B', *JEGP* 89 (1990), 155–65, which argues an identification between the servant and Guðlac's body, while Pega, the sister, represents the soul. The servant's incomprehension of the meaning of Guðlac's death can be linked to 'Soul and Body' dialogues.

14. *Hamðismál* 273–4.

15. 'Sē þe wel þenceð' refers to a moral quality, as well as the intellectual capacity to think things out. See in addition R. E. Kaske, 'The Coastwarden's Maxim in *Beowulf*: A Clarification', *NQ* NS 31 (1984), 16–18.

16. Cf. *Háv*. 18: 'Sá einn veit | er víða ratar . . .' (He alone knows, who travels widely . . .).

17. Saxo, i. bk. vi, pp. 183–95.

18. Hansen, *SC*, 63 identifies 1724b–1727 as a gnomic assertion; but the dependence of the assertion on 'Wundor is tō secganne' (it is a wonderful thing to say) converts it to a metalinguistic utterance.

19. Cf. the Babylonian *Advice to a Prince* in W. G. Lambert ed., *Babylonian Wisdom Literature* (Oxford, 1960), the Egyptian *Instruction of King Merikare*; and Ecclus. 10: 3, 10; 'An undisciplined king will ruin his people, but a city will grow through the understanding of its rulers . . . A long illness baffles the physician; the king of today will die tomorrow.' Cf. also Ecclus. 10: 26–7 on pride and Proverbs 20: 26 ff., 21: 1–4 for the role of the king and the dangers of arrogance.

20. Cf. the *Ruotlieb*, a Latin romance composed in South Germany in the mid-eleventh century, in which the hero, Ruotlieb, who has led a victorious army for the king, chooses to hear sage counsel from the king rather than taking a material reward. *Ruotlieb*, ed. and tr. E. H. Zeydel, University of North Carolina Studies in the Germanic Languages and Literatures, 23 (Chapel Hill, NC, 1959), 422–542, pp. 70–7.

21. The term is taken from Greenfield, 'The Authenticating Voice in *Beowulf*'.

22. Burlin, 'Gnomic Indirection', 48.

23. F. Klaeber, 'Die christlichen Elemente im *Beowulf*', *Anglia*, 25 (1912), 111–36; 249–70; 453–82 connects the 'wā bið þǣm þe . . .' gnomes with 'die biblischen weherufe' ('the biblical cries of woe') (265). The 'wel bið þǣm þe' gnomes are linked with the Beatitudes (ibid. 453).

24. *Ex. Max.* 111, for example.

25. *Muspilli* in *An Old High German Reader*, ed. C. C. Barber (Oxford, 1951).

26. For more on the role of the peace-weaver, see J. Hill, '"Þæt wæs Geomru Ides!" A Female Stereotype Examined', in *New Readings on Women in Old English Literature*, ed. H. Damico and A. Hennessey Olsen (Bloomington, Ind., 1990), 235–47.

27. Heremod is also the subject of *Beowulf* 901 ff.

28. For the formulaic nature of the 'Hero on the Beach' type-scene, see D. K. Crowne, 'The Hero on the Beach: An Example of Composition by Theme in Anglo-Saxon Poetry', *NM* 61 (1960), 362–72 and D. K. Fry, 'OE Formulaic Themes and Type-Scenes', *Neophilologus*, 52 (1968), 48–54.

CONCLUSION

COMMON AND DISTINCTIVE ELEMENTS IN OLD NORSE AND OLD ENGLISH WISDOM POETRY

The most striking characteristic of Germanic wisdom poetry is the apparently unstructured nature of its content: a ready flow of statements which nevertheless proceeds both by sharp breaks and contrasts, and by variations on a single theme. The resulting problems of coherence and unity which confront the scholar are inherent in the genre itself. On close reading, it is evident that the poems are not random agglomerations of gnomes: the constituent gnomes or maxims may be carefully shaped, then these units are integrated, sometimes by means of a large external framework, such as we find in *Precepts*, sometimes by a smaller 'local' structure, such as the enumerations in *Sigrdrífumál* or the *Ljóðatal* section of *Hávamál*. Elsewhere — the Gnomic Poem of *Hávamál*, the *Exeter Maxims* — the poem unfolds through verbal or thematic links, subtle modulations from one stanza to the next, or sometimes the range of thought is extended through unexpected juxtapositions of images. An aesthetic impulse is always at work in the organization of the wisdom poem: with no inherent logical or chronological order, its structure becomes symphonic in character. Themes are taken up, allowed to drop, returned to in a different key or tempo, modulated until resolution is finally reached.

The wisdom poems of Old Icelandic and Old English have many themes in common, for the preoccupations of both societies were similar: the dangers of travel, the nature of women, trust, friendship, and caution, among others. Yet each culture treats these themes distinctively: *Hávamál*'s spirited account of sexual game-playing between Óðinn and 'Billings mær' may be contrasted with the stately portrait of the nobleman's wife in the *Exeter Maxims*, or the cautionary and prohibitive maxims of *Sigrdrífumál*, warning the warrior against witches, women, and excessive drink, with the bold assertions and perfect heroic confidence of *Beowulf*: 'swā sceal man dōn!' (so should a man do!). In *Hávamál*, a persistent impulse towards realism manifests itself in vivid detail: two goats, a half loaf and tilted cup, two hams hanging up. In the hall, the foolish man is the butt of sly, mocking glances from more knowing fellows; no such mockery and gibing mars the perfect ritual of mead-drinking and gift-giving in the lady's hall in the *Exeter Maxims*. The emotions encountered in everyday life, loneliness, fear, the joy of good fellowship, are depicted in *Hávamál* with an unparalleled sharpness of observation. Against this, the Old English *Maxims* offer a generalized and static anatomization of the typical, rarely touched by feeling: none of the observations of the *Exeter Maxims* brings quite the shock of recognition, the immediate assent to a simple, if sardonic truth, as:

> blindr er betri   it is better to be blind
> en brendr sé —   than to be burnt —
> nýtr manngi nás.   a corpse is no good to anyone.

Wisdom in Old Norse is numinous: it is Óðinn's prize and his gift to mankind, hence his presence as originator is always felt. Unlike Óðinn, God is not the provider of wisdom in the Old English poems: although he too is a constant presence, his role is chiefly that of the Creator who has brought into being the wonderful profusion of creatures which walk, swim, and fly through the *Maxims*, according to divine ordinance. God's gift is life itself, he is Creator of the universe which teaches wisdom through cumulative experience: 'Forþon ne mæg weorþan wīs wer, ær hē āge | wintra dæl in woruldrīce.' (*The Wanderer* 64–5b: Thus no man may become wise before he has had his share of winters in the world).

The figure of God the Judge is also sensed in the more overtly moralizing *Precepts*: our eternal fate will be determined by our understanding and application of the wisdom the poem presents. By contrast, the final sanction of the Old Norse gnomes, epitomized in *Hávamál*, is social failure: becoming the fool scorned and mocked by his fellows, the man who cannot win 'lof' and 'dómr' (reputation and fame).

The paradox of the wisdom poem is that, while the Idea — the principle which can be extrapolated from experience —must be central, its expression must be firmly rooted in the actual. The demonstration of that Idea must be drawn from everyday life if it is to persuade us of the essential truth of the wisdom which it presents. Thus the poetry gives the illusion of concreteness: the *Fortunes of Men* depicts a range of skilled craftsmen, the Frisian's wife welcomes her man home. *Hávamál* sketches a landscape of open fields, apparently welcoming halls, rides to the Þing, the small cottage and the rudderless boat. Realism is built up through an accretion of small details, so gradually that the effect is scarcely noticeable. Only when the link to the actual is lost, as in *Hugsvinnsmál*, where the Roman background has been stripped away, but no spirit of 'Icelandicness' breathed into what remains, do we realize how necessary to the wisdom poems is the apprehension of a real, functioning society, behind the text. *Hugsvinnsmál* is colourless in comparison with the poems which spring from the native Germanic tradition.

Yet we should not make the mistake of believing that the wisdom poems constitute an actual record of how the societies really were. The texts are constructs: the Old English poems idealize and dramatize the Anglo-Saxon conception of how the world ought to be, the gnomes of *Fáfnismál* offer a version of the heroic worthy of a textbook. The Gnomic Poem of *Hávamál*, by contrast, is so firmly based in the pragmatic that its relevance is unaffected by the coming of Christianity, for its ethical standards are practical and its aims are spiritually modest. *Hávamál* does not deal in religious aspirations: getting by 'with a dry skin' is enough for the middling wise man.

Also distinct is the linguistic style of the poems. The Old Norse idiom is directed towards fine, precise observations: the man who sinks steadily deeper into a slough of 'dul' (self-delusion), or the powerful image of the fiery infatuation between friends which burns itself out in five days. The Norse texts offer few linguistic problems for the inflections and syntax are well-preserved; it is the content of the archaic mythological stanzas which render parts of *Hávamál* obscure. While the Old English wisdom poems are one of only two textual environments (the other being the *Charms*) where pagan references, to Woden and Ing (and, conceivably, to Ōs (ON Áss) (pagan god) and Þunor), persist, it is not these outcrops of ancient lore which offer difficulty so much as individual *hapax legomena* and ambiguous, perhaps colloquial syntax. The obscure 'tennaþ' (nurture?) and 'tǣtaþ' (coax?), for example, in *Fortunes of Men* 4 indicate the paucity of surviving words from a register of tenderness, while meaning is often slippery to interpret: 'Geara is hwær ārǣd' says *Exeter Maxims* 191: The resolute man is always ready? The man who is ready is resolute? Perhaps the ambiguity is intended. In parts of the *Maxims* we sense a language which eludes the scribe himself, imperfectly understood through the decay of the inflectional system or persistent miscopying. The antiquarian interests of Icelandic writers, who were more tolerant of pagan story than the monastic transmitters of culture in England, may have been instrumental in preserving *Hávamál* and the poems of Sigurðr's youth. The impact of the Conversion on the Icelanders was gradual; *Sturlunga saga* and the *Byskupa sǫgur* chronicle the struggle to impose Christian mores on an Icelandic society whose basic unit was still the farmhouse-hall realized in the opening stanzas of *Hávamál.* A neutral, non-dogmatic wisdom, generated by everyday experience rather than pagan belief and ritual, could survive without scholarly revisions, imparted to successive audiences in the isolated farmhouses out of reach of the newly established schools at Skálholt and Hólar. Imported Christian wisdom was embodied in poems like *Hugsvinnsmál* and *Sólarljóð*, new departures for Church-educated Icelandic poets who were able to assimilate both the new belief systems and new genres (the parental dialogue, the vision poem) to the metrical and structural patterns of the native tradition.

In England, the revision and assimilation process seems to have been more thoroughgoing. Just as Christian writers systematically omitted any record of Anglo-Saxon pagan practice from their histories, so the English poets reformed their wisdom tradition in the image of God the Creator, as in the *Exeter* and *Cotton Maxims*, and the *Rune Poem*, or of God the Judge, as in *Precepts*. Even the ancient Germanic preoccupation with the individual's fate and the larger operations of *wyrd*, explored in a Christian context in *Fortunes of Men*, is developed in the light of new Boethian philosophy in *Solomon and Saturn II*. The result was a Christian poetics, exulting, as we have seen in chapter 4, in the created world and highly conscious of the operations of a divine power ordering human existence.

Old Norse and Old English culture valued gnomic wisdom greatly: traditions were maintained and apparently readapted for succeeding generations and different genres. The poet of *Beowulf* refashions heroic gnomes to fit precisely the context of his digressions to ensure that their moral relevance is pointed by an epigrammatic conclusion; Eyvindr *skáldaspillir* sounds familiar gnomic themes with ironic resonance from *Hávamál,* with specific political intention in *Hákonarmál.* The applications may continually be new, but the absolute value of the wisdom remains unchanged: the distilled lessons of experience constitute a uniting ideology, as much part of the 'langue' of the community as the very words which the poets use.

BIBLIOGRAPHY

1. Reference Works

Old Norse Dictionaries

Ordbog over det gamle norske Sprog, ed. J. Fritzner, 3 vols. (Kristiania, 1883–96).
Norwegisch-dänisches etymologische Wörterbuch, ed. H. Falk and A. Torp, 2 vols. (Heidelberg, 1910–11).
Lexicon Poeticum Antiquæ Linguæ Septentrionalis (Ordbog over det norskislandske Skjaldesprog), ed. S. Egilsson; 2nd edn., ed. F. Jónsson (Copenhagen, 1916; repr. 1966).
Altnordisches etymologisches Wörterbuch, ed. J. de Vries (Leiden, 1961; repr. 1977).

Old English Dictionaries

An Anglo-Saxon Dictionary, ed. J. Bosworth and T. N. Toller (Oxford, 1882–98); *Supplement*, ed. T. N. Toller and A. Campbell (Oxford, 1921; repr. 1973).
Sprachschatz der angelsächsischen Dichter, ed. C. M. W. Grein (Heidelberg, 1912).

Other Reference Works

Deutsche Mythologie, J. Grimm, 4th edn., 4 vols. (Berlin, 1876).
Handwörterbuch des deutschen Aberglaubens, H. Bächthold-Stäubli (Berlin, 1927–42).
Kommentar zu den Liedern der Edda, H. Gering; nach dem Tode des Verfassers herausgegeben von B. Sijmons, 2 vols. (Halle, 1927–31).
Kulturhistorisk Lexikon for nordisk middelalder (Mälmo, 1956–78).
Medieval Scandinavia: An Encyclopedia, ed. P. Pulsiano *et al.* (New York, 1992).
Motif-Index of Early Icelandic Literature, ed. I. M. Boberg (Copenhagen, 1966).
Proverbs, Sentences and Proverbial Phrases from English Writings Mainly before 1500, edd. B. J. and H. W. Whiting (Cambridge, 1968).
Reallexikon der deutschen Literaturgeschichte, ed. P. Merker and W. Stammler (Berlin, 1926–8).
Reallexikon der deutschen Literaturgeschichte, ed. K. Kanzog and A. Masser, 2nd edn. (Berlin and New York, 1984).

2. *Editions of Major Texts*

Old Norse

Unless otherwise stated, all Eddic verse cited from Helgason, except *Sigurðarkviða in skamma* and *Brot af Sigurðarkviða* cited from Neckel and Kuhn, and *Atlakviða, Atlamál, Guðrúnarhvǫt,* and *Hamðismál,* cited from Dronke. Unless otherwise stated, all skaldic verse cited from Jónsson, *Skjaldedigtning.*

Edda, Die Lieder des Codex Regius nebst verwandten Denkmälern, i. *Text,* ed. G. Neckel, 5th edn., rev. H. Kuhn (Heidelberg, 1983).

Eddadigte, ed. J. Helgason, 3 vols. (Copenhagen, 1955)

Den norsk-islandske Skjaldedigtning, ed. F. Jónsson, 4 vols. (IA–IIA and IB–IIB) (Copenhagen, 1908–15); repr. 1967 (A) and 1973 (B).

The Poetic Edda, i. *Heroic Poems,* ed. U. Dronke (Oxford, 1969).

Old English

Andreas and The Fates of the Apostles, ed. K. R. Brooks (Oxford, 1961).

Beowulf, ed. F. Klaeber, 3rd edn. (Lexington, Mass., 1950).

Cotton Maxims, Menologium, in *The Anglo-Saxon Poetic Records,* vi. *The Anglo-Saxon Minor Poems,* ed. E. V. K. Dobbie (London and New York,1942).

Exeter Maxims, Fortunes of Men, Precepts, Wulf and Eadwacer, Deor, The Wife's Lament, in *The Anglo-Saxon Poetic Records,* iii. *The Exeter Book,* ed. G. P. Krapp and E. V. K. Dobbie (London and New York, 1936).

The Guðlac Poems of the Exeter Book, ed. J. Roberts (Oxford, 1974).

The Old English Rune Poem: A Critical Edition, ed. M. Halsall (Toronto, 1981).

The Seafarer, ed. I. L. Gordon (London, 1960).

The Wanderer, ed. T. P. Dunning and A. J. Bliss (London, 1969).

3. *Editions of Other Norse Works*

Austfirðinga saga, ed. J. Johannesson, ÍF xi (Reykjavik, 1950). (*Hrafnkels saga Freysgóa*).

Borgfirðinga sǫgur, ed. S. Nordal and G. Jónsson, ÍF iii. (Reykjavik, 1938). (*Hœnsa-Þóris saga* and *Gunnlaugs saga ormstunga*).

Brennu-Njáls saga, ed. E. Ó. Sveinsson, ÍF xii (Reykjavik, 1954).

Egils saga Skallagrímssonar, ed. S. Nordal, ÍF ii (Reykjavik, 1933).

Eyfirðinga sǫgur, ed. J. Kristjánsson, ÍF ix (Reykjavik, 1956). (*Þorleifs þáttr jarlsskálds*).

Eyrbyggja saga, Grœnlendinga saga, and *Eiríks saga inn rauða,* ed. E. Ó. Sveinsson and M. Þórðarson, ÍF iv (Reykjavik, 1935).

Fareyinga saga, ed. F. Jónsson (Copenhagen, 1927).

Fornmanna sǫgur, 12 vols. (Copenhagen, 1825–37).

Frostaþingslǫg, in *Norges Gamle Love*, ed. R. Keyser, P. A. Munch, and G. Storm, 4 vols. (Kristiania, 1846–85).

Fóstbrœðra saga, ed. B. Þórolfsson and G. Jónsson, ÍF vi (Reykjavik, 1943).

Gísla saga Súrssonar, ed. A. Loth (Copenhagen, 1956).

Grettis saga Asmundarsonar, ed. G. Jónsson, ÍF vii (Reykjavik, 1936).

Grágás etter der Arnamagnænske Handskrift, 334, *Staðarhólsbók*, ed. Vilhjálmur Finsen (Copenhagen, 1879).

Gull-Þóris saga eller Þorskfirðing saga, ed. K. Kålund, STUAGNL 26 (Copenhagen, 1898).

Heilagra manna sǫgur, ed. C. R. Unger, 2 vols. (Kristiania, 1877).

Heimskringla, ed. B. Aðalbjarnarson, ÍF xxxvi–xxxviii (Reykjavik, 1941–51).

Hervarar saga ok Heiðreks, ed. E. O. G. Turville-Petre (London, 1956).

Homiliubók, ed. T. Wisén (Lund, 1872).

Islendinga saga, in *Sturlunga saga*, i. ed. J. Johannesson, M. Finnbogason, and K. Eldjarn (Reykjavik, 1946).

Konungs skuggsjá, ed. L. Holm-Olsen (Oslo, 1983).

Landnámabók, ed. J. Benediktsson, ÍF i (Reykjavik, 1968).

Laxdœla saga, ed. E. Ó. Sveinsson, ÍF v (Reykjavik, 1934).

Oddr Snorrason, *Óláfs saga Tryggvasonar*, ed. F. Jónsson (Copenhagen, 1932).

Orkneyinga saga, ed. F. Guðmundsson, ÍF xxxiv (Reykjavik, 1965).

Postola sǫgur, ed. C. R. Unger (Kristiania, 1874).

Samling af Sweriges Gamla Lagar, ed. H. S. Collin and C. J. Schlyter, 12 vols. (Stockholm and Lund, 1827–77).

Snorri Sturluson, *Prologue to the Snorra Edda and Gylfaginning*, ed. A. Faulkes (Oxford, 1982) ; repr. (London, 1988).

——— *Skáldskaparmál; Háttatal*, ed. F. Jónsson (Copenhagen, 1931).

Sólarljóð, ed. B. Fidjestøl (Bergen, 1979).

Stjórn, ed. C. R. Unger (Kristiania, 1862).

Sverris saga, ed. G. Indrebø (Kristiania, 1920).

Þorsteins þáttr stangarhǫggs and *Þiðranda þáttr ok Þórhalls*, in *Íslendinga sögur*, 10, ed. G. Jónsson (Reykjavik, 1947).

Vǫlsunga saga, Gǫngu-Hrólfs saga, Norna-Gests þáttr, and *Ragnars saga loðbrókar* in *Fornaldar sögur Norðurlanda*, ed. G. Jónsson and B.Vilhjálmsson, 4 vols. (Reykjavik, 1943–54).

4. Other Works

Alexander, G., 'Studien über den *Hugsvinnsmál*', ZDA 68 (1931), 97–127.

Alexiou, M., *Ritual Lament in Greek Tradition* (London, 1974).

Alfred, *Old English Translation of Boethius*, ed. W. J. Sedgefield (Oxford, 1899).

Alster, B. ed., *The Instructions of Suruppak* (Copenhagen, 1974).

Amory, F., 'Kenning', in *Medieval Scandinavia: An Encyclopedia*, ed. P. Pulsiano *et al.* (New York, 1992.

Andersson, T. M., 'The Displacement of the Heroic Ideal in the Family Sagas', *Speculum*, 45 (1970), 575–93.

—— *The Legend of Brynhild*, Islandica, 43 (Ithaca, NY, and London, 1980).

Aristotle, *Rhetorica* II, tr. W. Rhys Roberts, *Collected Translated Works*, xi. (Oxford, 1946).

Arngart, O. ed., *Proverbs of Alfred*, Skrifter utgivna av kungl. humanistiska Vetenskapssamfundet i Lund (Lund, 1955).

—— *Durham Proverbs*, Lunds Universitets Årskrift, 52 (Lund, 1956), and *Speculum*, 56 (1981), 288–300.

Ball, C. J. E., and Cameron, A., 'Some Specimen Entries for the Dictionary of Old English', *A Plan for the Dictionary of Old English*, ed. R. Frank and A. Cameron (Toronto and Buffalo, NY., 1973), 329–47.

Barber, C. C. ed., *An Old High German Reader* (Oxford, 1951).

Barley, N. F., 'A Structural Approach to the Proverb and Maxim, with Special Reference to the Anglo-Saxon Corpus', *Proverbium*, 20 (1972), 737–50.

—— 'Anthropological Aspects of Anglo-Saxon Symbolism', D.Phil. thesis (Oxford, 1974).

—— 'Structure in the *Cotton Gnomes*', *NM* 78 (1977), 244–9.

Belanoff, P., 'Women's Songs, Women's Language: *Wulf and Eadwacer* and *The Wife's Lament*', in H. Damico and A. Hennessey Olsen ed., *New Readings on Women in Old English Literature* (Bloomington, Ind., 1990), 193–203.

Berkhout, C. T., 'Four Difficult Passages in the *Exeter Book Maxims*', *ELN* 18 (1981), 247–51.

Beyschlag, S., review of K. von See, *Die Gestalt der Hávamál*, 'Zur *Gestalt der Hávamál*, Zu einer Studie Klaus von Sees', *ZDA* 103 (1974), 1–19.

Biggs, F. M., 'Unities in the Old English *Guðlac* B', *JEGP* 89 (1990), 155–65.

—— and McEntire, S. 'Spiritual Blindness in the Old English *Maxims I* Part 1', *NQ* NS 35 (1988), 11.

Bjarni Guðnason,, 'Þankar um siðfræði Íslendingasagna', *Skírnir*, 139 (1965), 65–82.

Bloomfield, M., 'Understanding Old English Poetry', *AnM* 9 (1968), 5–25.

Boethius, *Theological Tractates and the Consolation of Philosophy*, ed. and tr. H. F. Stewart, E. K. Rand, and S. J. Tester, Loeb Classical Libarary (London and Cambridge, Mass., 1923; repr. 1973).

Bollard, J. K., 'The *Cotton Maxims*', *Neophilologus*, 57 (1973), 179–87.

Bouterwek, K. W. ed., *Die Vier Evangelien in altnorthumbrischer Sprache* (Gütersloh, 1857).

Brodeur, A. G., 'A Study of Diction and Style in Three Anglo-Saxon Narrative Poems.' in *Nordica et Anglica:, Studies in Honor of Stefán Einarsson*, ed. A. H. Orrick (The Hague, 1968).

Brown, C., '"Poculum Mortis" in Old English', *Speculum*, 15 (1940), 389–99.

Bühler, G., ed., *The Laws of Manu*, Sacred Books of the East, 25 (Oxford, 1886).

Burlin, R. B., 'Gnomic Indirection in *Beowulf*, in L. E. Nicholson and D. W. Frese, *Anglo-Saxon Poetry: Essays in Appreciation* (Notre Dame, Ind., 1975), 41–9.

Campbell, J., *The Hero with a Thousand Faces*, 2nd. edn. (New York, 1968).

Chadwick, H. M., and Chadwick, N. K., *The Growth of Literature*, 3 vols. (Cambridge, 1932–40; repr. 1968).

Clarke, D. M. ed., *The Hávamál*, (Cambridge, 1923).

Clover, C. J., 'Hildigunnr's Lament', in J. Lindow, L. Lönnroth and G.W. Weber edd., *Structure amd Meaning in Old Norse Literature*, (Odense, 1986), 141–83.

—— and Lindow, J. ed., *Old Norse-Icelandic Literature. A Critical Guide*, Islandica 45 (Ithaca, NY. and London, 1985).

Clunies Ross, M., 'An Interpretation of the Myth of Þórr's Encounter with Geirrøðr and his Daughters', in U. Dronke, G. Helgadóttir, G. W. Weber, and H. Bekker-Nielsen ed., *Speculum Norrœnum, Norse Studies in Memory of Gabriel Turville-Petre* (Odense, 1981), 370–91.

—— 'Voice and Voices in Eddaic Poetry', *Poetry in the Scandinavian Middle Ages*, 7th International Saga Conference (Spoleto, 1988), 43–53.

—— 'The Anglo-Saxon and Norse "Rune Poems": A Comparative Study', *ASE* 19 (1990), 23–40.

—— and Martin, B. K., 'Narrative Structures and Intertextuality in the *Snorra Edda*, the example of Þórr's Encounter with Geirrøðr.' in J. Lindow, L. Lönnroth, and G. W. Weber ed., *Structure and Meaning in Old Norse Literature*, (Odense, 1986), 56–72.

Colgrave, B. ed., *The Earliest Life of Gregory the Great*, by an anonymous monk of Whitby (Lawrence, Kan., 1968).

Costello, D. P., and Foote, I. P. ed., *Russian Folk Literature* (Oxford, 1967).

Cox, B. S., *Cruces of Beowulf* (The Hague, 1971).

Cox, R. S. ed., 'The Old English *Dicts of Cato*', *Anglia*, 90 (1972), 1–42.

Cross, J. E. and T. D. Hill ed., *The Prose Solomon and Saturn and Adrian and Ritheus* (Toronto, 1982).

Crowne, D. K., 'The Hero on the Beach: An Example of Composition by

Theme in Anglo-Saxon Poetry', *NM* 61 (1960), 362–72.

Crozier, A., 'Old West Norse "íþrótt" and Old English "indryhtu"', *Studia Neophilologica*, 58 (1986), 3–10.

Dane, J. A., 'The Structure of the Old English *Solomon and Saturn II*', *Neophilologus*, 64 (1980), 592–603.

——— '"On folce geþeon"', *NM* 85 (1984), 61–4.

Davidson, D., 'Earl Hákon and his Poets', D.Phil. thesis (Oxford, 1983).

Dhuoda, *Manuel pour mon fils*, ed. P. Riché Sources chrétiennes, 225 (Paris, 1975).

Dickins, B. ed., *Runic and Heroic Poems* (Cambridge, 1915).

Doht, R., *Der Rauschtrank im germanischen Mythos* (Vienna, 1974).

Dronke, U., '*Reginsmál* v. 8', *MM* (1960), 97–8.

——— '"Óminnis hegri"', *Festskrift til Ludwig Holm-Olsen* (Øvre Ervik, 1984), 53–60

Earl, J. W., '*Maxims I*, Part I', *Neophilologus*, 67 (1983), 277–83.

Einar Ólafur Sveinsson, 'Vísa í *Hávamálum* og írsk saga', *Skírnir*, 126 (1952), 168–77.

——— *Íslenzkar Bókmenntir í Fornöld* (Reykjavik, 1962).

Eiríkur Magnússon, '[on Háv. st. 4, 8, 13, 19, and 134]', *PCPhS* 16 (1887), 5–18.

——— 'Vilmǫgum or vílmǫgum?', *ANF* 15 (1899), 319–20.

Eliade, M., *Myth of the Eternal Return*, tr. W. Trask (Paris, 1949).

Eliot, T. S., *Collected Poems 1909–1962* (London, 1974).

Ellis Davidson, H., *Scandinavian Mythology* (London, 1969).

Eschenbach, Wolfram von, *Parzival*, tr. A. T. Hatto (London, 1980).

Evans, D. A. H. ed., *Hávamál* (London, 1986).

——— 'More Common Sense about *Hávamál*', *Skandinavistik*, 19 (1989), 127–41.

Faulkes, A., *Hávamál: Glossary and Index to D. A. H. Evans's Edition* (London, 1987).

Finnur Jónsson, 'Oldislandske ordsprog og talemåder', *ANF* 30 (1915), 61– 111; 170–217.

Fleck, J., 'Konr-Ottarr-Geirrøðr: A Knowledge-Criterion for Succession to the Germanic Sacred Kingship', *SS* 42 (1970), 39–49.

——— 'Óðinn's Self-Sacrifice, A New Interpretation. I: The Ritual Inversion', *SS* 43 (1971), 119–42; 'II: The Ritual Landscape' ibid., 385– 413.

——— 'The Knowledge-Criterion in the *Grímnismál*: the Case against Shamanism', *ANF* 86 (1971), 7–20.

Frank, R., 'Some Uses of Paronomasia in Old English Scriptural Verse.' *Speculum*, 47 (1972), 207–26.

——— 'Old Norse Memorial Eulogies and the Ending of *Beowulf*', in *The Early Middle Ages, Acta*, 6 (1979), 1–19.

Fry, D. K., 'OE Formulaic Themes and Type-Scenes', *Neophilologus*, 52 (1968), 48–54.

Fukuchi, M. S., 'Gnomic Statements in Old English Poetry', *Neophilologus*, 59 (1975), 610–13.

Genette, G., *Narrative Discourse: An Essay in Method*, tr. J. E. Lewin (Ithaca, NY, 1980) (Orig. publ. 1972).

Gennep, A. van, *Les Rites de passage* (Paris, 1909), tr. M. L. Vizedom and G. L. Cuffee (Chicago, 1960).

Gering, H. ed., *Hugsvinnsmál* (Kiel, 1907).

Godden, M., 'Anglo-Saxons on the Mind', *Learning and Literature in Anglo-Saxon England: Studies presented to Peter Clemoes on the Occasion of his Sixty-fifth Birthday* (Cambridge, 1985), 271–98.

Grattan J. H. G., and Singer, C., *Anglo-Saxon Magic and Medicine* (Oxford,1952).

Greenfield, S. B., *A Critical History of Old English Literature* (New York,1965).

—— 'The Authenticating Voice in *Beowulf*', *ASE* 5 (1976), 51–62.

—— and Calder, D. G., *A New Critical History of Old English Literature* (New York and London, 1986).

—— and Evert, R. '*Maxims II*, Gnome and Poem', in L. E. Nicholson and D. W. Frese, *Anglo-Saxon Poetry: Essays in Appreciation* (Notre Dame, Ind., 1975), 337–54.

Gruber, L. C., 'The Agnostic Anglo-Saxon Gnomes: *Maxims I* and *II*, *Germania*, and the Boundaries of Northern Wisdom', *Poetica*, 6 (1976), 23–45.

—— 'The Rites of Passage: *Hávamál* Stanzas 1–5', *SS* 49 (1977), 330–9.

Grünberg, M. ed., *The West-Saxon Gospels: A Study of the Gospel of St. Matthew, with the Texts of the Four Gospels*, (Amsterdam, 1967).

Gunnar Karlsson, 'Dyggðir og lestir í þjóðfélagi Íslendingasagna', *TMM* 46 (1985), 9–19.

—— 'The Ethics of the Icelandic Saga Authors and their Contemporaries: A Comment on Hermann Pálsson's Theories on the Subject', *Workshop Papers*, 6th International Saga Conference i. (Copenhagen, 1985), 381–400.

Hagman, N., 'Kring några motiv i *Hávamál*', *ANF* 72 (1957), 13–24.

Hall, J. R., 'Perspective and Word-Play in the Old English *Rune Poem*', *Neophilologus*, 61 (1977), 453–60.

Halsall, M., ed., *The Old English Rune Poem: A Critical Edition*. (Toronto, 1981).

Hansen, E. T., '*Precepts*: an Old English Instruction', *Speculum*, 56 (1981), 1–16.

—— 'Hroðgar's "Sermon" in *Beowulf* as Parental Wisdom', *ASE* 10 (1982), 53–67.

Hansen, E. T., *The Solomon Complex* (Toronto, 1988).

Harris, J., 'Elegy in Old English and Old Norse: A Problem in Literary History', in *The Vikings*, ed. R. T. Farrell (London, 1982).

—— 'Eddic Poetry', in C. Clover and J. Lindow ed., *Old Norse-Icelandic Literature. A Critical Guide*, Islandica 45 (Ithaca, NY. and London, 1985), 68–156.

Haugen, E. ed. and tr. , *Fyrsta Málfrœðiritgerðin* (tr. as *First Grammatical Treatise*), Linguistic Society of America Monograph, 25 (1950; repr. London, 1972)

Heaton, E. W., *The Hebrew Kingdoms* (Oxford, 1968).

Henry, P. L., *The Early English and Celtic Lyric* (London, 1966).

Hermann Pálsson, 'Áhrif Hugsvinnsmála á aðrar fornbókmenntir', Studia Islandica 43, (Reykjavik, 1985).

Herzfeld, G. ed., *Ane Old English Martyrology*, EETS OS 116 (London,1900).

Hesiod, *Works and Days*, ed. M. L. West (Oxford, 1978; repr. 1980).

—— *Works and Days*, ed. and tr. H. G. Evelyn-White (London, 1914; rev. 1936).

Heusler, A., 'Sprichwörter in den eddischen Sittengedichten', *Zeitschrift des Vereins für Volkskunde*, 25 (1915), 108–15; ibid. 26 (1916), 42– 54 (repr. in *Kleine Schriften* ii. (Berlin, 1969), 292–313).

—— 'Die zwei altnordischen Sittengedichte der *Hávamál* nach ihrer Strophenfolge', *Sitzungsberichte der Preußischen Akademie der Wissenschaften phil. hist. Klasse* (1917), 105–35 (repr. in Kleine Schriften ii. (Berlin, 1969), 195–22.

Hill, J., '"Þæt wæs Geomru Ides!" A Female Stereotype Examined', in *New Readings on Women in Old English Literature*, ed. H. Damico and A. Hennessey Olsen (Bloomington, Ind., 1990), 235–47.

Hill, T. D., 'Notes on the Old English *Maxims I* and *II*', *NQ* NS 17 (1970), 445–7.

—— 'The Falling Leaf and Buried Treasure: two notes on the imagery of *Solomon and Saturn*', *NM* 71 (1970), 571–6.

Holtsmark, A., 'Til *Hávamál* str. 52', *MM* (1959), 1

Horgan, A. D., '*The Wanderer*: A Boethian Poem?' *RES* 38 (1987), 40–6.

Howe, N., 'The Old English Catalogue Poems', *Anglistica*, 23 (Copenhagen, 1985).

Huppé, B., '*The Wanderer*: Theme and Structure.' *JEGP* 42 (1943), 516– 38.

Isaacs, N. D., 'Up a Tree: To See the Fates of Men', in L. E. Nicholson and D. W. Frese, *Anglo-Saxon Poetry: Essays in Appreciation* (Notre Dame, Ind., 1975), 363–75.

Jackson, K., *Studies in Early Celtic Nature Poetry* (Cambridge, 1935).

—— *Early Welsh Gnomic Poems* (Cardiff, 1935).

Jakob Benediktsson, *Sturlunga saga* Early Icelandic Manuscripts in Facsimile, i. (Copenhagen, 1958).

Jón Helgason, *MS AM 764 A4to,* Manuscripta Islandica, IV (Copenhagen, 1957).

Jónas Kristjánsson, 'Stages in the Composition of Eddic Poetry', in *Poetry in the Scandinavian Middle Ages,* 7th International Saga Conference (Spoleto, 1988), 145–60.

Karkov, C. and Farrell, R., 'The Gnomic Passages of *Beowulf, NM* 91 (1990), 295–310.

Kaske, R. E., '*Sapientia et Fortitudo* as the Controlling Theme of *Beowulf, SP* 55 (1958), 423–56.

—— 'The Coastwarden's Maxim in *Beowulf:* A Clarification.' *NQ* NS 31 (1984), 16–8.

Kershaw, N., ed., *Anglo-Saxon and Norse Poems* (Cambridge, 1922).

Kinsella, T. tr., *The Táin* (Oxford, 1969).

Klaeber, F., 'Die christlichen Elemente im *Beowulf, Anglia,* 25 (1912), 111–36, 249–70, 453–82.

Kleineke, W., *Englischen Fürstenspiegel vom Policraticus Johanns von Salisbury bis zum Basilikon Doron König Jacobs I,* Studien zur englischen Philologie, 90 (Halle, 1937).

Köhne, R., 'Zur Mittelalterlichkeit der eddischen Spruchdichtung', *BGDSL*(T) 105 (1983), 380–417.

Kragerud, A., 'De mytologiske spørsmål i *Fåvnesmål', ANF* 96 (1981), 9– 48.

Kramer, S. N., *The Sumerians* (Chicago, 1963).

Kristján Albertsson, 'Hverfanda hvel', *Skírnir,* 151 (1977), 57–8.

Kromer, G., 'The Didactic Tradition in Virgil's *Georgics',* Ramus, 8 (1979), 7–21.

Lambert, W. G., *Babylonian Wisdom Literature* (Oxford, 1960).

Langland, W., *The Vision of Piers Plowman: The B-Text,* ed. A. V. C. Schmidt (London, 1978).

Larrington, C. A., review of D. A. H. Evans ed., *Hávamál, SBVS* 22, (1987), 127–30.

—— 'Old Icelandic and Old English Wisdom Poetry: Gnomic Themes and Styles', D.Phil. thesis (Oxford, 1988).

—— review of E. T. Hansen, *The Solomon Complex, MÆ* 58 (1989), 319–20.

—— '*Hávamál* and Sources from Outside Scandinavia', *SBVS* 23 (1992), 141–57.

Lendinara, P., '*Maxims I* 146–51: A Hint of Funeral Lamentation', *NM* 74 (1973), 214–16.

Leslie, R. F., ed., *Three Old English Elegies* (Manchester, 1981).

Lie, H., 'Noen gamle tvistemål i *Hávamál',* in *Festskrift til Ludwig Holm-Olsen* (Øvre Ervik, 1984), 215–20.

Lindblad, G., *Studier i Codex Regius av äldre Eddan*, Lundastudier in nordisk språkvetenskap, 10 (Lund, 1954).

—— 'Snorre Sturluson och Eddadiktningen', *Saga och Sed*, (1978), 17–34.

Lindow, J., Lönnroth, L., and Weber, G. W., ed. *Structure and Meaning in Old Norse Literature* (Odense, 1986).

Lindquist, I., 'Ordstudier och tolkingar: *Hávamál*', *SNF* 9 (1917), 1–17.

—— *Die Urgestalt der Hávamál: Ein Versuch zur Bestimmung auf synthetischem Wege* Lunds Universitets Årsskrift, 52 (Lund, 1956).

Lönnroth, L., 'The Noble Heathen: A Theme in the Sagas', *SS* 41 (1969), 1–29.

McGregor Dawson, R., 'The Structure of the Old English *Gnomic Poems*', *JEGP* 61 (1962), 14–22.

Magoun, F. P., Jr. tr., *The Kalevala* (Cambridge, Mass., 1963).

Malone, K., 'Notes on *Gnomic Poem* B of the Exeter Book', *MÆ* 12 (1943), 65–7.

—— 'Words of Wisdom in *Beowulf*', in *Humaniora*, ed. W. D. Hand and G. O. Arlt (Locust Valley, NY, 1960), 180–94.

—— 'Two English *Frauenlieder*', *CL* 14 (1962), 106–17.

Mann, J., 'On Proverbial Wisdom in the *Ysengrimus*', *NLH* 16, (1984), 93–110.

Marquardt, H., *Die altenglischen Kenningar* (Halle, 1938).

May, H. G. and Metzger, B. M. ed., *The Oxford Annotated Bible with Apocrypha* (RSV) (New York, 1965).

Meaney, A. L., 'The "Ides" of the Cotton *Gnomic Poem*', *MÆ* 48 (1979), 23–39.

Menner, R. J. ed., *The Poetical Dialogues of Solomon and Saturn*, (New York, 1941).

Meyer, K. ed., *Instruction of Cormac*, Todd Lecture Series, Royal Irish Academy, 15 (Dublin, 1909).

Mitchell, B., *Old English Syntax*, 2 vols. (Oxford, 1985).

—— and Robinson, F. C., *A Guide to Old English*, 4th edn. (Oxford, 1986).

Mohr, W., 'Entstehungsgeschichte und Heimat der jüngeren Eddalieder süd-germanischen Stoffes', *ZDA* 75 (1938–9), 217–80.

—— 'Wortschatz und Motive der jüngeren Eddalieder mit südgermanischem Stoff', *ZDA* 76 (1939–40), 149–217.

Müllenhoff, K., *Deutsche Altertumskunde* v. (Berlin, 1891).

Mustanoja, T., 'The Unnamed Woman's Song of Mourning over Beowulf and the Tradition of Ritual Lament', *NM* 68 (1967), 1–27.

Neckel, G., 'Sigmunds Drachenkampf', *Edda*, 13 (1920), 122–40, 204–29.

Nelson, M., '"Is" and "Ought" in the *Exeter Book Maxims*', *Southern Folklore Quarterly*, 45 (1984 for 1981), 109–21.

Nicholson, L. E. and Frese, D. W. ed., *Anglo-Saxon Poetry: Essays in Appreciation. For John C. McGalliard* (Notre Dame, Ind., 1975).

Nordal, S., 'Átrúnaðar Egils Skallagrímssonar', *Skírnir*, 98 (1924), 152– 65.

—— '"Billings mær"', in *Bidrag till nordisk filologi tillägnade Emil Olson* (Lund, 1936), 288–95.

Noreen, E., 'Några anteckningar om ljóðaháttr och i detta versmått avfattade dikter', Uppsala Universitets Årskrift, 1 (Uppsala, 1915).

North, J. R. J., 'Words and Contexts: An Investigation into the Meanings of Early English Words by Comparison of Vocabulary and Narrative Themes in Old English and Old Norse Poetry', Ph.D. thesis (Cambridge, 1987).

—— 'The Pagan Inheritance of Egill's *Sonatorrek*', *Poetry in the Scandinavian Middle Ages*, 7th International Saga Conference (Spoleto, 1988), 289–300.

—— *Pagan Words and Christian Meanings*, Costerus New Series, 81, (Amsterdam and Athens, Ga. 1991)

Noth, M., and Winton, T. D. edd., *Wisdom in Israel and the Ancient Near East* (Brill, 1960).

Ohlmarks, Å., *Eddan Gudesånger, tolkade och försedda med inledning och kommentarer* (Stockholm, 1948).

Óláfur M. Ólafsson, 'Sigurðr duldi nafn síns', *Andvari*, NS 12 (1970), 182–9.

Ong, W. J., *Orality and Literacy* (London, 1982).

Osborn, M., 'Old English "Ing" and his Wain', *NM* 81 (1980), 388–9.

—— and Longland, S., 'A Celtic Intruder in the Old English *Rune Poem*', *NM* 81 (1980), 385–7.

Paris, G., *La Légende de Trajan*, Bibl. de l'école des hautes études, 35 (Paris, 1878).

Paulus Diaconus, *Historia Langobardorum*, ed. L. Bethman and G. Waitz, *MGH* SS (1878).

Pipping, R., '*Hávamál* 21 och ett par ställen hos Seneca', *APS* 20 (1949), 371–5.

Ploss, E., *Siegfried-Sigurd der Drachenkampfer, Untersuchung zur germanisch-deutschen Heldensage, Zugleich ein Beitrag zur Entwicklungsgeschichte des alteuropäischen Erzählsgutes*, (Cologne, 1966).

Plummer, C. ed., *Venerabilis Baedae Historiam Ecclesiam Gentis Anglorum*, 2 vols. (Oxford, 1896).

Polomé, E. C., 'Some Comments on *Vǫluspá* 17–18', in *Old Norse Literature and Mythology: A Symposium*, ed. E. C. Polomé (Austin, Tex., 1969), 265—90.

Pritchard, J. B. ed., *Ancient Near East Texts*, 3rd edn. (Princeton, NJ., 969).

Quirk, R., 'Langland's Use of *Kind Wit* and *Inwit*', *JEGP* 52 (1953), 182–9.

236 *Bibliography*

Remly, L. L., 'The Anglo-Saxon Gnomes as Sacred Poetry', *Folklore*, 82 (1971), 147–58.

Robinson, F. C., 'Understanding an Old English Wisdom Verse: *Maxims II* Lines 10 ff.', in *The Wisdom of Poetry*. *Studies in Early English Literature in Honor of Morton W. Bloomfield*, ed. L. D. Benson and S. Wenzel (Kalamazoo, Mich., 1982), 1–11.

Russom, G. R., 'A Germanic Concept of Nobility in *The Gifts of Men* and *Beowulf*, *Speculum*, 153 (1978), 1–15.

Saxo Grammaticus, *History of the Danes*, ed. and tr. P. Fisher and H. E. Davidson, 2 vols. (Cambridge, 1979).

Schlauch, M., 'Widsith, Víðfǫrull, and some other analogues', *PMLA* 46 (1931), 969–87.

Schneider, H., *Eine Uredda* (Halle, 1948).

Schneider, K., *Die Germanische Runennamen: Versuch einer Gesamtdarstellung* (Meisenheim am Glan, 1956).

—— 'Dichterisch getarnte Begriffsnamen in der AE. Spruchdichtung (*Maxims I* u. *II*)', *AION-SG* 15 (1972), 89–114.

See, K. von, 'Zwei Eddische Preislieder: *Eiríksmál* und *Hákonarmál*', in *Festgabe für U. Pretzel* (Berlin, 1963), 107–17.

—— 'Die Sage von Hamdir und Sorli', in *Festschrift Gottfried Weber zu seinem 70-Geburtstag berreicht von Frankfurter Kollegen und Schülern*, edd. H. O. Burger and K. von See, Frankfurter Beiträge zur Germanistik, 1 (Bad Homburg, 1967) (repr. in *Edda, Saga, Skaldendichtung, Aufsätze zur skandinavische Literatur des Mittelalters* (Heidelberg, 1981), 224–49.

—— '*Sonatorrek* und *Hávamál*', *ZDA* 99 (1970), 26–33.

—— '*Disticha Catonis* und *Hávamál*', *BGDSL*(T) 94 (1972), 1–18 (repr. in *Edda*, 27–44).

—— *Die Gestalt der Hávamál, Eine Studie zur eddischen Spruchdichtung* (Frankfurt on Main, 1972).

—— 'Probleme der altnordischen Spruchdichtung', *ZDA* 104 (1975), 91–118 (repr. in *Edda*, 45–72).

—— 'Das Herz in Edda und Skaldendichtung', *Skandinavistik*, 8 (1978), 16–26 (repr. in *Edda*, 73–83).

—— 'Common Sense und *Hávamál*', *Skandinavistik*, 17 (1987), 135– 47.

—— 'Duplik', *Skandinavistik*, 19 (1989), 142–8.

Seip, D. A., 'Har nordmenn skrevet opp Edda-diktningen?', *MM* 43 (1951), 3–33.

Seneca, *Epistulae Morales I and II*, ed. and tr., R. M. Gummere (London, 1918–20).

Shippey, T. A., *Poems of Wisdom and Learning in Old English* (Cambridge and Totowa, NJ., 1976).

—— 'Maxims in Old English Narrative: Literary Art or Traditional

Wisdom?', in *Oral Tradition, Literary Tradition: A Symposium*, ed. H.
Bekker-Nielsen *et al.* (Odense, 1977), 28–46.

Sieper, E., *Die altenglischen Elegien* (Strassburg, 1915).

Singer, S., *Sprichwörter des Mittelalters*, i. (Bern, 1944).

Sisam, K., review of R. J. Menner ed., *The Poetical Dialogues of Solomon and
Saturn* (New York, 1941), *MÆ* 13 (1944), 28–36.

Smyser, H. M., 'Ibn Fadlan's Account of the Rus, with some Commentary,
and some Allusions to *Beowulf*, in J. B. Bessinger and R. P. Creed
ed., *Medieval and Linguistic Studies in Honor of Francis Peabody
Magoun, Jr.* (London, 1965), 92–119.

Sorrell, P., 'Oaks, Ships, Riddles and the Old English "Rune Poem" *ASE*
19 (1990), 103–16.

Stanley, E. G., 'The Oldest English Poetry Now Extant', *Poetica*, 2 1974',
1–24 (repr. in *A Collection of Papers with Emphasis on Old English
Literature*, ed. E. G. Stanley (Toronto, 1987), 115–38.

—— 'Notes on the Text of *Christ and Satan*, and on the *Riming Poem*, and
the *Rune Poem*, chiefly on *wynn, wen* and *wenne*', *NQ* NS 31 (1984),
443–53.

Stefán Karlsson, 'Om norvagismer i islandske håndskrifter', *MM* (1978),
87–102.

Ström, F., *Den döendes makt och Odin i trädet*, Göteborg Högskolas Årskrift,
53 (1947).

Svava Jakobsdóttir, *Gunnlaðarsaga* (Reykjavik, 1987).

—— 'Gunnlǫð og hinn dýri mjǫður', *Skírnir*, 162 (1988), 215–45.

Sweet's Anglo-Saxon Primer, rev. N. Davis (Oxford, 1978).

Taylor, P. B., 'Heroic Ritual in the Old English *Maxims*', *NM* 70 (1969),
387–407.

Thorpe, B. ed., *The Anglo-Saxon Chronicle* i. (London, 1861).

Timmer, B. J., '*Wyrd* in Anglo-Saxon Prose and Poetry', *Neophilologus*, 26
(1941), 24–33, 213–28.

Toorn, M. C. van den, *Ethics and Morals in Icelandic Saga Literature* (Assen,
1955).

—— '*Egils saga* als dichterische Leistung', *ZfdPh* 77 (1958), 46–59.

Turville-Petre, E. O. G., *Scaldic Poetry* (Oxford, 1976).

Virgil, *The Georgics*, ed. R. S. Thomas, 2 vols. (Cambridge, Mass., 1988).

Vries, J. de, 'Om Eddaens Visdomsdigtning', *ANF* 50 (1934), 1–59.

—— *Altgermanische Religionsgeschichte*, 2nd edn., 2 vols. (Berlin, 1956).

—— *Altnordische Literaturgeschichte*, 2 vols. (Berlin, 1967).

Wender, D., 'From Hesiod to Homer by way of Rome', *Ramus*, 8, (1979),
59–64.

Wessén, E., '*Hávamál*: Några stilfrågor', Filologiskt Arkiv, 8, Kungl.
Vitterhets Historie och Antikvitets Akademien (Stockhom, 1959).

—— 'Ordspråk och lärodikt: Några stilformer i *Hávamál*', in

Septentrionalia et Orientalia: Studia Bernardo Karlgren dedicata, Kungl. Vitterhets Historie och Antikvitets Akademiens Handlingar, 91 (Stockholm, 1959), 455–73.

Whitelock, D., 'The Interpretation of *The Seafarer*', in C. Fox and B. Dickins ed., *The Early Cultures of North-West Europe: H. M. Chadwick Memorial Studies* (Cambridge, 1950) (repr. in J. B. Bessinger and S. J. Kahrl ed., *Essential Articles for the Study of Old English Poetry* (Hamden, Conn., 1968), 442–57).

Wight J. and Duff, A. M. ed., *Disticha Catonis*, (Loeb Classical Library; London, 1934).

Williams, B. C., *Gnomic Poetry in Anglo-Saxon* (New York, 1914) (repr. 1966).

Wolf, A., 'Zitat und Polemik in den *Hákonarmál* Eyvinds', in *Germanistiche Studien*, ed. J. Erben and E. Thurnher, Innsbrücker Beiträge zur Kulturwissenschaft, 15 (Innsbruck, 1969), 9–32.

Zeydel, E. H. ed. and tr., *Ruodlieb*, University of North Carolina Studies in the Germanic Languages and Literatures, 23 (Chapel Hill, NC., 1959).

INDEX